THE
WEST WING
SEASONS 3 & 4
THE SHOOTING SCRIPTS

THE
WEST WING
S E A S O N S 3 & 4
THE SHOOTING SCRIPTS

JOHN WELLS PRODUCTIONS

NEWMARKET PRESS • NEW YORK

The West Wing Script Book Production Team:

Melanie O'Brien, Manager of Sales
Skye Van Raalte-Herzog, Manager of Book Production
Warner Bros. Worldwide Publishing

Photo on page ii by Ron Jaffe. Photo on page 567 by Craig Mathew.

The West Wing Created by Aaron Sorkin

This book is published in the United States of America.

First Edition

10 9 8 7 6 5 4 3 2

ISBN 1-55704-612-3 (pb)

10 9 8 7 6 5 4 3 2 1

ISBN 1-55704-611-5 (hc)

Library of Congress Cataloging-in-Publication Data available upon request.

QUANTITY PURCHASES
Companies, professional groups, clubs, and other organizations may qualify for
special terms when ordering quantities of this title. For information, write Special
Sales Department, Newmarket Press, 18 East 48th Street, New York, NY 10017; call
(212) 832-3575; fax (212) 832-3629; or e-mail mailbox@newmarketpress.com.

www.newmarketpress.com

Manufactured in the United States of America.

CONTENTS

ACKNOWLEDGMENTS

Special thanks to: Allison Abner, Eli Attie, Aeden Babish, Patrick H. Caddell, Debora Cahn, Kevin Falls, Marlin Fitzwater, David Gerken, Laura Glasser, Mark Goffman, David Handelman, Stephen Hootstein, Frank Luntz, Dee Dee Myers, Melissa Myers, Peggy Noonan, Michael Oates Palmer, Paul Redford, Lauren Schmidt, Billy Sind, Gene Sperling, Felicia Willson, and Paula Yoo.

Additional thanks to: Dennis DeFrehn, Paula Hallin, Lauren Lohman, W.J. Rinier, and Stephen Scaia.

THE
WEST WING
SEASON THREE

SEASON THREE

Sid Caesar is making his way to a small stage in a banquet room at the Ritz-Carlton Hotel in Pasadena. The occasion is the annual Television Critics Association Awards and a few weeks ago when you heard Caesar was getting their Lifetime Achievement Award for his contribution to television, you took a moment to wonder, if the TV critics are just getting around to giving him the award this year, who the hell were they giving it to before?

Your Show of Shows, written by a team of unknowns with names like Mel Brooks, Carl Reiner, Neil Simon, Imogene Coca and Allen Stewart Konigsberg—a kid from Brooklyn who signed his checks Woody Allen—had been off the air for half a century and remained the gold standard. The only thing Caesar was better at than physical comedy was language. His characters, whether a world-renowned professor or a waiter in a snooty restaurant, frequently spoke rapid-fire languages of dubious origin and for years he'd ruled the airwaves like no one since.

You remember a story you once heard. During the height of *Your Show of Shows*, Caesar was shaving in his bathroom mirror when his seven-year-old daughter came in and took up a position in the doorway.

DAUGHTER

Dad, what's your name?

CAESAR

You know my name, sweetheart. It's Sidney.

DAUGHTER

Sidney Caesar.

<pre>
                    CAESAR
        Yeah.

                    DAUGHTER
            (pause)
        You're Sid Caesar?!
</pre>

But right now, as he makes his way to the stage in front of a banquet room full of people dressed in "festive business attire" as instructed on their invitations, Sid Caesar isn't looking like someone you want to be.

He's in very poor health. He needs an escort to help him to the podium and that's going to take a little while. You want to lean over to Tommy Schlamme, *The West Wing*'s principal director and your partner of three years and whisper, "I can't remember, has he had a stroke?" but you don't.

You think about whether it was hard for him to tie his necktie tonight and wonder how long it's been since he drove himself somewhere in a car and that he probably misses that.

You worry that this entertainer—for whom language was like a baseball coming to you from Satchel Paige—you worry that he probably can't get a clear sentence out of his mouth.

"Don't sweat it," you implore him telepathically, "all you have to do is make it to the podium and thank the TCA and then you'll get another standing ovation like the one you're getting now."

And now he's at the podium and his escort steps back out of the light and Caesar stands there silently for a long moment which has everyone a little tight until he raises his arms, opens his mouth and thanks the TCA.

In French.

But not really.

And you can't believe it, because he's thanking the TCA, with grand and precise gesticulation, as The Man Who Almost Speaks French.

You can't remember the last time you were with a group of people laughing this loud and this sincerely. He went on for a minute and a half (a lifetime on stage) and when he was done he started thanking the TCA all over again in Almost German.

Your table—Tommy and his wife Christine, Janel, Allison, Richard, Dulé, Martin, they've all completely lost control. You look a couple of tables over where Brad's sitting with his wife, Jane, and the guys from *Malcolm in the Middle* and Brad's looking back at you and holding an arm toward the stage—are you *seeing* this?—and just in case there was anyone left in the room who was feeling sorry for him 'cause he needed help walking to the stage or tying his tie, Caesar started all over again in Almost Italian.

And you're so happy that this summer hiatus is over. And that you still want to be Sid Caesar.

Later in the evening we accepted the TCA Award for Best Drama, we being Tommy, Co-Executive Producer Kevin Falls, Line Producer Lew Wells, myself and the entire principal cast save Rob Lowe.

"In the doldrums of summer re-runs and reality shows, a television critic needs something to write about," I said at the podium. "No need to thank us."

What had we given them to write about over the summer?

Well first there was the cast walking out.

The West Wing was a more expensive than usual show to make, and the pilot was the most expensive ever made.

Studios are mindful of the fact that the odds overwhelmingly say the pilot they're bankrolling isn't going to get picked up for series, so they want you to shoot as much as possible on existing sets like *ER*'s E.R. or the courtroom from *The Practice* or if you're *Third Watch* you shoot at any number of firehouses or if you're *The West Wing* you just go to the real White House and set up your cameras and shoot right in the—uh-oh.

Peter Roth is the President of Warner Bros. Television and a wise and gentle champion of our show. Peter green-lit the construction of the West Wing of the White House. (Part of it, the Oval Office set, Warner Bros. already owned, ironically, having a few years earlier purchased Castle Rock Entertainment, which made *The American President*, which I wrote. But even that needed some refurbishing as it was blown up in *Independence Day*. The rest would have to be designed and built from scratch.)

And Tommy wanted the best of the best at all the key positions and I wanted what Tommy wanted. (Tommy and I had begun our partnership a year earlier when he directed the pilot episode of *Sports*

Night, then at my urging—begging—came on as an Executive Producer. He would serve in the same capacity on *The West Wing* in its first four years—directing some of the series' most memorable episodes and being the overall field general for a team of 150 people.)

Tommy got Jon Hutman to design a White House you could walk through forever and see through for miles. Tom Del Ruth, Director of Photography on *Stand by Me* and *This Is Spinal Tap* came on board to light and shoot the show. Lyn Paolo, Emmy-winning, beautiful, brilliant and British would design the clothes and Lew Wells, younger brother of John, who'd been line producing features, came over to the dark side to line produce what we promised him was going to be a 41-minute feature every week.

And it wasn't like the cast was cheap. We weren't gonna find a lot of bargains in the group we wanted, all of them coveted by studios and networks and, moreover, writers and directors. But the cast was going to have to be where Warner Bros. made the budget work.

At the time, there were only five principal (main title) actors in the show: Allison Janney as C.J., Rob Lowe as Sam, Richard Schiff as Toby, John Spencer as Leo and Brad Whitford as Josh. Martin Sheen had only been signed to play a certain a number of episodes (a situation that would get renegotiated), Dulé Hill's Charlie wouldn't enter the show until the third episode and Janel Moloney's Donna wouldn't be paid as a regular until the second season.

So the five actors' contracts would have to be worked out, an area of the operation that, by design, neither Tommy nor I have anything at all do with. We're all employees of Warner Bros. and with the exception of our own assistants, we're not involved with payroll. In fact, until this second summer hiatus, when salaries were getting printed in the newspapers, I didn't know what anyone else was making on the show. It occurs to me at this writing that, in two years of *Sports Night* and four years of *The West Wing*, I still don't know what Tommy makes. Not enough.

Warner Bros. entered into a tough negotiation with the five actors. Deals were made with four of the five while Rob's representatives held firm. They reasoned that Rob was already taking a pay cut going from features to television, which was reasonable reasoning, but

Tommy and I were told to audition more actors for the role of Sam and so we did.

And found no one we liked as much as Rob or even close.

Tommy and I thought, well, maybe it'll be easier to find another actor we like as *Josh* and we called Brad Whitford, explained the situation and asked him if he'd play Sam. He said he wanted to do the show and he'd play Donna if we wanted but he wanted to play Josh.

And we wanted him to play Josh. And we wanted Rob to play Sam.

So we called John Wells and said you gotta get Warner Bros. to make Rob's deal. Look, we said, if the show doesn't go, it doesn't matter what they're paying him 'cause they're not gonna be paying it anymore, and if it works it works....

That night at Mr. Chow's, sometime before the arrival of the crispy, spicy beef, I got a call from John saying we bought you an actor and go to work.

It was 48 hours before the start of filming.

And now it was two years later and Allison, Richard, John and Brad had decided that the show had indeed worked and, looking around, there was certainly evidence to support that argument.

The show had finished 23rd at the end of its first season while the network was charging top-ten prices for ad buys due to what Madison Avenue was describing as the unusually upscale nature of its audience. It had won the Peabody Award and then broke the record for Emmy wins. By the end of the second season, it had won the Directors Guild Award, Producers Guild Award, Writers Guild Award and Screen Actors Guild Award and then became only the third series in history to win a second Peabody.

And the show was being praised for its ensemble. Nothing could have made Tommy and me happier. Ensemble was the religion we were asking for on the set. There was no star. Everyone passes, everyone shoots. Support each other and be good bench players.

(No one takes this more seriously than Martin, who's always been slightly embarrassed that because of his character's job title, he frequently gets singled out more than, say, John Spencer. On the other hand, no one gets happier for Martin's recognition than John Spencer. One morning toward the end of the first season, Tommy and I had to go to Martin's trailer to personally beseech him to submit himself for Emmy consideration in the Best Actor category rather than the Supporting Actor category, which we'd learned was his intention. Only after he was persuaded that he might be taking a spot away from one of the others did he change his submission.)

It was an acting company on television and it was the irreplaceable, indispensable centerpiece of whatever measure of success *The West Wing* was enjoying. So Brad, Allison, Richard and John decided to enter into a renegotiation and to do it as a team. The papers picked it up and we were off to the races.

A few days later there were four empty chairs at the voluntary table read of the season opener held a few days before the start of production.

The next morning we were nominated for 18 Emmy Awards, including Supporting Actor nominations for Allison, Richard, John and Brad. The actors had been instructed by their lawyer not to speak with anyone from the show so congratulations would wait.

And by now, Rob wasn't the happiest kid at the circus either, feeling that he'd spent the last few weeks being shown up by the other four in the press. (One problem at a time, I thought.)

Finally, on a Sunday, Brad called me in my room at the greatest hotel on earth, the Four Seasons Beverly Hills, where I'd been living the last six weeks after separating from the greatest wife on earth, entertainment lawyer Julia Bingham. (It was a happy time in my life, there was also back surgery.)

"We want to come over," Brad said, "the four of us."

They were there in about an hour and they walked me through their logic which was logical and said they understood there was really nothing I could do but was there anything I could do?

They were merciful enough not to ask me what I'm sure they wanted to ask me: Would I be willing to walk off the show if they did?

We talked for a few hours and I said I wanted to include Tommy in the conversation and we agreed to meet up again in my room that night.

Tommy came over, I ordered chicken wings from room service, we talked some more and I went into the bedroom and got Peter Roth on the phone at home.

ME

(into phone)

Good, thank you. Listen, Peter, Brad, Richard, John and Allison are up here along with Tommy. They called me this afternoon and asked if they could come over and we've now had two long conversations today which I know is news that isn't gonna make you happy.

PETER

It's an impossible situation.

Which Peter then made a possible situation. In the next few days—I really don't know how—all four actors got new deals that both they and the studio were happy with.

But that was the *third* story of the summer.

Just before the contract story, various outlets were picking up on a *New York Times* piece quoting several members of the show's writing staff expressing concerns over not being offered a raise at the end of the season. The *Times* story also added that, in accepting the Best Writing Emmy the year before, I'd failed to properly acknowledge a co-writer, and that the writer was understandably piqued.

But even those incidents combined wouldn't have registered as loud a media decibel level if only eight weeks earlier I hadn't been arrested at Burbank Airport on two counts of felony drug possession.

It was Sunday afternoon, April 15, and a thoroughly decent Burbank Police Officer said, "Everyone here really enjoys your work," as he lowered my head into a squad car.

I was booked by Taylor. Taylor the Jailer, though I didn't make that or any other joke since it was clearly Taylor who was gonna decide whether or not I had roommates.

I used my phone call to call Julia and got our answering machine. I talked Taylor into a second phone call and found my assistant, Lauren Carpenter—now Lauren Lohman—at the Staples Center watching a Laker game with her boyfriend—now husband—Eric. So I sat in the cell for a few hours, remembering how frustrated I was a few hours earlier when I looked up at an airport TV screen and saw that my Southwest flight to Las Vegas would be delayed 20 minutes.

Both Julia and Lauren showed up like superwomen with a bail

bondsman in tow, I posted a $1,000 bond against $10,000 bail and Julia drove us home.

After calling my father to tell him what happened, I called Tommy. Tommy, as always, was a friend before he was a partner so he waited until the end of the conversation to say this: "This is personal, this happened to you. I would tell John, but after that there's no reason anyone else needs to know."

Tommy's was a good plan but was not to be. Someone at the airport had picked up the red phone with a direct line to *Access Entertainment Inside Hollywood Scoop Tonight* so it looked like a couple of more people than Tommy had suggested were about to find out.

The next morning a hastily assembled meeting at my house with my agent, Ari Emanuel; my publicist, the long-suffering Tracy Shaffer; my two new friends, criminal lawyers Steve Sitkoff and Mike Nassiter; and Julia and myself produced a statement for the press but before that I had to call my bosses, NBC President Jeff Zucker, Warner Bros. Television President Peter Roth, and Peter's bosses Barry Meyer and Alan Horn, all of whom were more supportive than they ought to have been.

I got in my car and drove over to Stage 23 on the Warner Bros. lot where we were shooting a scene in the Oval Office where Bartlet imagines he's talking to his secretary, Mrs. Landingham, who'd been killed in a car accident two days before by a drunk driver, and asked Tommy to stop shooting after the next take and bring everyone in.

I told them I'd been arrested the night before for drug possession and that I was guilty. I apologized for embarrassing the show (the greatest assault on the religion of ensemble) and went back to my office where I had to peel Ari off of NBC because someone at the five o'clock taping of *The Tonight Show* about a half-mile down the road had just called to say that Jay had led off his monologue with the arrest.

Then came the gun-to-your-head interviews. "*US Weekly*'s doing a feature whether you talk to them or not and they say it'll be better if you go on the record." "*TV Guide* is gonna do it and they're saying it'll be better for you if you cooperate." (TV Guide?)

After being given a DEJ (Deferred Entry of Judgement) by the Judge and sentenced to 18 months probation, summer vacation was over.

Shooting had begun on our season opener, a two-parter called *Manchester*. I hadn't been entirely happy with it while I was writing but in series TV you don't have the luxury you have with a play or a screenplay. You can't stick it in a drawer and wait for your head to straighten out, you have to get it as good as you can get it in the time you've got. I wrote the next three episodes—*Ways and Means, On the Day Before, War Crimes*—feeling a little better about each one, or at least there was a moment in each one where I felt a little bit better, and then sat down with the staff to talk about Episode Six which, as Kevin Falls was eager to point out, would air on Halloween.

Kevin was Co-Executive Producer in charge of the writing staff on *Sports Night* and came over to *The West Wing* to take over that job after *Sports Night* ended. Kevin is instantly likable, a strong leader and a wonderful writer. To see him in action with our staff was to be reminded of Hoover, the president of the Deltas in *Animal House*.

And he'd wanted to do a Halloween show ever since *Sports Night*. I wasn't wild about the idea—paper cut-outs of ghosts and goblins at Margaret's desk?—but lacking any ideas of my own, I turned to Kevin and the staff and said what I usually say when I have nothing at all, "Okay, that's it for a while," and went back in my office to play with my Darren Dreifort baseball bat. Dee Dee Myers, former Press Secretary to President Clinton and a consultant on the show since its first season, called at Kevin's request.

"On Halloween," she told me, "the children of the reporters in the press corps can take their kids to the White House for trick-or-treating."

Well...okay.

Okay. Wait a second, okay, maybe there's a teaser at least. Maybe Bartlet had a comically Scrooge-like attitude toward Halloween and was giving these kids a hard time. If I could do that while introducing the actual story (which we hadn't thought of yet) it could be fun. I pieced a few things together and wrote a six-page teaser (the cold opening before the main titles). I passed it out to Kevin and Tommy and a few minutes later was told that it was funny.

Funny was good, *The West Wing* scripts always being at their best when approached as comedy and discovered as something more. Let the emotional hit stay hidden in the tall grass 'til the release in Act 4.

I went back to my room at The Four Seasons, ordered a cheeseburger, watched Sports Center and went to bed knowing tomorrow was going to be a good writing day.

And that was September 10th.

"We're being attacked, a plane just flew into the World Trade Center and they're saying—"

It was Julia and it was around 7:00. The cast/crew call wasn't until nine that morning because of the late shooting the night before so I was just sitting in bed with a glass of grapefruit juice and the sports section.

"Wait, wait, what do you mean a plane flew—"

I started rummaging through the sheets to find the spot where I'd dumped off the TV remote the night before.

"They're saying it isn't an accident, somebody's attacking us. I'm telling you, the plane, a passenger plane, a jet, just flew right into the—"

Giving up on the remote, I jumped up to the TV and hit the on/off button, then manually clicked it up 32 channels to CNN, for some reason not thinking that CBS, NBC, ABC and Fox would probably be carrying the story as well.

"Julia, you have to start at the beginning 'cause I can't understand what you're—"

I'm sure she knew from the sudden stop that I'd just seen it.

"Is Roxy all right?" Our ten-month-old daughter was playing on the bed, wondering why *Blue's Clues* wasn't on the TV anymore.

On the drive over to Julia's, I called Tommy.

"Do you know anyone in the buildings?" he asked.

"No," I said, "my brother's on Wall Street and my dad's at Rockefeller Plaza but I don't know anyone in the buildings."

I was wrong. My friend Laura from college who'd tell you she battled a weight problem but who was beautiful at any weight, who had the singing voice of Julie Andrews and who housed half the homeless animals in Manhattan in her one-bedroom in the West 80s, was between acting gigs and so went early to her temp job that morning at Windows on the World.

"Well, we should cancel shooting today," I said, stating the obvious to Tommy.

The next day at noon there was a prayer service on the Warner Bros. back lot for all employees. A few hundred actors, directors, writers, technicians, painters, builders, executives, secretaries, cafeteria workers and maintenance staff gathered at, purely coincidentally, a town square in middle America used in dozens of Warner Bros. movies and TV shows from *The Music Man* to *Gilmore Girls*. Everyone was there but the studio security staff, which had quadrupled itself in the last 24 hours. Studio heads Barry Meyer and Alan Horn spoke briefly and beautifully. The colors were presented. We sang *God Bless America*.

Back at the stage we'd set up a shuttle van to a nearby hospital, where the line to donate blood ran down the block.

Two days later I called Peter Roth.

> ME
>
> I want to postpone our premiere.

Premiere week for NBC was a week away but all the networks had already postponed a week. (Among the much lesser damages of 9-11 is that the TV networks lost huge sums of money. The news coverage was expensive to produce, there was no money coming in from commercials and there was no promotional platform in the final two weeks before premiering brand new shows that no one was yet familiar with.) I had called Peter because at our weekly producers' meeting—which in the last week had become a daily producers' meeting—it was the strong feeling of everyone around the table that it was too early to go on the air.

> PETER ROTH
>
> Well everyone's already postponed a week.

> ME
>
> I think we have to wait longer. Democrats and
> Republicans and the White House versus Congress and
> running for re-election...it's just all in bad taste right now.

> PETER ROTH
>
> Well, how long did you want to wait?

ME

I don't really know.

PETER ROTH

They're not gonna program re-runs.

ME

I don't think they should.

PETER ROTH

Well what do you think they should do?

ME

I don't know. *Dateline*?

No.

Peter, and then Jeff Zucker, voiced the argument that people were going to want diversion and heroes. I answered that while I thought people would soon welcome diversion, it was going to be hard to root for fake heroes when there were so many real ones to root for. Let's delay the start of our season.

Can't do it.

There was brief discussion of simply not delivering the final cut of *Manchester*, the season premiere, which was in various stages of the post-production process, but that didn't seem a very good way to treat either the network or the studio, partners who'd been good to us.

I went to an A.A. meeting on Ventura Blvd. and listened to a Chapter 5 reading alongside two strippers and a man who lives in a shrub.

Back at the hotel I turned on CNN and watched the images of people screaming and running for their lives, rescue workers shoving boulders and still-smoldering steel in a cold rain, parents and children, husbands and wives holding up snapshots of missing family members, Arab children cheering, Osama bin Laden looking beatific and President Bush with a bullhorn.

(I remembered when I finally found my brother, Noah, that day. After successfully prosecuting organized crime bosses for the Brooklyn District Attorney's office, Noah had taken a job as counsel to a Wall Street investment house. He's always had a distaste for drama and when I was able to get him on the phone he said, "Oh yeah, I'm fine. I'm fine." And then he burst out crying and said, "I can't describe what I saw." He didn't need to. I knew he'd seen people jumping out windows.)

Two weeks from now these images would be replaced by Josh and Donna flirting and Sam and Toby wisecracking and Leo and C.J. stampeding down a corridor and a fake President whose primary fear was that his failure to disclose his health would fatally damage his bid for a second term as fake President.

In a government of gridlock and bickering and interns, the fictional West Wing government was quixotic. But now the real guys were fighting a battle against an evil like we'd never seen up close, they were trying to protect us from a palpable day-to-day threat and moreover they were avenging the murder of 4,000 of our friends. Suddenly watching C.J. snipe with the press corps makes me not that crazy about C.J. anymore, and you've got to hit your head pretty hard to not be crazy about Allison Janney.

The attacks had profoundly affected everyone in the country except these characters, who suddenly were living in a world that no longer existed. They weren't one of us. The show's juice had always been wish fulfillment but now there was only one wish that we shared collectively as a nation and that was that 19 twisted cocksuckers had never woken up on September 11. And soon I'd be longing for the halcyon days of the Burbank Jail.

The next morning at seven I asked Lew Wells, Mike Hissrich (in charge of post production), Chris Misiano and Tommy to meet with me. I reiterated that I was extremely uncomfortable starting our season with the *Manchester* episode as if skyscrapers may fall but hit shows go on. But since we didn't have a choice but to go on, I wanted to delay *Manchester* a week and do a new show in its place. One with no fireworks, no running through the halls, no snappy one-liners, no flirting and no mention of politics. It would have no connection or relation to the rest of the series—*Manchester* began a moment after the Season II finale had ended and this episode would ignore that. It would be the show's version of bowing its head. It would never reference the World Trade Center or the Pentagon or Pennsylvania or airplanes, but we'll know something happened recently and everyone's been on edge. Terrorism's crowded out all other topics. We wouldn't run main titles or theme music.

Ordinarily, from the time I start writing a script to the time it goes on the air is about six weeks. We needed to do this in twelve days.

Yes, we'll do it was the answer.

I called the writing staff into the conference room and told them the new plan. The trick-or-treaters were gonna be high school kids now. They're getting a White House tour when there's a security lockdown which has been happening a lot lately. Stuck in the building, our characters would talk to the high school kids about the same things we were all talking about at the coffee machine and in our kitchens, they'd talk about terrorism. In our case, the history of terrorism.

"So," I asked them, "what's the history of terrorism?"

"Well...it's been around for a while."

That came from Eli Attie, who you'll hear more about later.

I called Jeff Zucker and told him the plan and he signed off on it. I asked that the show not be promoted as "very special" or really even promoted at all. We could point a camera at two of our actors and have them tell the audience we were delaying our season premiere for a week and substituting something else. We'd just give them the information. We'd pass on all publicity requests and it would be taken out of the re-run rotation.

I called John Wells.

"You're gonna get killed and you should absolutely do it."

John was right on both counts.

Here's *Isaac and Ishmael*.

The West Wing

Isaac and Ishmael

BLUE 2 REVISIONS:	10/11/01
WHITE 2 REVISIONS:	9/28/01
CHERRY REVISIONS:	9/28/01
SALMON REVISIONS:	9/28/01
BUFF REVISIONS:	9/27/01
GREEN REVISIONS:	9/26/01
YELLOW REVISIONS:	9/26/01

THE WEST WING

"Isaac and Ishmael"

Written by
Aaron Sorkin

Directed by
Christopher Misiano

PRODUCTION #227 206
Episode Six

JOHN WELLS PRODUCTIONS
in association with
WARNER BROS. TELEVISION
4000 Warner Blvd.
Burbank, CA 91522

Final Shooting Draft (PINK)
September 22, 2001
Copyright © 2001
Warner Bros Television
All Rights Reserved

THE WEST WING

"Isaac and Ishmael"

Script Revision History

DATE	COLOR	PAGES
9/21/01	BLUE PAGES	1,3,11,12,13,13A,14,14A, 15,20,29,32
9/22/01	FULL PINK	1-47
9/26/01	YELLOW PAGES	29,33,33A
9/26/01	GREEN PAGES	12,13,14,15
9/27/01	BUFF PAGES	1
9/28/01	SALMON PAGES	10,10A,10B,11
9/28/01	CHERRY PAGES	14,15,45,45A
9/28/01	WHITE 2 PAGES	9,10,10A,10B
10/11/01	BLUE 2 PAGES	TITLE PAGE

SET LIST

INTERIORS

EXTERIORS

FBI FIELD OFFICE/COMPUTER
    ROOM

WHITE HOUSE
    Josh's Office
    Josh's Bullpen
    Lobby
    Mess
    Leo's Outer Office
    Leo's Office
    Ali's Bullpen Area

OEOB/FILE ROOM

THE WEST WING
"Isaac and Ishmael"
CAST LIST

PRESIDENT JOSIAH BARTLET
LEO McGARRY
JOSH LYMAN
SAM SEABORN
TOBY ZIEGLER
C.J. CREGG
CHARLIE YOUNG
DONNA MOSS
ABIGAIL BARTLET

RON BUTTERFIELD

AGENT
JOAN
ADULT (Marjorie Mann)
SECRET SERVICE AGENT
AGENT #1
AGENT #2
GIRL #1
BOY #1
GIRL #2
BOY #2
GIRL #3
BOY #3
BOY #4
GIRL #4
RAQIM ALI
CLEARY
FBI AGENT

Isaac and Ishmael

<u>INTRODUCTION</u>

MARTIN

Good evening, I'm Martin Sheen and I'm
with the cast of The West Wing. For those
of you who tuned in tonight to see our
season premiere, you won't. That'll be
next week.

ROB

We're eager to get back to our continuing
story lines, but tonight we wanted to
stop for a moment and do something
different.

ALLISON

You'll notice a few things different
about the show tonight. For instance, in
place of our usual main title sequence,
we'll be putting phone numbers up on the
screen where you can pledge donations to
groups that are able to help with
victims' assistance.

JOHN

By now, nobody needs to be convinced that
when they named New York's Finest and New
York's Bravest, they knew what they were
talking about. That's why we're pleased
to tell you that the profits from
tonight's episode will be donated to the
New York Firefighters 911 Disaster Relief
Fund and the New York Police and Fire
Widows' and Children's Benefit Fund.

DULE

A helping hand from our family to theirs.

BRAD

Now don't panic, we're in show business
and we'll get back to tending our egos in
short order, but tonight we offer a play.
It's called *Isaac and Ishmael*. We suggest
you don't spend a lot of time trying to
figure out where this episode comes in
the timeline of the series. It doesn't.
It's a storytelling aberration, if you'll
allow.

                    RICHARD
Next week we'll start our third season.
That's when you'll see stories about a re-
election campaign, an MS disclosure, an
embassy in Haiti--

                    STOCKARD
Repealing the estate tax--

                    ROB
A fight against Big Tobacco--

                    DULE
A fight to get our friends back--

                    JOHN
Funding the NEA--

                    ALLISON
A veto override--

                    STOCKARD
A marriage in trouble--

                    JANEL
And I get a boyfriend.

                    MARTIN
That's all for us. Thank you for
listening. And may God bless the United
States of America.

                    END OF INTRODUCTION

Isaac and Ishmael

<u>TEASER</u>

FADE IN:

1   **INT. COMPUTER ROOM - DAY**   1

Several technicians are sitting at computer monitors going
through routine work.

TITLE:

                    FBI Field Office
                    Burlington, VT

After a moment, an agent comes through the door and up to one
particular technician.

                    AGENT
          Joan, run a search in the NICK. Yaarun
          Nabi. Y-A-A-R-U-N N-A-B-I.

The technician, JOAN, starts feeding it in. While she's doing
this--

                    JOAN
          Yaarun Nabi is a Persian name.

                    AGENT
          Yeah?

                    JOAN
          It means friend of the prophet.

                    AGENT
          You getting anything?

                    JOAN
          Four AKAs. Yaquin Kashani, Raqim Ali,
          Yamin Bandari and Yawar Aryanpur.

                    AGENT
          Run 'em.

While she's doing that--

                    JOAN
          I wonder if they all mean friend of the
          prophet. I guess that would be silly. Or
          at least remarkably coincidental.
                    (MORE)

                                        (CONTINUED)

4.

1   CONTINUED: 1

                         JOAN (cont'd)
              That the aliases would mean the same
              thing as the actual name. I mean you
              gotta ask what good would an alias be if--

And then she sees something on the screen--it's horrifying and
it takes a moment to sink in--

                         JOAN
                    (to the AGENT)
              Greg.

She points to the screen. The AGENT looks at it for a moment
then grabs a phone and punches two numbers.

                         AGENT
                    (into phone)
              Get me the Secret Service Joint
              Operations Center at the White House.

                                                         CUT TO:

2   **INT. JOSH'S OFFICE/BULLPEN - DAY**   2

JOSH is packing up his knapsack with work--

                         JOSH
              Donna.

DONNA comes in--

                         DONNA
              Yeah.

                         JOSH
              I'm going home.

                         DONNA
              It's only five.

                         JOSH
              Yeah, I'm heading home.

                         DONNA
              You can't go yet, you have to talk to the
              students.

                         JOSH
              What students?

                         DONNA
              From Presidential Classroom.

                                                      (CONTINUED)

>   JOSH
> What are you talking about?

>   DONNA
> They're high school kids from across the
> country who are accepted for, I don't
> know they come to Washington for four
> days and they get to meet with
> interesting people and you're one of
> them.

>   JOSH
> What did--when did this get on my
> schedule?

>   DONNA
> It's been there.

>   JOSH
> No it hasn't, it just--there isn't
> anybody else who can do this?

>   DONNA
> It's supposed to be you.

>   JOSH
> I have to work.

>   DONNA
> You can work in the office.

>   JOSH
> No, I can't work in the office. We've
> crashed five times in three weeks. When
> I'm not being evacuated from the building
> I'm not being allowed to <u>leave</u> the
> building and now the one night, *God,
> Donna, I wanna go home*!

>   DONNA
>   (pause)
> Josh, it was on your schedule.

>   JOSH
>   (beat--calmer)
> All right. I'll give 'em a few minutes
> and then I've gotta go, okay?

>   DONNA
> Yeah.

(CONTINUED)

2   CONTINUED: (2)   2

                         JOSH
              When am I supposed to do this?

                         DONNA
              Now.

                         JOSH
              Where are they?

                         DONNA
              They're right in the Northwest Lobby.

DONNA follows JOSH as he walks out into--

3   **INT. LOBBY - CONTINUOUS**   3

Maybe 30 high school students with a few adult chaperones are
waiting in a group in the lobby. They're all dressed in blue
blazers and khaki pants.

                         JOSH
              Good evening, good to see you. You're
              the group from Presidential...Something?

                         DONNA
              Classroom.

                         JOSH
              Classroom?

                         ADULT
              I'm their supervisor, Marjorie Mann.

                         JOSH
              Josh Lyman.

                         ADULT
              Thank you for taking the time.

                         JOSH
              How'd you all get here?

                         STUDENTS
              Bus/We took the bus/By bus.

                         JOSH
                   (pause)
              I meant--

(CONTINUED)

3   CONTINUED:

> ADULT
> They qualify with essays,
> recommendations, grades in history and
> government, it's very competitive.
>
> JOSH
> Well all right. I'm Josh Lyman, I'm the
> Deputy White House Chief of Staff. I
> joined the Bartlet campaign shortly
> before the Iowa caucus and served as the
> campaign's political director. Before
> that I worked for then <u>Senator</u> John
> Hoynes, for a while as his floor manager,
> and I'll explain what that means, but
> before that--
>
> DONNA
> Josh.
>
> JOSH
> Yeah.

JOSH sees that DONNA's looking at the phones on the security
desk. All the lights are blinking red and a special red light
is blinking.

A uniformed Secret Service Agent hurries back to the desk,
picks up the phone and punches two numbers--

> SECRET SERVICE AGENT
> (into phone)
> Station 1, Code Black. Crash.

JOSH shakes his head slightly...then--

> JOSH
> All right. Sorry. Listen. Something's
> about to happen. Don't let it frighten
> you. They need to seal the building.

And now SECRET SERVICE begin filling the lobby--

> AGENT #1
> Stay where you are please.
>
> AGENT #2
> Everybody please stay where you
> are.
>
> SECRET SERVICE AGENT
> Mr. Lyman, are these kids with you?

(CONTINUED)

3   CONTINUED: (2)   3

                          JOSH
               I--yeah, I guess they are.

And JOSH watches as the room fills with security and agents take positions at the doors and talk into radios and code this and eagle that and secure the other thing and he turns to the group of students and says...

                          JOSH
            Something's happened.

                                        FADE OUT:

END OF TEASER

ACT ONE

FADE IN:

4   **INT. MESS - DAY**   4

The students are being filed into the mess.

>   DONNA
>   Right in here. Just grab a seat anywhere.
>   Right in here. This is the mess. This is
>   where we eat lunch. We'll just wait here.

>   JOSH
>   What's going on?

>   DONNA
>   How should I know?

>   JOSH
>   Would you call Leo's office, find out
>   what's going on and more important how
>   long it's gonna be going on for?

>   DONNA
>   They're probably scared, you might try
>   lightening up a little bit.

>   JOSH
>   Yeah, I'll definitely give that a try.

JOSH joins the STUDENTS as they take seats around the room.

>   JOSH
>   Okay, well this is called a crash. It
>   means there's been some kind of security
>   breach and no one's allowed in or out of
>   the building.
>   (to DONNA)
>   Would you call Leo's office?

DONNA heads to a phone in the corner.

>   JOSH
>   So I guess we should use this time. This
>   is the White House. Home of the President
>   and the Executive Branch, the most
>   powerful of the three branches of the
>   Federal Government.

(CONTINUED)

BOY #1 raises his hand.

                    JOSH
          Yeah.

                    BOY #1
          Actually, Mr. Lyman, isn't it true that
          the Framers made sure that the Executive
          Branch was the weakest of the three
          branches because we were breaking off
          from the Royalist model that put absolute
          power in one place? I mean isn't that why
          they made the Legislative Branch or
          People's Branch the most powerful?

                    JOSH
               (pause)
          What's your name?

                    BOY #1
          I'm Billy Fernandez.

                    JOSH
          Okay, I'll call you Fred. A little
          knowledge can be a dangerous thing. I
          don't know how long you're gonna be here,
          but you just made my list.
               (to the group)
          Yes, I suppose technically,
          Constitutionally, the Legislative Branch
          is the most powerful. But we get a
          motorcade, so back off.
               (beat)
          All right you already know about the
          branches of Government and I assume you
          know how a bill becomes a law, what do
          you wanna talk about?
               (beat)
          I'm stuck here, I can't go anywhere, you
          can ask me anything.
               (beat)
          Guys, seriously, it's nothing to worry
          about, we've been having these crashes
          once a week. We can talk about anything
          you want. The Strategic Petroleum
          Reserve? Oooooh, SPR anybody?
               (beat)
          Let's go, somebody ask me something.

There's an excruciatingly long pause before--

                                                        (CONTINUED)

4   CONTINUED: (2)   4

                    GIRL #2
          So what's the deal with everybody trying
          to kill you?

                    JOSH
               (pause)
          Well it's not everybody...and they're
          trying to kill you too.

                    GIRL #2
          But mostly you.

                    JOSH
          No both of us the same. Let's go, it
          doesn't have to be about politics. You're
          off to college, I'm the guy who knows
          what you need to know. Sophomore year my
          roommates and I got a fish registered for
          18 credits and she made the Dean's List.
          My roommates and I made a Dean's List of
          a different sort but that doesn't matter.

                    BOY #2
          Do you get scared coming to work at the
          White House?

                    JOSH
          Do we get--no. Like I said, I mean...it's
          not really cool to talk about it 'cause
          we're just, I mean, we're bystanders
          basically and we work around a lot of
          people who routinely put themselves in
          harm's way. The Secret Service and
          military. You know on the protection
          detail they practice a thousand different
          scenarios for a gun. Who tackles the
          President, who opens the car, who's
          covering the perimeter and there's one
          guy whose job it is to stand in front of
          the bullets. Not get the shooter. Stand
          in front of the bullets. I've seen them
          do it.

                    GIRL #2
          Do you ever think about quitting?

                                              (CONTINUED)

4   CONTINUED: (3)   4

                         JOSH
          Nah, well my mother wants me to. My
          family members have a habit of dying
          before you're supposed to and it's just
          me and my mom now and you guys know I
          guess I got accidentally shot a little
          bit in Rosslyn or something and...she'd
          like to see me in the private sector but
          I tell her that my Government salary may
          not be a lot but I still get paid more
          than the guy whose job it is to stand in
          front of the bullets so how do I tell <u>him</u>
          I'm quitting?
               (beat)
          So she made this box that I'm supposed to
          keep in the trunk of my car. It's got a
          super-powered flashlight and five gallons
          of water and a transistor radio and some
          first aid. But she keeps thinking of
          things to add to it every week. She'll
          call and say, "I ran across that Yankees
          cap that Dad got Joe Peppitone to sign
          for you on your birthday. You wore it to
          school every day in seventh grade. Do you
          want me to send it to you so you can put
          it in the box?"

JOSH turns around and faces away...not dramatically or
anything...but in the middle of telling a funny nothing story
he realizes he was about to cry...he's just casually looking
at whatever might be on the other side of the room...the kids
know what's going on and the moment is awkward...DONNA watches
but doesn't interfere...

JOSH turns back...

                         JOSH
          So, I say, "Yeah, Mom, let's put it in
          the box."
               (beat)
          So, anyway, I don't know against who and
          I don't know what it's gonna look like,
          but one of these days we're gonna have a
          big win. And for a lot of us who've seen
          what we've seen, we're not leaving till
          we do. I'm still gonna be here six
          Presidents from now in my office, Wile E.
          Coyote and a map.

                         GIRL #3
               (pause)
          So why <u>is</u> everybody trying to kill us.

                                              (CONTINUED)

4   CONTINUED: (4)

> JOSH
> It's not everybody.

> GIRL #3
> It seems like everybody.

> BOY #3
> It's just the Arabs.

> BOY #2
> Saying the Arabs is too general.

> BOY #3
> It's Islamics.

> JOSH
>   (pause)
> Okay, wait, wait, wait. This is crucial,
> this is more important than the fish
> thing. It's not Arabs and Islamics. Don't
> leave this room without knowing this.
> It's not Arabs. It's not Islamics.
>   (to DONNA)
> They're juniors and seniors?

> DONNA
> Yes.

As JOSH speaks, he goes to a magic marker board on an easel
and wipes off today's lunch specials.

> JOSH
> You're juniors and seniors. In honor of
> the SATs you're about to take, answer the
> following question: Islamic Extremist is
> to Islamic as "blank" is to Christianity.
> Islamic Extremist is to Islamic as
> "blank" is to Christianity.

> BOY #3
> Christian Fundamentalists.

> JOSH
> No.

> BOY #4
> Jehovah's Witnesses?

(CONTINUED)

4   CONTINUED: (5)   4

                         JOSH
          No. Guys. The Christian Right may not be
          your cup of tea but they don't blow
          things up. Islamic Extremist is to
          Islamic as "blank" is to Christianity.

And then JOSH writes the answer on the board: KKK.

                         JOSH
          That's what we're talking about. It's the
          Klan. Gone medieval and global. It
          couldn't have less to do with Islamic men
          of faith, of whom there are millions upon
          millions. Muslims defend this country in
          the Army, Navy, Air Force, Marine Corps,
          National Guard and Police and Fire
          Departments.
               (to GIRL #2)
          So let's ask the question again.

                         GIRL #2
          Why are Islamic Extremists fighting with
          us?

                         JOSH
          That's a reasonable question if ever I
          heard one. Why are we targets of war?

                         BOY #3
          Because we're Americans.

                         JOSH
          That's it?

                         GIRL #4
          It's our freedom?

                         JOSH
          No other reasons?

                         BOY #4
          Freedom and Democracy.

                         JOSH
          I'll tell you, right or wrong, and I
          think they're wrong, it's probably a good
          idea to acknowledge that they do have
          specific complaints, I hear 'em every
          day. Troops in Saudi Arabia, sanctions
          against Iraq, support for Egypt, it's not
          just that they don't like Irving Berlin.

                                          (CONTINUED)

4   CONTINUED: (6)   4

                         DONNA
          Yes it is.

                         JOSH
          No it's not.

                         DONNA
          I don't know about Irving Berlin, but
          your ridiculous search for rational
          reasons why somebody straps a bomb to
          their chest is ridiculous.

                         JOSH
          You just called me ridiculous twice in
          one sentence.

                         DONNA
          That's hardly a record for me.

                         JOSH
          And you just made my list.

                         DONNA
               (to the STUDENTS)
          Nothing happens on the list.

                         JOSH
          It's a serious list, but she does have a
          point, albeit college girlish.

                         DONNA
          Watch now as he's going to put me down
          and make my point at the exact same time.

                         JOSH
          Hardly a record for me. What's Islamic
          Extremism. It's strict adherence to a
          particular interpretation of 7th Century
          Islamic law as practiced by the prophet
          Muhammad. When I say strict adherence,
          I'm not kidding around. Men are forced to
          pray, grow their beards a certain length.
          Among my favorites is that there's only
          one acceptable cheer at a soccer match.
          It's Allah-u-Akbar, God is great. If your
          guys are getting creamed then you're on
          your own. Things are a lot less comic for
          women, who aren't allowed to attend
          school or have jobs. They're not allowed
          to be unaccompanied and oftentimes get
          publicly stoned to death for crimes like
          not wearing a veil.
                         (MORE)

                                                       (CONTINUED)

4   CONTINUED: (7)   4

                              JOSH (cont'd)
        I don't have to tell you they don't need
        to shout at a soccer match, they're never
        gonna go to one. So what bothers them
        about us? Well the variety of cheers
        alone coming from the cheap seats at
        Giants Stadium when they're playing the
        Cowboys is enough for a jihad. To say
        nothing of street corners lined church
        next to synagogue next to mosque,
        newspapers that can print anything they
        want and women who <u>do</u> anything they want,
        including taking a rocket ship to outer
        space, vote and <u>play</u> soccer.
              (beat)
        This is a plural society, that means we
        accept more than one idea. It offends
        them. So yes, she has a point, but that
        certainly doesn't mean you should listen
        to her.

                              GIRL #4
              (pause)
        So what do we do now?

                              JOSH
        What?

                              GIRL #4
        What do we do now?

                              JOSH
              (beat)
        Well... I think for help with that
        question we're gonna need some people
        smarter than I am.

                              DONNA
        Yes.

                              JOSH
        The thing is, that's pretty tough to
        find. But I'm gonna go upstairs and see
        if I can get some of my friends to come
        down and join us. Listen, I don't know
        what's going on or how long we're gonna
        be here. Are you guys hungry? Freddy why
        don't you grab a couple of people and go
        to the back of the kitchen and get apples
        and peanut butter. Guys, I've gotten
        entire pieces of legislation through
        Congress on apples and peanut butter.
        I'll be back in a little bit.

                                                          (CONTINUED)

4   CONTINUED: (8)   4

JOSH heads out. As he passes DONNA at the door--

                    DONNA
          How you doin'?

And JOSH smiles at her as he exits.

                                                        CUT TO:

5   **INT. OEOB/FILE ROOM - DAY**   5

The room is dark and nondescript. A YOUNG MAN sits on a carton
near an open window and blows cigarette smoke out. He takes
another drag, blows the smoke out the window.

Title:
                          5:22 pm
                Old Executive Office Building

After a moment, he suddenly hears the sound of someone trying
the knob on the other side of the locked door.

Then silence.

Then BAM! The door's kicked open and seven SECRET SERVICE
AGENTS, including BUTTERFIELD, rush into the room with their
guns drawn.

                    AGENTS
          Secret Service, don't move/Put your hands
          in the air/FBI, step away from the
          window/etc.

The YOUNG MAN is terrified and shaking--

                    BUTTERFIELD
          Are you Raqim Ali?

                    ALI
          Yes, there's--what.

                    BUTTERFIELD
          Stay calm. I'm Special Agent Ron
          Butterfield of the United States Secret
          Service. Keep your hands in the air and
          step away from the window, we're gonna
          ask you some questions.

                                              FADE TO BLACK

                    END OF ACT ONE

ACT TWO

FADE IN:

6   **INT. LEO'S OUTER OFFICE - DAY**   6

BUTTERFIELD waits. LEO comes in and BUTTERFIELD follows him into--

7   **INT. LEO'S OFFICE - CONTINUOUS**   7

LEO closes the door and--

> BUTTERFIELD
> Five hours ago Khuram Sharif was taken into custody while crossing from Ontario into Vermont. There was a warrant for his arrest in connection with an attempted bombing at La Guardia. Turning state's evidence over to the U.S. Attorney, he named several coconspirators, one of whom is Yaarun Nabi. A preliminary check in the NCIC kicked out five aliases, one of which is Raqim Ali. There are three Raqim Ali's. One's a software designer in Spokane. Another's a caterer in Los Angeles.

> LEO
> Who's the third.

> BUTTERFIELD
> He works in the White House.

And LEO's chilled by this...he rubs his eyes...

> LEO
> It was only a matter of time, huh?

BUTTERFIELD doesn't say anything...

> LEO
> I want to sit in on his questioning.

> BUTTERFIELD
> Yeah.

They exit and we

                                                          CUT TO:

8 **INT. FILE ROOM - EVENING**   8

The young man, RAQIM ALI, is sitting in a chair surrounded by
FBI and SECRET SERVICE AGENTS. An FBI Agent, CLEARY, is doing
the questioning.

                         CLEARY
Have you ever heard of Khuram Sharif.

                         ALI
Yes. He was arrested in connection with
an attempted bombing of...uhm... one of
the New York airports. I think he may
have also been arrested once in Paterson,
New Jersey.

                         CLEARY
Paterson mean something to you?

                         ALI
I was born there.

                         CLEARY
Where did you go to school?

                         ALI
The Massachusetts Institute of
Technology. I have a Bachelor's Degree in
Applied Mathematics.

The door opens and LEO and BUTTERFIELD walk in. CLEARY
suspends his questions. ALI's looking at LEO.

                         LEO
                       (pause)
You know who I am?

                         ALI
                       (beat)
Of course I know who you are.

LEO pulls a chair up. Sits. And nods to CLEARY to continue.

                         CLEARY
Let's go over your employment history for
the six months prior to last April 2nd.

                         ALI
I was a staff assistant at the Institute
for Middle East Policy.

                                        (CONTINUED)

8   CONTINUED: 8

                         CLEARY
            For six months?

                         ALI
            For about ten months.

                         BUTTERFIELD
            Excuse me, what were you doing in this
            room? Your office is downstairs and on
            the other side of the building.

                         ALI
            I was smoking a cigarette.

                         CLEARY
            Can you tell us your whereabouts on April
            2nd of last year?

ALI stops for a moment...LEO's eyes are burning a hole in the
side of his head...he finally turns to LEO--

                         ALI
            Why are you looking at me?

LEO says nothing.

                                                    CUT TO:

9   **INT. MESS - NIGHT**   9

TOBY's sitting in a chair, eating an apple.

                         GIRL #1
            Okay, so I've got a question and this is
            totally un-PC.

                         JOSH
            So are we, so--

                         GIRL #1
            Isn't it time to just go in and wipe out
            the place? There's never gonna be peace
            in the Middle East, instability <u>anywhere</u>
            in the world is bad for us. Doesn't there
            come a time when you just go in and--

                         TOBY
            Kill 'em all, yeah.

                         BOY #3
                 (beat)
            All the Islamic Extremists?

                                             (CONTINUED)

9   CONTINUED:

                        TOBY
No, no, I mean everyone. You're all
bothering me. I want to be left alone and
clearly the only way that's gonna happen
is to <u>be</u> alone. So I'm sorry, but I'm
gonna have to let you all go.
        (pause)
Except the Yankees and the Knicks.
        (beat)
And the Yankees and the Knicks are gonna
need someone to play, so keep the Red Sox
and the Lakers.
        (beat)
And the Laker Girls.
        (beat)
And The Palm. And we'll need to keep the
people who work at The Palm. That's it
though. The Yankees, the Red Sox, the
Knicks, the Lakers, the Laker Girls and
anyone who works at The Palm. Sports,
Laker Girls and well prepared steak,
that's all I need.
        (beat)
Sometimes I like to mix it up with
Italian.
        (beat)
And Chinese, all right you can all stay,
but don't bug me. You're on probation,
don't forget that I was this close to
banishing you.

                        JOSH
        (pause)
This is Toby Ziegler. And, actually, he's
in charge of crafting our message to the
public.

                        TOBY
        (to BOY #2)
And today that message is?

                        BOY #2
        (pause)
Don't bug me?

                        TOBY
That's right.

                        GIRL #2
Nice beard.

                                (CONTINUED)

> TOBY
> My choice, sister. By the way, there's
> nothing wrong with a religion whose laws
> say a man's gotta wear a beard or cover
> his head or wear a color...It's when
> violation of these laws becomes a crime
> against the State and not your parents
> that we're talking about lack of choice.

TOBY looks over at the lunch board...

> TOBY
> Islamic Extremist is to Islamic as KKK is
> to Christianity. That's about right,
> that's a good religious analogy, but
> what's a political analogy, what's an
> analogy using governments?

> BOY #4
> They don't have a government.

> BOY #2
> They have the Taliban, they have the
> government of Afghanistan.

> TOBY
> The Taliban isn't the recognized
> government of Afghanistan, the Taliban
> took <u>over</u> the recognized government of
> Afghanistan and there's your political
> analogy.

> GIRL #2
> What do you mean?

> TOBY
> When you think of Afghanistan, think of
> Poland. When you think of the Taliban,
> think of the Nazis. When you think of the
> citizens of Afghanistan, think of Jews in
> concentration camps.

He lets it sink in...

> TOBY
> A friend of my dad's was at one of the
> camps. He used to come over to the house
> and he and my dad would shoot some
> pinochle. He said he once saw a guy at
> the camp kneeling and praying. He said,
> "What are you doing?" The guy said he was
> thanking God.
>   (MORE)

(CONTINUED)

9   CONTINUED: (3)

                    TOBY (cont'd)
My dad's friend said, "What could you
possibly be thanking God for?" He said,
"I'm thanking God for not making me like
them." Bad people can't be recognized on
sight, there's no point in trying.

                    JOSH
Actually we already covered that.

                    TOBY
It's worth covering twice, don't you
agree?

                    JOSH
I do.

                    TOBY
Yeah, I changed my mind again, kill 'em
all.

                    JOSH
Laker girls.

                    TOBY
No, all right.

                    GIRL #4
So come on, we're all smart, we need a
solution.

                    JOSH
No, we need more information. I'm a freak
for information. I move slowly. I move
deliberately. Sometimes even not at all.

                    DONNA
I was about to say.

                    JOSH
Have I fired you yet today?

                    DONNA
Couple a times.
    (to the STUDENTS)
It didn't take.

                    BOY #3
What was the first act of terrorism?

                    TOBY
    (to JOSH)
What was the first act of terrorism.

                                    (CONTINUED)

9   CONTINUED: (4)   9

> JOSH
> I could answer, but I think he was asking
> you, man.

> TOBY
> I know it's not new. I know in the 11th
> Century--I'm gonna have trouble
> pronouncing this--in the 11th Century,
> secret followers of al-Hasan ibn-al-
> Sabbah, who were taught to "believe in
> nothing and dare all," carried out these
> very swift and very treacherous murders
> of fellow Muslims and they did it in a
> state of religious ecstacy.

SAM wanders in as TOBY speaks.

> TOBY
> As a matter of fact, young men between 12
> and 20 were given hashish and smuggled
> into...I don't really know what to call
> it, they were smuggled into a kind of
> specially designed pleasure garden
> complete with concubines. They were told
> that this was paradise and that the
> Master's angels would carry them back if
> they carried out murders of the Master's
> enemies.

> SAM
>   (to the GIRLS)
> Ahhhhhh, temptation I have named thee and
> thy name is Woman.
>   (then to the ADULTS in back)
> I'm okay.

> JOSH
> This is Sam Seaborn, Deputy
> Communications Director. Now don't be
> frightened by what I'm gonna tell you
> now, but in this room, Sam is the
> knowledgable terrorism expert. The good
> news is that in this Government we have
> some extremely knowledgable terrorism
> experts...

> SAM
> I heard I was needed. I came.

> TOBY
> We're talking about al--am I pronouncing
> this right--al-Hasan ibn-al-Sabbah?

                                            (CONTINUED)

                              SAM
                    Yeah, from the 11th Century. By the way,
                    the Arabic name for their secret order
                    has survived until today, can anybody
                    guess what it was? The Arabic name?
                         (to BOY #1)
                    You know, I can see it in your face.
                    C'mon, guess.

                              BOY #1
                    Assassins.

                              SAM
                    Assassins, that's right.

                              JOSH
                    Yeah, we don't call on him.

                              TOBY
                    Do you know what's going on?

                              SAM
                    The crash?

                              TOBY
                    Yeah.

                              SAM
                    No.

                              GIRL #4
                    You know a lot about terrorism?

                              SAM
                    I dabble.

                              GIRL #4
                    What are you struck by most?

                              SAM
                    Its 100% failure rate.

                              BOY #4
                    Really?

                              SAM
                    Not only do terrorists always fail at
                    what they're after, they pretty much
                    always succeed in strengthening whatever
                    it is they're against.

                                                    (CONTINUED)

9   CONTINUED: (6)

                          JOSH
          Talk about the Russian group.

                          SAM
          1881, a group called *The People's Will*
          sought constitutional reforms in Russia
          so they killed Czar Alexander II with a
          home-made bomb. The result was an end to
          constitutional reforms in Russia to say
          nothing of 40 years of crackdowns against
          groups like *The People's Will*.

                          BOY #3
          What about the IRA?

                          SAM
          The Brits are still there, Protestants
          are still there, Basque extremists have
          been staging terrorist attacks in Spain
          for decades with no result, left wing Red
          Brigades from the '60s and '70s from
          Baader-Meinhof Gang in Germany to the
          Weathermen in the U.S. have tried to
          overthrow capitalism, you tell me, how's
          capitalism doing?

                          BOY #4
          What about non-violent protest?

                          SAM
          What about it?

                          BOY #4
          Well it worked for Gandhi.

                          SAM
          Yes it did, who else did it work for?

                          BOY #3
          The Civil Rights movement?

                          SAM
          That's right.

                          GIRL #4
          Yeah, but weren't we terrorists at the
          Boston Tea Party?

                                                    (CONTINUED)

9   CONTINUED: (7)   9

                         SAM
          Nobody got hurt at the Boston Tea Party.
          Only people who got hurt were some fancy-
          boys didn't have anything to wash down
          their crumpets with. We jumped out from
          behind bushes while the British came down
          the road in bright red jackets, but never
          has a war been so courteously declared.
          It was on parchment with calligraphy and
          "Your Highness, we beseech on this day in
          Philadelphia to bite me if you please."

                         GIRL #2
          Can I go back to what you said at the
          beginning?

                         SAM
          Yeah.

                         GIRL #2
          About it being a hundred percent
          ineffective?

                         SAM
          Yeah.

                         GIRL #2
          They keep doing it anyway.

                         SAM
          Yeah.

                         GIRL #2
          They're not frustrated by the failure.

                         SAM
          No.

                         GIRL #2
          Well what do you call a society that has
          to just live every day with the idea that
          the pizza place you're eating in can just
          blow up with no warning?

                         SAM
          Israel.

                                                        CUT TO:

10   **INT. FILE ROOM - NIGHT**   10

     The interrogation continues.

                                                     (CONTINUED)

10   CONTINUED:

                  CLEARY
Can you tell us about the wire in your
backpack?

                  ALI
It's for my computer. My apartment is in
an older building and I needed the older
telephone wires so I could upgrade the
M-Wave on the motherboard.

                  LEO
You're an expert in circuitry and wiring?

                  ALI
My father works for the phone company.

                  LEO
I want to talk about the Applied
Mathematics degree.

                  ALI
Yeah.

                  LEO
What are you doing working for a White
House Staff Secretary.

                  ALI
I--What do you mean?

                  LEO
We don't do a lot of math around here.

                  ALI
My interests shifted, I became interested
in policy.

                  LEO
You're aware that the intelligence
agencies routinely recruit top
mathematicians, oftentimes out of MIT,
and train them to be cryptographers?

                  ALI
Sure.

                  LEO
And those cryptographers are the ones
who, on a daily basis, code and decode
messages sent between the White House,
the State Department and the Pentagon?

                  (CONTINUED)

                        ALI
Yes.

                        LEO
Last year your father made a contribution
to something called the Holy Land
Defenders, were you aware of the
contribution?

                        ALI
        (pause)
Mr. McGarry, I understand the need for
these questions and I hope you've noticed
I've been cooperating but if you drag my
father into this pitiful exercise I'm
afraid I'm going to get angry.

                        LEO
I don't think you understand the
seriousness of what's happening right
now.

                        ALI
I don't think you do.

                                              FADE TO BLACK

                        END OF ACT TWO

ACT THREE

FADE IN:

11 **INT. MESS - NIGHT**   11

>   JOSH
> No. No. No, no, no. You've walked into
> quicksand.

TOBY and SAM are still there, having found nesting places, and
C.J. has joined the group.

>   TOBY
> You don't ask C.J. about the CIA.

>   SAM
> You just don't do it.

>   JOSH
> C.J. has a bizarre affection for the
> intelligence community that we just
> don't--

>   C.J.
> Bizarre? How 'bout <u>right</u>.

>   JOSH
> Okay.

>   C.J.
> This song is called "The CIA: Our
> Maligned Little Brother."

>   SAM
> Oh God.

>   C.J.
> We need spies. Human spies. Spy
> satellites are great if you're trying to
> detect whether or not Kruschev's put
> missiles in Cuba, but you want to
> overhear a conversation over Turkish
> coffee in Kyhber Pass, you need a spy.
> And the café in Kyhber Pass is where it's
> going down. You guys want to get great
> jobs after college and serve your
> country? Study Arabic, Chinese and Farsi.

(CONTINUED)

11   CONTINUED:

> TOBY
> Maybe this'd be a good time for a chorus
> of Our Maligned Little Brother, Civil
> Liberties.

> C.J.
> Liberties Shmiberties.

> TOBY
> C.J. Cregg, ladies and gentlemen.

> C.J.
> You know of a way to do this without
> tapping some phones?

> TOBY
> What about illegal searches? What about
> profiling? You know what Benjamin
> Franklin said?

> C.J.
> (pause)
> He said, "Hey, look, I've invented the
> stove."

> BOY #1
> He said, "They that can give up essential
> liberty to obtain a little temporary
> safety deserve neither liberty nor
> safety."

> C.J.
> (to BOY #1)
> I know that.

> TOBY
> Well?

> C.J.
> Well I don't think we're talking about a
> little temporary safety and it's not like
> we need to search high and low for clear
> and present danger.

> TOBY
> Well what would you say the point in
> fighting terrorism is?

> C.J.
> It's to insure freedom, Pokey, I don't
> need the brochure.

(CONTINUED)

                        TOBY
        I think you do, because during times of
        great crisis and threat, America has used
        draconian measures before, and I think
        you've forgotten just how effective
        they've been. Can you name some?

                        GIRL #2
        The blacklist?

                        TOBY
        I want her to name them.

                        C.J.
        The blacklist.

                        TOBY
        Thank you, and speaking of shameful
        periods in our history, who knows what
        Manzanar was?
                (pause)
        Nobody?

                        C.J.
                (beat)
        All right, we gotta work on that. It's
        where they locked up about 100,000
        Japanese-Americans after Pearl Harbor.

                        TOBY
        You can go back to Lincoln suspending
        habeas corpus during the Civil War, our
        national past has deep scars where there
        was a periodic rush to bad judgement due
        to fear.

BOY #4 raises his hand.

                        C.J.
                (pause)
        What?

                        BOY #4
        Yeah Ms. Cregg, I was wondering if you
        were in favor of suspending the 1976
        order prohibiting assassinations.

                        C.J.
        I am.
                (to TOBY)
        Shut up.
                (to BOY #4)
                (MORE)

                                                    (CONTINUED)

11   CONTINUED: (3)   11

                          C.J. (cont'd)
          I am. Look, I take civil liberties as
          seriously as anybody, okay, I've been to
          the dinners. And we haven't even talked
          about free speech yet and somebody
          getting lynched by the patriotism police
          for voicing a minority opinion. That said
          Tobus, we're gonna have to do some stuff,
          and we're gonna have to tap some phones.
          And we're gonna have to partner with some
          people who are the lesser of evils. As
          for assassinations, I'm sorry, but
          terrorists don't have armies and navys.
          They don't have capitals. Some of these
          guys, we're gonna have to walk up to them
          and shoot them. Yeah, we can root
          terrorist nests, but some of these guys
          aren't gonna be taken by the 105th
          Armored Tank Division, some of these guys
          are gonna be taken by a busboy with a
          silencer. So it's time to give the
          intelligence agencies the money and the
          manpower they need. We don't hear about
          their successes. Guess what, the Soviets
          never crossed the Elbe, the North Koreans
          stayed behind the 38th parallel. During
          the Millennium? Not one incident. You
          think that's because the terrorists
          decided that'd be a good day to take off?
          Not much action that day? End of song.

                                                        CUT TO:

12   **INT. FILE ROOM - NIGHT**   12

The questioning continues.

                          CLEARY
          You were arrested two years ago.

                          ALI
          Yes, but the charges were dropped.

                          CLEARY
          You were arrested for holding a rally
          without a permit.

                          ALI
          I had the permit, it hadn't processed and
          the charges were dropped.

                          LEO
          What were you protesting?

                                                        (CONTINUED)

12   CONTINUED: 12

                         ALI
         The presence of U.S. troops in Saudi
         Arabia.

                         LEO
         What exactly is your concern with our
         troops in Saudi Arabia.

                         ALI
         Saudi Arabia's the home of two Holy
         Mosques. How'd you like it if I camped
         out at the Vatican with a stockpile of
         M-16s?

                         LEO
         I'd like it fine if you were there to
         protect the Vatican.

                         ALI
         Mr. McGarry--

                         LEO
         We sent troops down there to make sure
         our friends didn't cross the Kuwaiti
         border and seize Saudi territory.

                         ALI
         You mean Saudi oil. It's Arab blood for
         American oil. It wasn't a strategic
         deployment, it was the world's biggest
         utility bill.

                         LEO
         Yes, we have oil interests in the Gulf.
         So does the rest of the world. And in '73
         when the Arab countries cut off the
         West's oil supply, it wreaked havoc on
         the _entire_--

                         ALI
         And that entitles you to trample on a
         nation's religious beliefs? You sent an
         army composed of women as well as men to
         protect a Muslim dynasty where women
         aren't allowed to drive a car.

                         LEO
         Maybe we can teach 'em.

And ALI just stares at LEO...

                                              (CONTINUED)

12   CONTINUED: (2)

>   ALI
>   (pause)
>   Anyway. That's what I was protesting.

After a moment...

>   CLEARY
>   You went to Edison High School in
>   Paterson, correct.

>   ALI
>   Correct.

>   CLEARY
>   On December 3rd, 1994, someone called in
>   a bomb threat to the school.

>   ALI
>   I remember there were bomb threats, I
>   remember there was more than one, I don't
>   remember the exact dates.

>   CLEARY
>   According to your transcripts, police
>   questioned you.

>   ALI
>   Yeah, it's on my <u>school</u> transcript 'cause
>   I wasn't arrested.

>   CLEARY
>   What'd they ask you?

>   ALI
>   They asked me if I called in a bomb
>   threat, which I didn't.

>   CLEARY
>   Did you know who did?

>   ALI
>   It was a couple of football players who
>   didn't want to take a chem final.

>   CLEARY
>   Did you tell the authorities that?

>   ALI
>   I wanted to live to see graduation.

(CONTINUED)

                        CLEARY
          So it was a couple of football players
          but they called you in anyway.

                        ALI
          It's not uncommon for Arab-Americans to
          be the first suspected when that kind of
          thing happens.

                        LEO
          I can't imagine why.

                        ALI
          Look--

                        LEO
          No, I'm trying to figure out why anytime
          there's terrorist activity people always
          assume it's Arabs, I'm racking my brain.

                        ALI
          Well I don't know the answer to that, Mr.
          McGarry, but I can tell you that it's
          horrible.

                        LEO
          Well that's the price you pay.

                        ALI
          Excuse me?

          And something in LEO knows he went way too far but it's out
          there and he can't get it back...There's a terrible silence...

                        ALI
                   (pause)
          The price I pay for what?

                        LEO
                   (pause--then to CLEARY)
          Continue the questions.

                        ALI
          The price I pay for what?

                                        FADE TO BLACK

                        END OF ACT THREE

ACT FOUR

FADE IN:

13   **INT. MESS - NIGHT**   13

> C.J.
> There's nothing more American than
> coalition building. The first thing John
> Wayne always did was put together a
> posse.

> JOSH
> (beat)
> That's a hell of an example, C.J.

> C.J.
> Shouldn't you be thinking of ways to find
> aid and comfort for our boys in
> intelligence?

> JOSH
> You know some of them may need comforting
> right now. When this crash is over you
> best get into some fishnets and head to a
> bar.

> C.J.
> I will.

BOY #3 has his hand raised.

> JOSH
> (calling on him)
> Yeah.

> BOY #3
> Where do terrorists come from?

> JOSH
> Where do they come from?

> SAM
> Everywhere. Iran, Iraq, Lebanon, Sudan,
> Syria, Libya -- mostly they come from
> exactly where you'd expect. Places of
> abject poverty and despair. Horribly
> impoverished places are an incubator for
> the worst kind of crime.

> CHARLIE
> Which is the same as it is right here.

(CONTINUED)

13   CONTINUED: 13

CHARLIE's been sitting in the back of the room for a while.
They look at him.

                    CHARLIE
          It's the same as it is here. I live in
          Southeast D.C. If you don't know the
          area, think Compton or South Central
          L.A., Detroit, the South Bronx,
          dilapidated schools, drugs, guns and what
          else?

                    GIRL #3
               (pause)
          Gangs?

                    CHARLIE
          Gangs. Where I come from there are a lot
          worse alternatives than gangs.

                    GIRL #3
          Why?

                    CHARLIE
          Gangs give you a sense of belonging and
          usually an income. But mostly they give
          you a sense of dignity. Men are men and
          men'll seek pride. Everybody here's got a
          badge to wear. "I'm the Deputy
          Communications Director," "I made
          Presidential Classroom," "I know the
          answer, I'm going to Cornell." You think
          bangers are walkin' around with their
          heads down saying, "Oh man, I didn't make
          anything outa my life, I'm in a gang." No
          man, they're walkin' around saying "Man,
          I'm in a <u>gang</u>. I'm with <u>them</u>, I wear
          colors."

                    BOY #3
          But you didn't join a gang.

                    CHARLIE
          No. And lotsa my friends didn't, either.

                    BOY #3
          You think we need more welfare?

CHARLIE takes in the question and its possible racist
overtones and lets it go 'cause kids are kids...

                                              (CONTINUED)

13   CONTINUED: (2)   13

                      CHARLIE
Look, I think people should overcome
obstacles. I don't think people should
have things handed to them, I think work
is good. I just think for some people it
shouldn't be this hard. <u>This</u> hard. I think
for kids it shouldn't be this hard. And I
think people should recognize that every
neighborhood in the country is their
neighborhood.

BARTLET's come in with ABBEY--

                  JOSH/TOBY/SAM/C.J./DONNA
Good evening, Mr. President/Good evening,
sir/ Good evening/etc.

BARTLET turns to the STUDENTS--

                      BARTLET
Hello.

And C.J. motions gently and mouths--"On your feet."

All the STUDENTS stand up.

BARTLET turns to ABBEY--

                      BARTLET
What the hell is going on?

                      C.J.
Sir, this is a group of high school
students from Presidential Classroom.

                      BARTLET
    (pause)
You women seem bright and lovely. The
men, disturbingly dense.

                      ABBEY
Ignore him. God knows the rest of us do.

                      BARTLET
Excuse me one moment.
    (turning to the staff)
Was anybody gonna come check how I was?

                      JOSH
    (pause)
I wasn't, were you?

(CONTINUED)

13   CONTINUED: (3)   13

                      SAM
No.

                      BARTLET
I could've been dead.

                      TOBY
Word gets around pretty fast, sir, I
think we would've heard if you were dead.

                      BARTLET
I could've just wanted somebody to talk to.

                      ABBEY
Hon, you may have put your finger on it.

                      BARTLET
        (to CHARLIE)
Weren't you coming down to get me some
apples and peanut butter?

                      CHARLIE
We're out of apples, sir.

BARTLET turns just in time to see SAM putting the last piece
of an apple in his mouth.

                      BARTLET
        (to BOY #3)
So we're stuck here, huh?

                      BOY #3
Yes sir.

                      BARTLET
Well I *live* here.

                      BOY #3
Yes sir.

                      BARTLET
I'm going back to my office, it was nice
meeting you all.

                      ABBEY
I'm gonna stay here a few minutes.

                      BOY #4
Sir?

                      BARTLET
Yeah.

(CONTINUED)

13 CONTINUED: (4)   13

>   BOY #4
> Do you consider yourself a man of
> principle?

>   BARTLET
> I try to be.

>   BOY #4
> Well don't you consider, I mean I know
> they're our enemy but I'm just trying to
> see it from their point of view, don't
> you consider there's something noble
> about being a martyr?

>   BARTLET
>   (beat)
> Are you stupid?

>   JOSH
> Yeah.
>   (to BARTLET re: BOY #1)
> Get that kid next.

BARTLET looks at JOSH, then back at BOY #4--

>   BARTLET
> A martyr would rather suffer death at the
> <u>hands</u> of an oppressor than renounce their
> beliefs. Killing yourself and innocent
> people to make a point is sick, twisted,
> brutal dumbass murder. And let me leave
> you with this thought before I go
> searching for the apples that were
> rightfully <u>mine</u>. We don't need martyrs
> right now. We need heroes. A hero would
> die for his country, but he'd much rather
> live for it. It was good meeting you all.

>   C.J.
> Thank you, Mr. President.

>   ALL
> Thank you.

BARTLET and CHARLIE exit and we

                                                          CUT TO:

14 **INT. COMPUTER ROOM - NIGHT**   14

Where we were in the first scene. The AGENT is standing next
to JOAN, who's seated at her computer monitor.

                                                     (CONTINUED)

14   CONTINUED: 14

                         AGENT
                      (pause)
              You know. When you said Friend of the
              Prophet before...for a second I thought
              it was F-I-T and I couldn't figure out--

                         JOAN
              P-H.

                         AGENT
              Yeah, I know that now, I'm just saying--

A phone rings and the AGENT grabs it--

                         AGENT
                      (into phone)
              Yeah.
                      (listens)
              I'll get to the J.O.C. right away, thank
              you.

He hangs up--

                         AGENT
                      (to JOAN)
              It's over.

                                                    CUT TO:

15   **INT. FILE ROOM - NIGHT**   15

The questioning continues. LEO is a little more detached than
he was before.

                         CLEARY
              Why were you in Uzbekistan?

                         ALI
              It was my Russia trip. I went there with
              some friends after graduation.

                         CLEARY
              Can you tell me about the Islamic League
              of Allston?

                         ALI
              It used to be my mosque.

An FBI AGENT's stepped in and motions to BUTTERFIELD and
CLEARY. They head over to the doorway and speak privately.

                                                    (CONTINUED)

15   CONTINUED: 15

                    FBI AGENT
          We found him.

                    BUTTERFIELD
          Where?

                    FBI AGENT
          Germany.

There's a pause for a moment...CLEARY looks at BUTTERFIELD--

                    BUTTERFIELD
          I'm fine.

                    CLEARY
          Mr. Ali, you're free to go, thank you.

                    ALI
          Thank you.

The room begins packing up and clearing out. ALI stops by LEO
on his way out.

                    ALI
          You know what, Mr. McGarry, you've got
          the memory of a gypsy moth. When you and
          the President and the President's
          daughter and about a hundred other
          people, including me, by the way, were
          met with a hail of .44 calibre gunfire in
          Rosslyn, not only were the shooters
          white, they were doing it because one of
          us wasn't.

And ALI heads out the door, leaving LEO alone before we

                                                    CUT TO:

16   **INT. MESS - NIGHT**   16

                    GIRL #1
          How did this all start?

TOBY, SAM and C.J are gone. ABBEY's lurking on the side.

                    ABBEY
          How did what all start?

                    GIRL #1
          Well...this.

                                               (CONTINUED)

16   CONTINUED: 16

                              ABBEY
                    Sarah. God said to Abraham, Look toward
                    the heaven, and number the stars, and so
                    shall your descendants be. In other
                    words, however many stars you can count,
                    that's how many kids you'll have. But
                    Abraham's wife, Sarah, was getting older
                    and God wasn't coming through on his
                    promise.
                         (beat)
                    I was very young when I had my kids.
                    Very, very, very, very young. I was
                    barely even born yet when I had my oldest
                    daughter, Elizabeth.
                         (beat)
                    Anyway, Sarah was getting older and she
                    was getting nervous 'cause she didn't
                    have any children so she sent Abraham to
                    the bed of her maid, Hagar. And Abraham
                    and Hagar had Ishmael. And not long after
                    they did, God kept his promise to Sarah
                    as he always intended to, and Abraham and
                    Sarah had Isaac. And Sarah said to
                    Abraham, "Cast out this slave woman with
                    her son; for the son of this slave woman
                    shall not be heir with my son Isaac." And
                    so it began. The Jews, the sons of Isaac,
                    and the Arabs, the sons of Ishmael. But
                    what most people find important to
                    remember is that in the end, the two sons
                    came together to bury their father.

                              JOSH
                    I think most people also find it
                    important to remember that the whole
                    thing happened about 73 million years
                    ago.

                              ABBEY
                    Yeah.

          DONNA hangs up the phone--

                              DONNA
                    Excuse me, ma'am, we're clear.

                              ABBEY
                    Well that's that, then. Good talking to
                    you guys. Hang in there.

          ABBEY exits.

                                                    (CONTINUED)

16   CONTINUED: (2)

> JOSH
> (pause)
> Well. All right. That's it then.

> GIRL #1
> Can I ask one more question?

> JOSH
> Yeah.

> GIRL #1
> Do you favor the death penalty?

> JOSH
> No.

> GIRL #1
> But you think we should kill these
> people?

> JOSH
> Well you don't have the kinds of choices
> in a war that you do in a jury room, but
> I wish we didn't have to. I think death
> is too simple.

> GIRL #1
> What would you do instead?

> JOSH
> I would put them in a small cell and make
> them watch home movies of the birthdays
> and baptisms and weddings of every person
> they killed. Over and over, every day for
> the rest of their lives.
> (beat)
> And then they would get punched in the
> mouth every night at bedtime.

Everyone laughs...

> JOSH
> By a different person every night. That's
> gonna be a long list of volunteers. But
> that's all right. We'll wait.
> (beat)
> But listen, don't worry about all this
> right now, we've got you covered. Worry
> about school, worry about what you're
> gonna tell your parents when you break
> curfew.
> (beat)
> (MORE)

(CONTINUED)

16   CONTINUED: (3)   16

                         JOSH (cont'd)
               Learn things, be good to each other, read
               the newspapers, go to the movies, go to a
               party, read a book.
                    (beat)
               In the meantime, remember pluralism. You
               want to get these people, I mean you
               wanna really reach in and get 'em where
               they live? Keep accepting more than one
               idea. Makes 'em absolutely crazy. Go.

As the kids file out, they thank him "nice meeting you," "that
was great," "I'm gonna write to you." JOSH motions over to BOY
#1--

                         JOSH
                    (quietly)
               Billy.

It's as if JOSH didn't want anybody to hear him calling Fred
by his real name--

JOSH takes him aside...

                         JOSH
               Listen.

JOSH wants to impart some profound advice on how to spend the
next few years in the way that best realizes his potential,
but then remembers that the kid seems to be doing fine on his
own.

                         JOSH
                    (beat)
               Nothing. Just keep doing what you're
               doing.

                         BOY #1
               Okay.

                                                    CUT TO:

17   **INT. ALI'S BULLPEN AREA- NIGHT**   17

ALI's working at his desk. Maybe one or two other people are
there, but most have gone home.

LEO comes in...

                         LEO
               Good evening.

ALI looks up and sees him...

                                                    (CONTINUED)

17   CONTINUED:

>   LEO
> That's the price you pay...for having the
> same physical features as criminals,
> that's what I was gonna say.

>   ALI
> No kidding.

>   LEO
> I'm sorry about that. Also about the
> crack I made about teaching Muslim women
> how to drive, I think if you talked to
> people who know me they'd tell you that
> that was unlike me.

ALI's looking at him but not saying anything...

>   LEO
> You know, we're obviously all under a...a
> greater than usual amount of, you
> know...and like you pointed out with the
> shooting and everything...

And ALI still isn't letting him off the hook...

>   LEO
> Yeah, all right. Well. That's all.

LEO heads off to leave and then when he gets to the door turns
around--

>   LEO
> Hey kid.

ALI looks up...We HEAR Buffalo Springfield's haunting "For
What it's Worth"--

>   LEO
> Way to be back at your desk.

And LEO exits as the song plays and we

>   FADE TO BLACK

ROLL CREDITS

<u>END OF SHOW</u>

BARTLET FOR AMERICA

As Brad Whitford stood up to accept the Emmy Award he'd just won for Best Supporting Actor for our second season, he turned to John Spencer and said, "You're next."

He didn't mean it as empty graciousness to one of the nominees he'd beaten (another of whom was the previous year's winner, Richard Schiff). Four days earlier, Tommy had started making *Bartlet for America* and while Brad had only played three scenes with John so far, he was ready to call it.

Here's *Bartlet for America*.

The West Wing

Bartlet for America

CHERRY REVISIONS:	12/03/01
SALMON REVISIONS:	11/28/01
BUFF REVISIONS:	11/27/01
GREEN REVISIONS:	11/26/01
YELLOW REVISIONS:	11/21/01
PINK REVISIONS:	11/20/01
BLUE REVISIONS:	11/19/01

THE WEST WING

"Bartlet for America"

Written by
Aaron Sorkin

Directed by
Thomas Schlamme

PRODUCTION #227 210
Episode Ten

JOHN WELLS PRODUCTIONS
in association with
WARNER BROS. TELEVISION
4000 Warner Blvd.
Burbank, CA 91522

Final Shooting Draft
November 16, 2001
Copyright © 2001
Warner Bros. Television
All Rights Reserved

THE WEST WING

"Bartlet for America"

Script Revision History

DATE	COLOR	PAGES
11/19/01	BLUE PAGES	CAST,SETS,12,12A,13,14, 15,16,17,18,20,21,31,33, 34-35,36-37,38,39,40-41, 45,49,50,51-54,59,60,61, 62,62A,74,74A,76,77,77A, 78,79,80,81
11/20/01	PINK PAGES	CAST,SETS,18-21,33,34-35
11/21/01	YELLOW PAGES	15,16,17-21,55,77,77A
11/26/01	GREEN PAGES	70,71,73,74,74A
11/27/01	BUFF PAGES	SETS,48,49
11/28/01	SALMON PAGES	77,78
12/03/01	CHERRY PAGES	51-54

SET LIST

INTERIORS

CAPITOL BUILDING
- Ante Room
- Main Hall
- Hearing Room
- Ante Room C
- Cloak Room

WHITE HOUSE
- Oval Office
- Lobby
- Josh's Bullpen
- Corridors
- Mrs. Landingham's Office
- Sam's Office
- Josh's Office
- Leo's Office

GOVERNOR BARTLET'S OFFICE
- Office
- Waiting Area

BARTLET CAMPAIGN HEAD-
QUARTERS

PRESIDENTIAL SUITE
- Foyer

HOTEL SUITE

TUNNEL

DEBATE SITE

EXTERIORS

WASHINGTON STREET – DAY

NEW HAMPSHIRE STREET - NIGHT

THE WEST WING

"Bartlet for America"

CAST LIST

PRESIDENT JOSIAH BARTLET
LEO McGARRY
JOSH LYMAN
SAM SEABORN
TOBY ZIEGLER
C.J. CREGG
CHARLIE YOUNG
DONNA MOSS
ABIGAIL BARTLET

MARGARET
CLIFF CALLEY
MRS. LANDINGHAM
JOHN HOYNES

MIKE CASPER
JORDON KENDALL
CHAIRMAN
ALAN
ALLEN
RATHBURN
PRATT
CONGRESSWOMAN
DEARBORN
REV. ALGISS SKYLER
ERICKSON
NEWSCASTER (V.O.)
CALHOUN
GIBSON
DONOR #1
DONOR #2
EVENT PLANNER
CONGRESSIONAL STAFFER

"Bartlet for America"

<u>TEASER</u>

FADE IN:

1   **INT. AN ANTE ROOM - DAY**   1

It's small but well-appointed in the style of the Capitol,
which is where we are. LEO sits alone in the room, thinking
his thoughts for a moment. Actually he's not alone, MARGARET's
there too. The door opens and AGENT CASPER walks in--

                    LEO
          Mike, come on in.

                    CASPER
          I was on the other side, they told me to--

                    LEO
          Yeah, Margaret, could you--

                    MARGARET
          Yeah.

MARGARET steps out.

                    CASPER
          Lotta people out there.

                    LEO
          Yeah. So listen, there were more threats?

                    CASPER
          Seven churches in five Tennessee
          counties.

                    LEO
          How many guys do you have on the ground?

                    CASPER
          We've got 25 and ATF's sending in a team.

                    LEO
          25 FBI agents, that's enough?

                    CASPER
          No.

                    LEO
          Has the Governor been briefed?

                                        (CONTINUED)

1   CONTINUED: 1

                         CASPER
                Right now.

                         LEO
                All right, listen, I gotta be here, I'm
                stuck with this thing, will you stay with
                Josh today.

                         CASPER
                Yeah.

                         LEO
                Okay.

MARGARET comes in to hand LEO a cell phone--

                         MARGARET
                Josh.

                         LEO
                And can you do me a favor and get me a
                secure phone hookup so I can monitor this
                thing, all I've got is the cell.

                         CASPER
                Good luck today.

                         LEO
                Go.

CASPER exits--

                         LEO
                    (into phone)
                Josh.

                                                  INTERCUT WITH:

2   **EXT. WASHINGTON STREET - SAME TIME**   2

                         JOSH
                There were new threats made in Tennessee
                this morning.

                         LEO
                Mike Casper was just here, he's gonna be
                with you today.

                         JOSH
                Good.

                                                  (CONTINUED)

> LEO
> You'll be all right?

> JOSH
> Yeah.

> LEO
> 'Cause I gotta be here all day, it's
> gonna take all day.

> JOSH
> Yeah and keep your head there, would you,
> don't call during every break and check
> in, keep your head there.

> LEO
> I'll keep my head where I want.

> JOSH
> Leo?

> LEO
> Yeah.

> JOSH
> There are ways.

> LEO
> Don't start again.

> JOSH
> There are ways to get the guy out of the
> room.

> LEO
> Hey I'll keep my head here, you keep your
> head there, huh.

> JOSH
> I used to do this for a living, Leo, he
> gets the floor for 5 minutes, I can get
> him outa the room.

> LEO
> Don't help me.

> JOSH
> I'm gonna help you 'cause you know why?

(CONTINUED)

> LEO
>
> 'Cause you walk around with so much guilt
> about everybody you love dying that
> you're a compulsive fixer?

> JOSH
>
> No. Leo, no. It's 'cause a guy's walking
> down the street when he falls into a
> hole, see.

> LEO
>
> Yeah.

> JOSH
>
> Yeah.

And JORDON KENDALL enters. She's 50ish, attractive and LEO's
attorney.

> LEO
>
> It's my day, Josh, I gotta take the hit.

> JOSH
>
> Leo--

> LEO
>
> I'll see you.

> JORDON
>
> They're waiting for us.

> LEO
>
> You wanna go get breakfast or something?

> JORDON
>
> No.

> LEO
>
> Breakfast is my favorite meal to eat out.
> I love tomato juice.

> JORDON
>
> They're waiting for us, Leo.

> LEO
>
> They can wait.

> JORDON
>
> No they really can't.

(CONTINUED)

CONTINUED: (3)

> LEO
> Yeah they really can. Seven new threats
> on black churches, the Governor's coming
> up, we might have to federalize the
> Tennessee National Guard and that's just
> the stuff I know about that's gonna
> happen and here I am today.

> JORDON
> You shouldn't be nervous.

> LEO
> I swear to God, Jordon, the last thing I
> am right now is nervous. Let's go.

They walk out into--

3   **INT. MAIN HALL - CONTINUOUS**   3

And LEO and JORDON are met by a near blinding spray of
flashbulbs and camera lights as they walk between the press on
either side.

> LEO
> Did I win a Grammy for something?

> JORDON
> Were you nominated?

> LEO
> No.

> JORDON
> That's ridiculous.

> LEO
> Well those things are so political.

> JORDON
> Leo is there something you haven't told
> me?

> LEO
> There's lots of things I haven't told
> you, Jordon.

> JORDON
> About today.

They walk through the huge double doors and into--

4   **INT. HEARING ROOM - CONTINUOUS**   4

Packed to the rafters. The Committee and the lawyers are
already in place. Michael Corleone is testifying today.

LEO takes it all in with a poker face...

                    JORDON
            What's gonna happen today that I don't
            already know about?

MARGARET comes to him with the cell phone--

                    MARGARET
        Leo?

                    JORDON
        He can't take any calls right now.

                    MARGARET
        It's the President.

                    LEO
        Good morning, sir.

                                            INTERCUT WITH:

5   **INT. OVAL OFFICE - DAY**   5

BARTLET's talking on the speaker phone. A TV has been set up
which is now tuned to MSNBC which is covering the hearings.

                    BARTLET
            Listen, I don't care that much about your
            ass but if you need to perjure yourself
            to protect _me_ you're gonna damn well do
            it.

                    LEO
            Sir, this isn't a secure call so I'm
            gonna say to the 17 global intelligence
            agencies that are listening in that he
            was kidding just then.

                    BARTLET
            Whatever it is Josh does you're gonna let
            him do it.

                    LEO
            I don't need to--

                                            (CONTINUED)

5   CONTINUED: 5

                    BARTLET
          Yeah yeah, how does she look?

                    LEO
          Who?

                    BARTLET
          Her.

                    LEO
          She looks good.

                    BARTLET
          What's she wearing?

                    LEO
             (to JORDON)
          What are you wearing?

                    JORDON
          What does it matter?

                    LEO
             (handing her the cell)
          Why don't you ask the President that.

                    JORDON
          A gray Armani suit.

                    LEO
             (into phone)
          Spandex.

                    BARTLET
          I like you and her. It's like a '50s
          screwball comedy.

                    LEO
             (to himself)
          You're like a '50s screwball--

                    BARTLET
          What was that?

                    LEO
          Nothing. We should do gifts and
          charitable donations tomorrow night.

                    BARTLET
          I'm not doing anything tomorrow night.

                                        (CONTINUED)

5   CONTINUED: (2)   5

                         LEO
              What's tomorrow night?

BARTLET takes a moment and rubs his eyes 'cause he still can't
believe this guy...

                         BARTLET
              It's Christmas Eve.

                         LEO
              I forgot, and you don't work then, right?

                         BARTLET
              Yeah, actually nobody does.

                         LEO
              All right, the Governor's gonna be there
              at noon but I'll be talking to you before
              then.

                         BARTLET
              You got about a thousand people in this
              building standing with you right now.

The CHAIRMAN bangs the gavel several times to bring the room
to order.

                         LEO
              I'll be back when I'm done.

                         BARTLET
              Okay.

LEO and JORDON take their place at the witness table.
MARGARET's sitting behind them.

                         JORDON
              Leo, what's going on?

                         CHAIRMAN
              Will the first witness rise, raise your
              right hand to God and swear the oath
              that's written in front of you?

LEO and JORDON stand and LEO raises his right hand. As soon as
he does there's a spray of flashbulbs from the front.

                         JORDON
              Leo--

                                                    (CONTINUED)

5   CONTINUED: (3)   5

> LEO
> (to JORDON--not at all
> kidding around)
> Ain't nothin' but a family thing.
> (to the Committee)
> I solemnly swear that the testimony today
> will be the truth, the whole truth and
> nothing but the truth so help me God.

SMASH CUT TO:

MAIN TITLES

END OF TEASER

<u>ACT ONE</u>

FADE IN:

6   **INT. HEARING ROOM - MORNING**   6

> CHAIRMAN
> Would you state your full name, please.

> LEO
> Leo Thomas McGarry.

> CHAIRMAN
> And would you identify counsel, please.

> LEO
> We've never met.

> JORDON
> Jordon Kendall, Mr. Chairman.

> CHAIRMAN
> Mr. McGarry, the Committee thanks you for
> your appearance today. Why are we here,
> what are we after? Many, if not most of
> us, were surprised by the President's
> announcement that he's been diagnosed
> with relapsing/remitting multiple
> sclerosis for seven years and never
> mentioned it while asking us to vote for
> him for President. But more surprising
> still, if not stunning, is that his
> medical condition could have been kept a
> secret from those campaign aides closest
> to him. In this age when the most minute
> details of a candidate's life are brought
> into the light, in a business where
> secrets aren't kept secret very long,
> this Committee would like to know, quite
> candidly, how it was pulled off. Did
> people lie, were people told to lie, are
> people lying now. You'll be questioned by
> Majority Counsel, then Minority Counsel,
> then each member will have five minutes
> to question, alternating back and forth
> between the majority and the minority.
> Mr. Calley.

> CLIFF
> Mr. McGarry, I'm Clifford Calley, I'm the
> Majority Counsel, good morning.

(CONTINUED)

6   CONTINUED: 6

                    LEO
          Good morning.

                    CLIFF
          What is your current job title?

                    LEO
          White House Chief of Staff.

                    CLIFF
          And what's your previous job title?

                    LEO
          General Chairman, Bartlet for America.

          How long have you known the President?

                    LEO
          We met for the first time about 32 years
          ago, but I would say our friendship began
          11 years ago.

                    CLIFF
          Can you describe how that friendship
          began?

                    LEO
          I was Labor Secretary and he was the
          Governor of New Hampshire and asked for
          my help in reforming his state's labor
          laws and...I guess we hit it off.

                    CLIFF
          You're the person in the White House
          who's known him the longest?

                    LEO
          No, the First Lady's known him the
          longest.

                    CLIFF
          Fair enough. Mr. McGarry, it was you who
          first approached Jed Bartlet about
          running for President, is that right?

                    LEO
          Yes.

                    CLIFF
          Where and when did that happen?

                                              (CONTINUED)

6   CONTINUED: (2)   6

                              ALAN (VO)
                    New Hampshire: It's What's New.

                              LEO
                    Four years ago last month at the State
                    House in Manchester.

                                                        CUT TO:

7   **INT. GOVERNOR BARTLET'S OFFICE - DAY**   7

Two young aides, ALAN and ALLEN are standing in front of an
easel that's covered with a sheet. BARTLET, in jeans and a
sweater, has his feet up on his desk and doesn't really
understand what's just been said to him, but neither does he
really care.

                              BARTLET
                        (pause)
                    Heh?

ALAN and ALLEN take the sheet off the easel with a flourish.
There's a board with an ad slogan that says--

                    NEW HAMPSHIRE: IT'S WHAT'S NEW

                              ALLEN
                    New Hampshire, it's what's new.

                              BARTLET
                    Thomas Hilton started a fishing colony
                    here in 1623, Allen.

                              ALAN
                    That's the point, Governor, people think
                    of us as a crusty New England relic and
                    tourism's our second largest industry.

                              BARTLET
                    I know what our second largest industry
                    is, Alan, and could one of you please
                    change your name.

                              ALLEN
                    We spell it differently.

                              BARTLET
                    Yeah.

                                                        CUT TO:

7A   **INT. BARTLET'S WAITING AREA - SAME TIME**   7A

LEO's standing there in his coat as we hear the meeting going
on through the open door. He sits. Sees a stray cocktail
napkin sitting on the coffee table. He can't help himself. He
takes out a pen and scribbles something on it.

                                    CUT BACK TO:

7B   **INT. GOVERNOR BARTLET'S OFFICE - SAME TIME**   7B

                    ALAN
The point is that if we don't find a way
to be fresh and new--

                    ALLEN
While obviously still retaining our
charm.

                    ALAN
Yeah, we'll never be able to stem the
fall off in revenue.

                    BARTLET
And a slogan's gonna do that?

                    ALAN
Well that's just the beginning, we've got
an aggressive strategy.

                    BARTLET
Yeah?

                    ALAN
The Office of Travel and Tourism is gonna
run print ads throughout New England
encouraging people to drive here and view
the fall foliage.

                    BARTLET
    (beat)
Whoa, whoa, slow down, you're going too
fast.

                    ALLEN
There's also our new toll free number
with up-to-the-minute reservation
information.

                                  (CONTINUED)

7B   CONTINUED: 7B

                          ALAN
          Now this is separate from the campaign
          we'll be doing for snowmobiling, which
          brings 367 million into the state.

                          BARTLET
          367 million in snowmobiling?

                          ALAN
          That includes the 1.1 million in
          registration fees and 717,000 in gas
          taxes.

                          BARTLET
          And the goggles, does it include the
          goggles.

                          ALAN
          I'm not sure.

                          BARTLET
          Okay. Thanks, guys.
              (calling)
          Mrs. Landingham!
              (to ALAN and ALLEN)
          Thanks.

They exit as MRS. LANDINGHAM comes in--

                          MRS. LANDINGHAM
          Yes sir.

                          BARTLET
          Speaking of crusty New England relics.

                          MRS. LANDINGHAM
          Governor, does it frustrate you to
          constantly aim for humor yet miss so
          dramatically.

                          BARTLET
          Nah. Abbey wants to eat at Patsy's
          tonight, would you let 'em know we're
          coming.

                          MRS. LANDINGHAM
          Yes sir.

                          BARTLET
          What's next?

                                            (CONTINUED)

7B   CONTINUED: (2)

> MRS. LANDINGHAM
> That's all for the schedule but Leo
> McGarry's here and would like a minute.

> BARTLET
> Leo's here?
> (calling)
> Leo!

> MRS. LANDINGHAM
> I'm happy to get him myself, as they do
> in a civilized world.

> BARTLET
> Yeah yeah--

LEO's come in.

> LEO
> Governor.

> BARTLET
> Hey.

The two friends embrace.

> LEO
> New Hampshire: It's what's new?

BARTLET takes the ad board and tosses it off the easel.

> BARTLET
> Jenny and Mallory are okay?

> LEO
> Yeah.

> BARTLET
> What are you doing here?

> LEO
> I don't know, what do you got? You got
> leaves, I came to look at the leaves.

> BARTLET
> What are--

> LEO
> I came to talk to you.

> BARTLET
> Everything's okay?

(CONTINUED)

7B   CONTINUED: (3)

                    LEO
Yeah.

                    BARTLET
Why didn't you call?

                    LEO
'Cause you would've asked me what I
wanted to talk to you about.

                    BARTLET
Where are you staying?

                    LEO
At the Marriott.

                    BARTLET
What <u>do</u> you want to talk to me about?

                    LEO
I've been thinking about getting back
into politics.

                    BARTLET
     (pause)
I think that's great, man, I think it's
about time. You probably mean the House
but I think you should consider the
Senate seat in Illinois in two years, I
can help raise money.

                    LEO
No I wasn't thinking about the Senate, I
was thinking about the White House.

                    BARTLET
     (pause)
Hey, Leo, I swear to God there's no one
I'd rather see in the Oval Office than
you, but if you run there's gonna be a
lot of discussion about valium and
alcohol, I mean it's gonna come out, this
is the world.

                    LEO
Yeah, see I wasn't thinking about me.

                    BARTLET
Who?

(CONTINUED)

7B   CONTINUED: (4)

                    LEO
I've been walking around in a kind of
daze for two weeks. And everywhere I go,
planes, trains, restaurants, meetings, I
find myself scribbling something down.

                    BARTLET
What?

LEO takes a napkin out of his pocket, licks the back of it,
and slaps it on the easel--

                Bartlet for America

BARTLET stares at it for a long time before we

                                  CUT TO:

8   **OMITTED**   8

9   **INT. HEARING ROOM - DAY**   9

LEO's being questioned by a Committee member.

                    RATHBURN
He never mentioned his health.

                    LEO
No.

                    RATHBURN
Not during the first meeting in his
office?

                    LEO
No.

                    RATHBURN
And not during the second meeting at the
Marriott.

                    LEO
No.

                    RATHBURN
And you never asked him about his health.

                    LEO
No.

                              (CONTINUED)

9   CONTINUED: 9

                         RATHBURN
          Not during the first meeting in his
          office?

                         LEO
          No.

                         RATHBURN
          Nor during the second meeting at the
          Marriott.

                         LEO
          No.

                         RATHBURN
          Well then I'd like to ask you this: If he
          had told you about his condition, would
          you still have thought it was a good idea
          that he run?

                         LEO
          I don't know.

                         RATHBURN
          Well think about it and try answering.

LEO covers the microphone and leans in to JORDON--

                         LEO
          Listen I'm gonna talk a little and you
          nod and talk a little bit back to me.

                         JORDON
          What are you doing?

                         LEO
          Good.

                         JORDON
          I'm really asking you.

                         LEO
          I think Rathburn's being a little snotty,
          I think he's gonna have to wait and I
          think he's gonna have to wait with the
          camera on me.

                         RATHBURN
          Mr. McGarry.

                                           (CONTINUED)

9   CONTINUED: (2)

                    LEO
          One second please.
                    (to JORDON)
          Listen, what are you doing for lunch?

                    JORDON
          I don't know.

                    LEO
          'Cause I thought maybe we could have
          lunch or something.

                    JORDON
          Leo, you've gotta answer the question.

                    LEO
          Congressman, could you repeat the
          question please.

                    RATHBURN
          If Jed Bartlet had told you about his
          health, either at the first meeting or
          the second meeting, would you still have
          thought it was a good idea for him to
          run.

                    LEO
          Yeah, I don't know.

                                        FADE TO BLACK

                    END OF ACT ONE

ACT TWO

FADE IN:

10   **INT. LOBBY - DAY**   10

MIKE CASPER stands in his overcoat as DONNA comes out.

                    DONNA
          Mike?

                    CASPER
          Yeah.

                    DONNA
          Come on back.

                    CASPER
          Thanks. Listen, churches are burning
          down, otherwise I'd be hitting on you.

                    DONNA
          I appreciate that.

                    CASPER
          Sure.

                    DONNA
          Maybe when it's a better time.

They walk into--

11   **INT. JOSH'S BULLPEN - CONTINUOUS**   11

As JOSH comes out of his office--

                    JOSH
          Let's go.

                    CASPER
          Where are we going?

                    JOSH
          A 17 month investigation, 34 black
          churches, how can there be no evidence of
          a conspiracy?

                    CASPER
          I don't know, it's probably because we're
          stupid.

They walk into--

12   **INT. CORRIDOR - CONTINUOUS**   12

                    JOSH
          Mike--

                    CASPER
          The FBI could invent a pattern but then
          that would be against the law.

                    JOSH
          Yeah.

                    CASPER
          Okay?

                    JOSH
          You saw Leo this morning?

                    CASPER
          Yeah, listen, that was big for me. I
          don't brief the White House Chief of
          Staff.

                    JOSH
          All right, well let's listen in on this
          meeting for a minute.

                    CASPER
          Hang on.

                    JOSH
          What.

CASPER's stopped walking when he realizes he's outside the
Oval Office.

                    CASPER
          This wall is curved.

                    JOSH
          Yeah. Let's go.

They go into--

13   **INT. MRS. LANDINGHAM'S OFFICE - CONTINUOUS**   13

                    CASPER
          I don't have to go in there, I can wait
          out here.

                    JOSH
          Charlie?

                                        (CONTINUED)

13   CONTINUED: 13

                              CHARLIE
                         (go on in)
                    Yeah.

                              JOSH
                    Let's go.

JOSH opens the door and they walk into--

14   **INT. THE OVAL OFFICE - CONTINUOUS**   14

Where BARTLET's in a meeting with Governor PRATT and about a
dozen AIDES. JOSH and CASPER stand in the back.

                              BARTLET
                    Well the phone calls have been coming all
                    morning, Governor, you should know that
                    Algiss Skyler called.

                              PRATT
                    Skyler wants you to call up the Guard?

                              BARTLET
                    Skyler wants to know why the hell you
                    haven't.

                              PRATT
                    Because local law enforcement is doing
                    plenty.

                              BARTLET
                    Was Eisenhower wrong in '57? Kennedy in
                    '61?

                              PRATT
                    This is a different situation.

                              BARTLET
                    Well we don't know what the situation is,
                    do we Josh?

                              JOSH
                    No sir. Mr. President, this is Special
                    Agent Mike Casper who's acting as the
                    FBI's White House liaison during the
                    situation.

                              BARTLET
                    Do we know what's going on, Agent Casper?

                              CASPER
                    No sir.

                                                      (CONTINUED)

> BARTLET
> (to PRATT)
> Edward, so far the churches have been
> empty, there've been no fatalities, but
> tomorrow night's Christmas Eve, they're
> gonna be packed, so why shouldn't I send
> troops in?

> PRATT
> Because due respect, Mr. President, but
> you do it without my consent and it's a
> clear violation of state's rights and you
> would've said the same thing when you
> were the Governor of New Hampshire.

> BARTLET
> This doesn't happen in New Hampshire.

> PRATT
> You got a pretty big black population in
> New Hampshire, do you?

BARTLET looks at PRATT for a moment, then kinda shrugs off his
insolence with a casual laugh.

> BARTLET
> We'll meet again this afternoon. Thank
> you, Governor.

> ALL (EXCEPT PRATT)
> Thank you, Mr. President.

> BARTLET
> Josh, stick around.

> JOSH
> Yes sir.

> CASPER
> (to JOSH)
> I'll be in the bullpen.

Everyone's exited.

> BARTLET
> What do you have cooking?

> JOSH
> I'm sorry?

> BARTLET
> I said what do you have cooking?

(CONTINUED)

14   CONTINUED: (2)   14

                         JOSH
                I don't understand.

                         BARTLET
                Yes you do.
                    (pause)
                I know what happened at the third debate.
                He told me. I know what's gonna happen
                this afternoon. What are you gonna do,
                you gonna try and get Gibson out of the
                room when it's his turn to question?

                         JOSH
                I don't think you and I should discuss
                it, sir.

    BARTLET looks at him for a moment and then nods his head
    "yeah." JOSH follows him out into--

15   **INT. MRS. LANDINGHAM'S OFFICE - CONTINUOUS**   15

    --where CHARLIE and a few others are watching the hearings on
    TV.

                         BARTLET
                Where are we?

                         CHARLIE
                Dearborn'll be next.

                         CONGRESSWOMAN (ON TV)
                --and the red light is on so I'll yield
                the floor back to the Chairman.

                         CHAIRMAN (ON TV)
                Congressman Dearborn, you have five
                minutes.

                         DEARBORN (ON TV)
                Mr. McGarry, I'd like to use my time to
                talk about Edith Wilson. Excuse me one
                moment.

    DEARBORN turns to consult quietly with a staffer...

                         BARTLET
                Abbey's about to get spanked.
                    (pause)
                Guys, there are things we do to
                women...my wife's a world class
                scientist.

                                                    (CONTINUED)

15   CONTINUED: 15

                           DEARBORN (ON TV)
            Do you know who Edith Wilson was?

                                            CUT TO:

16   **INT. HEARING ROOM - DAY**   16

                              LEO
            Edith Wilson was Edith Galt before she
            became the second wife of Woodrow Wilson.

                         DEARBORN
            And with the help of doctors, ran this
            country for months while her husband was
            incapacitated by a stroke.

                              LEO
            Yes.

                         DEARBORN
            Do you believe that the President having
            a stroke falls within the scope of the
            25th Amendment?

                         JORDON
            Excuse me, but with the Wilsons being
            dead for 80 years, I don't believe it
            falls within the scope of this hearing.

                         DEARBORN
            Abbey Bartlet knew of her husband's
            condition.

                                LEO
            Yes.

                         DEARBORN
            And she kept it to herself.

                                LEO
            Well I don't know who she kept it to,
            Congressman.

                         DEARBORN
            She didn't tell you.

                              LEO
            No.

                         DEARBORN
            Or anyone else in the high command of the
            Bartlet campaign.

                                     (CONTINUED)

16   CONTINUED: 16

LEO smiles...

                    DEARBORN
You're smiling.

                    LEO
Yes sir.

                    DEARBORN
Why?

                    LEO
Because at this point there wasn't much
of a high command. All we'd done is show
a strong third in Iowa, we were working
out of a storefront.

                    TOBY (VO)
Pop it.

                    DEARBORN
You had Toby Ziegler?

                    LEO
Yeah.

                    DEARBORN
You had Josh Lyman and Sam Seaborn?

                    TOBY (VO)
Pop it, pop it.

                    LEO
Yeah.

                    DEARBORN
C.J. Cregg?

                               CUT TO:

17   **INT. BARTLET CAMPAIGN HEADQUARTERS - DAY**   17

The same place we saw last year. A converted storefront.
BARTLET FOR AMERICA posters on the walls. Volunteers at desks
on the phones. And spread out in a triangle around the room
are TOBY, SAM and C.J. who are tossing a basketball.

                    TOBY
You gotta pop the ball, you gotta pop it.

                    C.J.
I'm popping it.

                          (CONTINUED)

17   CONTINUED:

                         TOBY
              No you're not.

                         SAM
              So my feeling?

                         TOBY
              Yeah?

                         SAM
              Is that we're fine playing this song in
              South Carolina.

                         C.J.
              I agree.

                         TOBY
              Pop it.

                         SAM
              As long as all he's doing is running
              against Wiley, it's fine that he doesn't
              seem like a real candidate.

                         TOBY
              It's when Wiley drops out and he's
              running against Hoynes.

                         SAM
              Right.

                         TOBY
              They're gonna cover us all the way to
              South Dakota, suddenly we don't want to
              be quaint anymore. People want to know is
              this guy for real.

                         SAM
              We've gotta show 'em we're an honest to
              God alternative, we've gotta show 'em
              we're big time.

CRASH! The basketball, which C.J. had pretty good pop on,
sails past SAM who was in mid-thought and crashes through the
storefront window.

They all look at it for a moment before...

                         C.J.
              Can we get an intern over here.

They gather at a desk...

                                        (CONTINUED)

17   CONTINUED: (2)

                          SAM
          What about this: A series of major
          national policy addresses, we work with
          Josh and pick three issues.

                          TOBY
          Yeah, and we should start projecting the
          image that <u>he</u> thinks he's for real.

                          C.J.
          We'll release his tax returns, put all
          his stocks in a blind trust.

                          SAM
          You know what else?

                          TOBY
          Yeah.

                          SAM
          He should take a physical.

                          C.J.
          Absolutely, he's got ten years on Hoynes,
          we should release a medical report.

                          TOBY
          I'll take it to Leo.

                          SAM
              (to the volunteers)
          Guys, let's go, let's be working.
          Somebody wanna get the ball?

                                          CUT TO:

18   **EXT. NEW HAMPSHIRE STREET - NIGHT**   18

BARTLET and ABBEY are strolling on the sidewalk. It's cold
outside. Where there used to be one State Trooper, now there's
two.

                          ABBEY
          I like some of these new people.

                          BARTLET
          Yeah?

                          ABBEY
          Josh Lyman's special. And Sam Seaborn's
          very funny.

                                          (CONTINUED)

18   CONTINUED:

                         BARTLET
                 Which one's he?

                         ABBEY
                 The young one.

                         BARTLET
                 Listen, they'd like me to do some things
                 before South Dakota.

                         ABBEY
                 South Carolina's next.

                         BARTLET
                 Yeah, we're looking past that.

                         ABBEY
                 What do they want you to do?

                         BARTLET
                 Full financial disclosure.

                         ABBEY
                 I don't have a problem with that.

                         BARTLET
                 And they want me to take a physical.

         ABBEY doesn't say anything...

                         BARTLET
                 What's a physical right now gonna show?

                         ABBEY
                 It'll--nothing. I'll--you're in
                 remission.

                         BARTLET
                 I'm not lying to anybody, Abbey, I'm
                 taking a physical. A physical which I'm
                 under no legal obligation to take, I'm
                 doing it voluntarily.

                         ABBEY
                 Yeah.

                         BARTLET
                 Now is when people are listening. I'll
                 make my speeches, get whomped on Super
                 Tuesday and we'll all go home.

                                        (CONTINUED)

18   CONTINUED: (2)

> LEO (VO)
> Congressman, I don't believe Mrs. Bartlet
> had a sinister plot to rule the empire if
> that's what you're suggesting.

CUT TO:

19   **INT. MRS. LANDINGHAM'S OFFICE - DAY**   19

Everyone's gone but BARTLET and CHARLIE.

> DEARBORN (ON TV)
> I'm suggesting--

> LEO (ON TV)
> Like all she has to do is show her
> husband the Queen of Diamonds and he'll
> shoot John McGiver?

> BARTLET
> That one'll be in the papers tomorrow for
> all the John Frankenheimer fans.

> CHARLIE
> Yeah.

> DEARBORN (ON TV)
> We've had the Iowa caucus, we've had the
> New Hampshire caucus, we're headed to
> South Carolina, we're planning for South
> Dakota and Mrs. Bartlet, excuse me, Dr.
> Bartlet has yet to mention to anyone that
> her husband has multiple sclerosis.

> BARTLET
> The things we do to women...

FADE TO BLACK

<u>END OF ACT TWO</u>

ACT THREE

FADE IN:

20   **OMITTED**   20

20A **INT. ANTE ROOM - DAY (FORMERLY SCENE 24)**   20A

DONNA's sitting alone with a newspaper. After a moment the door opens and CLIFF comes in and without seeing DONNA tosses some thick files on the couch. Then he sees her.

> CLIFF
> Hey, I didn't see you. What are you doing here?

> DONNA
> I have to drop something off for Leo. You're not supposed to be in here.

> CLIFF
> Why not?

> DONNA
> Ante Room B is for witnesses, Ante Room C is for counsel.

> CLIFF
> This is Ante Room C.

> DONNA
> (pause)
> All right.

She starts to gather up her things...

> DONNA
> Could you guys possibly take a few more breaks, by the way, we've only had three so far this afternoon.

> CLIFF
> This day has had a lot of votes they can't miss.

> DONNA
> Enjoy Ante Room C.

> CLIFF
> I think he's doing well.

(CONTINUED)

20A   CONTINUED:

> DONNA
> He'll be happy to hear you think so.

> CLIFF
> What did I do today?

DONNA makes an exaggerated gesture that says "what could it POSSIBLY be?"

> CLIFF
> Hey you know what? It's not like these are questions that nobody has a right to ask, I think they're important and 69 percent of the public agrees with me.

> DONNA
> Not a bad break for an ambitious young lawyer who gets to be the star of his own television show for a month.

CLIFF takes a very long moment...He wants to stay calm 'cause he'd always rather stay calm but also 'cause he's in the middle of pitching a game.

> CLIFF
> You know I'm hoping for a third date with you one day, Donna. So I'm gonna go ahead and assume that your choice of the word ambitious just then wasn't your way of describing someone who's both hardworking and Jewish at the same time.

> DONNA
> (beat)
> That's ridiculous.

> CLIFF
> Good.

> DONNA
> Cliff, it's ridiculous.

And now we see that CLIFF's tired and under a lot of pressure.

> CLIFF
> It's not a little thing, it's a big thing. He lied, we're living with it, don't get pissy with me for asking <u>questions</u> about it. First of all, it's my <u>job</u>. Second of all it's my <u>vote</u>!

(CONTINUED)

20A CONTINUED: (2)

                DONNA
       (beat)
   You're right.
       (beat)
   Okay.

DONNA exits.

                            CUT TO:

21 **INT. SAM'S OFFICE - DAY**   21

SAM is watching the hearings on TV as JOSH comes in--

                JOSH
   Listen--

                SAM
   They're coming back from the break.

                JOSH
   Yeah.

                SAM
   You know what I was thinking about? I was
   thinking about when we threw that
   basketball through the window at the
   first campaign headquarters in
   Manchester.

                JOSH
   I heard about it, I wasn't there.

                SAM
   Weren't you throwing the ball around with
   us?

                JOSH
   It was you and Toby and C.J.

                SAM
   What that must've looked like from the
   point of view of somebody coming down the
   sidewalk.

                JOSH
   I need somebody in the steel lobby to
   speak to Darren Gibson right away,
   sometime toward the end of this hour.

                SAM
   Jim Jericho.

                        (CONTINUED)

21   CONTINUED: 21

                              JOSH
          Jim Jericho is who I had, he had to leave
          town, his wife is sick. Who else do we
          have, one of our people?

                              SAM
          Nick Grindell?

JOSH shakes his head "no."

                              SAM
          Well I'll get to somebody, what's this
          about?

                              JOSH
          Nothing.

                              SAM
          It's not about nothing, you want Gibson
          out of the room.

                              JOSH
          I'd like 'em all out of the room.

                              SAM
          What's Gibson got?

                              JOSH
          You'll get the guy for me?

                              SAM
          Yeah.

JOSH exits. SAM opens a drawer and pulls out a little black
book basically as the hearings start up on TV. The CHAIRMAN
gavels the room to order.

                         CHAIRMAN (ON TV)
          I would like our 10 minute breaks to be
          closer to 15 minutes than they are to a
          half hour.

                                                           CUT TO:

22   **INT. HEARING ROOM - SAME TIME**   22

                              CHAIRMAN
          And with that, the Chair recognizes the
          Gentleman from Pennsylvania.

                                                      (CONTINUED)

> ERICKSON
> Thank you, Mr. Chairman, and I'd like to
> compliment you on your leadership of this
> Committee. Mr. McGarry, you're familiar
> are you not with Article II, Section 1,
> Clause 6 of the US Constitution.

LEO considers this, then covers the microphone and leans into
JORDON--

> LEO
> We're gonna have to do this again.

> JORDON
> He's being snotty.

> LEO
> Yeah. So I was thinking maybe, you know,
> dinner.

> JORDON
> Listen to me. I don't like this. You pay
> me $650 an hour. You tell me everything.

> LEO
> Well what do I have to pay to only tell
> you some things.

> JORDON
> I don't know, but you have to pay it to
> another lawyer.

> LEO
> So what are you saying about dinner?

> JORDON
> I'm not kidding around.

> LEO
>   (into microphone)
> Yes I am.

> ERICKSON
> It says that if something happens
> to the President, the Vice President
> will assume his duties.

> LEO
> No, it says the Vice President assumes
> his duties if the President dies.
>   (MORE)

(CONTINUED)

22   CONTINUED: (2)   22

> LEO (cont'd)
> Short of that, impeachment, or the 25th
> Amendment being invoked, the Vice
> President stays the Vice President.

> ERICKSON
> Who picked John Hoynes to be the running
> mate on the ticket?

> LEO
> The President did.

> ERICKSON
> Did he have help?

> LEO
> Yes.

> ERICKSON
> From whom?

> LEO
> Bill Trillin led the search committee. A
> number of people weighed in on the
> decision.

> ERICKSON
> Do you think Bill Trillin and the people
> who weighed in on the decision might've
> benefited from knowing about the
> President's health condition?

> LEO
> I don't see how.

> ERICKSON
> You don't?

> LEO
> No.

> ERICKSON
> With the possibility that the President
> might die in office--

> LEO
> Hold it--

> ERICKSON
> --considerations such as winning Texas
> might've taken--

(CONTINUED)

22   CONTINUED: (3)

                         LEO
          Hold it. Because for a refreshing change
          of pace, the Gentleman from Pennsylvania
          doesn't know what he's talking about. To
          begin with, there's a possibility that
          any President will die in office.

                         ERICKSON
          A greater possibility with this
          President.

                         LEO
          No sir, that's not true. MS isn't fatal
          and while on national television it is
          criminal to imply otherwise in an offer
          to score some cheap points. You owe an
          apology to fathers of children who are
          suffering from this disease.

                         ERICKSON
          Mr.--

                         LEO
          Finally, the President chose his running
          mate using the only yard stick that means
          anything: Ability to assume the duties of
          the Presidency, and in John Hoynes we got
          our man. And the Vice President was
          immediately told of the President's
          condition.

                         ERICKSON
          Well finally we found somebody. When and
          where was the Vice President told?

                         LEO
          From what I understand, he was told in
          the Presidential Suite of the Sheraton
          Hotel in Miami on the first night of the
          convention.

                         ERICKSON
          From what you understand.

                         LEO
          Yeah.

                         ERICKSON
          You weren't in the room.

                         LEO
          Not for that part of the meeting.

                                        (CONTINUED)

22   CONTINUED: (4)   22

                        NEWCASTER (VO)
          I can tell you that when Jed Bartlet
          takes this stage 72 hours from now, these
          delegates are gonna go absolutely crazy.

                                              CUT TO:

23   **INT. PRESIDENTIAL SUITE - NIGHT**   23

BARTLET, LEO, TOBY, SAM, JOSH, ABBEY and C.J. are sitting.
Nobody's talking. Televisions are showing a live feed from the
convention, but nobody's watching the television either. All
eyes are on BARTLET.

                        NEWCASTER (VO)
          They've scheduled 20 minutes for a
          demonstration but I don't think that's
          gonna be enough.

                        BARTLET
          Toby?

                        TOBY
          Yeah.

                        BARTLET
          Josh?

                        JOSH
          Yeah.

                        BARTLET
          Sam?

                        SAM
          Yeah, I think so.

                        BARTLET
          C.J.?

                        C.J.
          Yeah.

                        BARTLET
               (pause--then to LEO)
          All right, let's do it.

                        LEO
               (to an AIDE)
          All right, send him in.

                                              (CONTINUED)

23   CONTINUED: 23

The staff looks at each other and exhales quietly. The deal's done.

HOYNES comes in--

                         BARTLET
               Senator.

                         HOYNES
               Good evening.

                         BARTLET
               I'd like you to be the Vice President.

HOYNES and BARTLET just look at each other for a moment...it's the end of a long war and possibly the beginning of a new one...

                         BARTLET
               Why don't you sit with Abbey and me for a
               few minutes. Can I have the room, please?

People start to file out...

                         BARTLET
               You want anything, coffee or anything?

                         HOYNES
               No.

Once everyone has left the room...

                         BARTLET
               You ran a good campaign. You're a young
               man, you'll be back.

                         HOYNES
               Thank you.

                         BARTLET
               There's something you need to know, it's
               why I had everyone leave the room. A few
               years ago I was diagnosed with a
               relapsing/remitting course of MS.

                         HOYNES
                    (pause)
               I'm sorry?

                         BARTLET
               Multiple Sclerosis.

                                                    (CONTINUED)

                       HOYNES
              (pause)
Did you just tell me that you have MS?

                       BARTLET
Yeah.

                       HOYNES
              (pause)
Which you never mentioned during the
campaign.

BARTLET shakes his head "no."

                       BARTLET
I told you because it's something you're
gonna need to know. But also because I
wanted to show that I trust you.

                       HOYNES
You do?

                       BARTLET
Yeah.

                       HOYNES
              (pause)
That's supposed to be me accepting the
nomination Thursday night. But I suppose
your trusting me is consolation prize
enough.

                       BARTLET
              (pause)
Well what do you say?

                       HOYNES
I'd like to think about it for a few
days.

                       BARTLET
I'd like your answer now, John.

                       HOYNES
You'll have it when I give it, Jed. Good
evening, Abbey.

HOYNES walks out.

BARTLET is silently fuming...he waits a long time before--

(CONTINUED)

23   CONTINUED: (3)

> BARTLET
> I'm gonna stretch my legs.

BARTLET exits. ABBEY sits there alone in her thoughts. She gets up and steps out into--

23A   **INT. FOYER - CONTINUOUS**   23A

--where BARTLET's still huddling with some staff.

> ABBEY
> Jed?

> BARTLET
> Yeah.

> ABBEY
> (beat)
> Nothing.

BARTLET and the STAFF head out the door. ABBEY stands in the foyer alone until a voice turns her around.

> VOICE (OS)
> Mrs. Bartlet?

ABBEY turns to see MRS. LANDINGHAM standing in the open doorway to one of the bedrooms. She's almost shaking...

> ABBEY
> I didn't know you were here.

> MRS. LANDINGHAM
> (pause)
> What does relapsing/remitting mean?

ABBEY stares at her for a moment...then walks into the main suite and closes the door behind her as we

> FADE TO BLACK

<u>END OF ACT THREE</u>

ACT FOUR

FADE IN:

24   **OMITTED (MOVED TO SCENE 20A)**   24

25   **INT. THE OVAL OFFICE - DAY**   25

CHARLIE steps in--

> CHARLIE
> Sir, Governor Pratt and Rev. Skyler are
> on their way.

> BARTLET
> Good, I want Josh in the meeting too.

> CHARLIE
> Yes sir.

PRATT, SKYLER and a few AIDES are being led in--

> BARTLET
> Come on in.

> SKYLER
> Good afternoon, Mr. President.

> BARTLET
> Good afternoon, Reverend. In 15 minutes
> we're gonna make a decision. It'd be nice
> if everybody was happy with the decision
> but it's only important that I am. Let's
> go.

                                                    CUT TO:

26   **INT. JOSH'S OFFICE - DAY**   26

--as DONNA comes in.

> JOSH
> (on the phone)
> If you could please give him that message
> as soon as he gets in, or, you know, or
> when he returns the page.
> (beat)
> Cindy, if I could tell you what it was
> regarding I'd have told you. Sorry. Thank
> you.

                                              (CONTINUED)

26   CONTINUED: 26

JOSH hangs up--

                         DONNA
               They want you.

                         JOSH
               Where have you been?

                         DONNA
               You sent me to the Hill.

They go out into--

27   **INT. BULLPEN - CONTINUOUS**   27

                         JOSH
               Has Sam called?

                         DONNA
               No.

                         JOSH
               He didn't maybe drop off a piece of paper
               with a name on it?

                         DONNA
               No. They want you in the Oval Office.

                         JOSH
               Okay.

JOSH heads into--

28   **INT. LOBBY - CONTINUOUS**   28

--as CASPER's coming through the front doors.

                         CASPER
               Josh.

                         JOSH
               And where have <u>you</u> been?

                         CASPER
               We got it.

                         JOSH
               The President's gonna make a decision
               right now, we gotta--
                    (beat)
               What?

                                              (CONTINUED)

                    CASPER
          We got it.

                    JOSH
          What do you mean?

                    CASPER
          Gilbert Murdock, a 17 year old high
          school drop-out was pulled over outside
          Chattanooga for a failing left brake
          light. When the officers approached his
          car, he sped off and led them in high
          pursuit.

                    JOSH
          Why?

                    CASPER
          'Cause he thought he was being pulled
          over for planning to make a Molotov
          cocktail.

                    JOSH
          Why?

                    CASPER
          'Cause he was planning to make a Molotov
          cocktail.

                    JOSH
          Did he name friends?

                    CASPER
          He was a tough nut to crack, it took
          almost 20 minutes.

                    JOSH
          We got ourselves a conspiracy.

                    CASPER
          Yeah.

                    JOSH
          Let's go.

                    CASPER
          Where?

                    JOSH
          To brief the President.

                                                        (CONTINUED)

28   CONTINUED: (2)   28

                         CASPER
          No the Director'll brief the President.

                         JOSH
          Mike, that's your task force out there.
          The only reason you're not out there with
          'em is 'cause, I don't know, 'cause
          you're a woman or something.

                         CASPER
          I am temporarily <u>desk</u> assigned for <u>health</u>
          reasons, a decision I appealed
          vigorously.

                         JOSH
          Let's go.

                         CASPER
          We don't take curtain calls.

                         JOSH
          You'll take a handshake, let's go.

                                                          CUT TO:

29   **INT. THE OVAL OFFICE - DAY**   29

                         SKYLER
          Of course there's a legal basis.
          Religious freedom is a civil right, the
          Civil Rights Act of 1964 raises these
          threats to a Federal level.

                         PRATT
          Credible threats and no one in this room
          is trying to take away your Civil Rights.

          JOSH and CASPER enter.

                         SKYLER
          A sin of omission by any other name.

                         JOSH
          Mr. President.

                         BARTLET
          Yeah.

                         JOSH
          Your decision just got a lot easier.

                                                     (CONTINUED)

29   CONTINUED: 29

                              BARTLET
               Tell me.

                              JOSH
                    (to CASPER)
               Go ahead.

                              CASPER
                    (quietly to JOSH)
               Um, well you can tell him that the FBI is
               willing to designate this--

                              JOSH
               You can talk directly to him.

                              CASPER
               Sir, the FBI is ready to call this a
               credible threat, we have one of the
               conspirators in custody.

                              BARTLET
               Conspirators?

                              CASPER
               Yes sir.

                              BARTLET
               All right! Here come the Tennessee
               Volunteers. Reverend, have the Pastors
               encourage the women to bake those guys
               something nice, they're all spending
               Christmas Eve where they don't wanna be.
               Ed, you get to be a hero to the black
               folks, anybody in your state doesn't like
               it, the FBI called the shots, what could
               you do. Anything else?

                              SKYLER
               No sir.

                              PRATT
               No sir.

                              BARTLET
               Thank you.

                              ALL
               Thank you, Mr. President/Thank you, sir/
               etc.

                                                        (CONTINUED)

> BARTLET
> (to CASPER)
> I'm sorry, I've forgotten your name.

> CASPER
> Michael Casper.

> BARTLET
> How'd you catch him?

> CASPER
> He was pulled over for a bad brake light
> and he thought it was something else.

> BARTLET
> A two year investigation gets its first
> crack from a broken tail light?

> CASPER
> In 13 years with the Bureau I've
> discovered that there's no amount of
> money, manpower or knowledge that can
> equal the person you're looking for being
> stupid.

> BARTLET
> God, well some of the stupidest criminals
> in the world are working right here in
> America, I've always been very proud of
> that.

> CASPER
> Yes sir.

> BARTLET
> Thank you, Agent Casper.

> CASPER
> Thank you, Mr. President.

JOSH and CASPER exchange a look as Casper exits.

> BARTLET
> So what's goin' on?

> JOSH
> I gotta call him and tell him you know--

> BARTLET
> It's not gonna happen?

(CONTINUED)

29   CONTINUED: (3)   29

                          JOSH
             I don't think so.

                          BARTLET
             It was a long shot anyway.
                  (beat)
             Look, I wanted to see him spared this
             but...Leo's made outa leather. His face
             has a map of the world on it. Leo comes
             back.

                          JOSH
             Okay.

                          BARTLET
             All right.

     JOSH exits.

                          BARTLET
             Damn it.

                                                           CUT TO:

30   **INT. HEARING ROOM - DAY**   30

     CALHOUN, a Democrat, is finishing up his questioning.

                          CALHOUN
             At no point did he lie.

                          LEO
             No.

                          CALHOUN
             At no point did you lie.

                          LEO
             No.

                          CALHOUN
             At no point did he encourage others to
             lie.

                          LEO
             No.

                          CALHOUN
             At no point has he been unable to
             discharge his duties.

                                                        (CONTINUED)

              LEO
No.

              CALHOUN
Thank you. Thank you, Mr. Chairman.

              CHAIRMAN
The Chair recognizes the Gentleman from
Michigan, Mr. Gibson for five minutes.

              GIBSON
Thank you, Mr. Chairman. Two years ago
January the President collapsed in the
Oval Office, is that correct?

              LEO
I'm not sure what the medical term would
be.

              GIBSON
He involuntarily fell to the ground.

              LEO
Yes.

              GIBSON
Will Minority Counsel stipulate that we
can call that collapsing.

The MINORITY COUNSEL nods his head "yes."

              GIBSON
Let the record reflect Minority Counsel
has nodded his head up and down so as to
indicate an affirmative response.

              CHAIRMAN
So ordered.

              GIBSON
Is this the only time since the President
took the oath of office that he's
collapsed.

              LEO
So far as I know.

              GIBSON
Is this the only time since the beginning
of the campaign that he's collapsed.

              (CONTINUED)

30   CONTINUED: (2)

                              LEO
                         (pause)
                    No it's not.

                              GIBSON
                    I'd like to take you back to 30 October
                    in St. Louis, Missouri, Jed Bartlet is
                    the Democratic nominee for President and
                    is about to participate in the third and
                    final debate.

                              JORDON
                    Mr. Chairman, I'd like to request a short
                    recess.

                              CHAIRMAN
                    We just got back from a recess.

                              JORDON
                    Sir, we've taken breaks at the request of
                    nearly every member of this Committee
                    while the witness has asked for a total
                    of none. One time, Mr. Chairman.

                              CHAIRMAN
                    We'll take a five minute break, please
                    let's keep it to ten minutes.

Bangs his gavel--

                              JORDON
                         (to LEO)
                    Come with me.

JORDON heads up the aisle without even seeing if this is okay
with LEO.

                              MARGARET
                    Leo?

MARGARET hands him the cell phone--

                              LEO
                    Yeah.

                                             INTERCUT WITH:

30A   **INT. JOSH'S OFFICE - SAME TIME**   30A

Josh is on the phone.

                                             (CONTINUED)

30A   CONTINUED: 30A

> JOSH
> I couldn't make it happen.

> LEO
> (beat)
> Don't worry about it.

LEO closes the phone and heads off. In the meantime, CLIFF's made his way over to where GIBSON is now conferring with the CHAIRMAN.

> CLIFF
> Excuse me, what's goin' on?

> CHAIRMAN
> I was just asking the same thing.

> CLIFF
> I don't know anything about testimony from October 30th.

> GIBSON
> It's okay, I got it.

> CLIFF
> No, you don't got it.

> CHAIRMAN
> We better go someplace and talk.

The three of them head out and we

                                                    CUT TO:

31   **INT. ANTE ROOM - DAY**   31

JORDON waits as LEO comes in a moment later.

> JORDON
> You have to tell me what's going on now or I'm walking out the door.

> LEO
> Look--

> JORDON
> *Tell me now!*

> MAN (VO)
> Leo McGarry.

                                          (CONTINUED)

31   CONTINUED: 31

                          LEO
               On the day of the final debate I was
               meeting with two potential donors.

                                                          CUT TO:

32   **INT. HOTEL SUITE - DAY**   32

     LEO's letting two men into the room plus a third who we don't
     really see. Firm handshakes all around.

                          JORDON (VO)
               You meet with donors personally?

                          LEO (VO)
               When they're this big I do. It was nine
               days till the election, we were too close
               to call and I didn't want to be the guy
               who ran outa money first.

                          DONOR #1
               You look nervous, Leo, don't worry about
               it, I brought my wallet.

                          LEO
               Let's siddown, anybody want to eat? I've
               got steak sandwiches on the way.

                          DONOR #2
               I wouldn't mind a drink.

                          LEO
               Margaret'll call downstairs.

                          DONOR #1
               I've got it.

                                                     CUT BACK TO:

33   **INT. ANTE ROOM - DAY**   33

                          LEO
               The President was at the debate site
               walking the stage.

                                                          CUT TO:

34   **INT. TUNNEL - DAY**   34

     BARTLET, with JOSH, SAM, C.J. and TOBY, is being led through a
     tunnel.

                                                     (CONTINUED)

34   CONTINUED: 34

> LEO (VO)
> A podium is a holy place for him, he
> makes it his own like it's an extension
> of his body. You ever see a pitcher work
> the mound so the dirt does exactly what
> his feet want it to do? That's the
> President. His opponent isn't his
> opponent, he's his straight man.
> Involuntarily deputized.

The tunnel spills them out onto the stage where crews are
working to prepare for the event that night. It's like he's
walked into the sunshine.

> EVENT PLANNER
> I can walk the stage with you Governor.

> BARTLET
> Thank you, I can walk it.

> C.J.
> He'll walk it.

CUT BACK TO:

35   **INT. ANTE ROOM - DAY**   35

> LEO
> He sees it as a genuine opportunity to
> change minds. Also as his best way of
> contributing to the team. He likes teams.
> I love him so much.

LEO's starting to unravel ever so slightly. Talking just a
little too fast maybe.

> JORDON
> What was going on in your room.

LEO says something inaudible.

> JORDON
> I didn't hear you.

> LEO
> I said I like the little things. The way
> a glass feels in your hand. A good glass.
> Thick, with a heavy base. I love the
> sound an ice cube makes when you drop it
> from just the right height.

CUT TO:

36   **INT. HOTEL SUITE - DAY**   36

    Clink. An ice cube is dropped into the glass.

>   LEO (VO)
>   Too high and it'll chip when you drop it.
>   Chip the ice and it'll melt too fast in
>   the scotch.

>   DONOR #1
>   You don't have to call Margaret, Frank
>   brought his own.

>   DONOR #2
>   You ever try this, Leo, it's Johnny
>   Walker Blue. Bartenders are selling it
>   for 30 bucks a shot.

                                                 CUT TO:

37   **INT. ANTE ROOM - DAY**   37

>   LEO
>   Good scotch sits in a charcoal barrel for
>   12 years. Very good scotch gets smoked
>   for 29 years. Johnny Walker Blue is 60
>   year old scotch.

>   JORDON
>   I don't care, what happened in the room,
>   Leo.

>   LEO
>   I'm trying to tell you what happened.

38   **INT. HOTEL SUITE - DAY**   38

>   LEO
>   Should we get to it?

>   DONOR #2
>   You don't want to find out what a $30 sip
>   of scotch tastes like?

>   LEO
>   No, I gotta stay sharp for tonight.

>   DONOR #2
>   You sayin' I'm not sharp?

                                              (CONTINUED)

38   CONTINUED: 38

                    LEO
          No.

CUT TO:

39   **INT. ANTE ROOM - DAY**   39

                    JORDON
          Why don't you just say I'm an alcoholic?

                    LEO
          They're two CEOs, I'm trying to get 'em
          to gimme half a million dollars apiece
          right now, it's not really the best time
          to mention it. The President's still at
          the debate site.

CUT TO:

40   **INT. DEBATE SITE - DAY**   40

                    EVENT PLANNER
          How do you feel about the temperature,
          sir?

                    BARTLET
          It's good.

                    EVENT PLANNER
          It's not too cold?

                    BARTLET
          It won't be later. This is a 550 seat
          theatre and they'll be seated a half hour
          prior to the start so the temperature'll
          be up 4 to 6 degrees.

CUT TO:

41   **INT. ANTE ROOM - DAY**   41

                    JORDON
          The hotel room, Leo.

CUT TO:

42   **INT. HOTEL ROOM - DAY**   42

                    DONOR #1
          We already gave to the RNC but we're
          worried we may have backed the wrong
          horse.

(CONTINUED)

42 CONTINUED: 42

> LEO
> Wanna hedge your bet?

> DONOR #1
> That's why we're here.

> LEO
> Good.
> (to DONOR #2)
> Gimme a sip of that.

LEO takes a little sip and hands back the glass--

> LEO
> That's what I remember.

                                                              CUT TO:

43 **INT. DEBATE SITE - DAY**   43

> SAM
> There's no lip on the podium.

> EVENT PLANNER
> Excuse me.

> SAM
> His pen's gonna slide down to the floor,
> I don't want him bending down picking
> things up.

> EVENT PLANNER
> I suppose we could attach some velcro.

> SAM
> Ripping sound.

> BARTLET
> Yeah, you need to build a lip. Three
> quarter inch, it's gotta match the color
> of the podium in case the camera catches
> it.

> EVENT PLANNER
> Well the camera won't be--

> TOBY
> We're inside the margin with nine days to
> go, same color as the damn podium.

                                                              CUT TO:

44   **INT. HOTEL SUITE - DAY**   44

Clink. LEO drops an ice cube into a glass and pours himself a
proper drink.

> DONOR #2
> If he wins this thing--

> LEO
> When he wins this thing.

> DONOR #2
> There'll be an aggressive high dollar
> program at the DNC so we don't have to go
> through this every four years?

> LEO
> Count on it.

                                                        CUT TO

45   **INT. ANTE ROOM - DAY**   45

> JORDON
> You had a drink?

> LEO
> I'm an alcoholic, I don't have one drink.
> I don't under<u>stand</u> people who have one
> drink. I don't understand people who
> leave half a glass of wine on the table.
> I don't understand people who say they've
> had enough. How can you have enough of
> feeling like this? How can you not want
> to feel like this longer? My brain works
> *differently*!

> JORDON
> Who was the third person in the room?

> LEO
> Well now we've arrived at our problem.

> JORDON
> Who was the third person in the room?

> LEO
> A prominent Republican lawyer who was
> palling around with the two donors.

                                                        CUT TO:

46   **INT. HOTEL SUITE - DAY**   46

And he speaks, we discover that the prominent Republican
lawyer is GIBSON.

                          GIBSON
               Whoa, you wanna be careful there, you're
               not the big money party, we are.

                          DONOR #1
               Did I mention he's thinking about running
               for Congress?

                          GIBSON
               I'm thinking about it.

                                                    CUT TO:

47   **INT. ANTE ROOM - DAY**   47

                          JORDON
               You were drunk in front of Gibson?

                          LEO
               I don't get drunk in front of people, I
               get drunk alone.

                                                    CUT TO:

48   **INT. HOTEL SUITE - DAY**   48

As a hand dives into an open mini-bar and pulls out two
bottles.

                          LEO
               I'm late.

                                                    CUT TO:

49   **INT. ANTE ROOM - DAY**   49

                          LEO
               They were going over something at the
               debate site.

                          JORDON
               I don't want to hear about the debate
               site.

                                              (CONTINUED)

49   CONTINUED:

                    LEO
The debate site is what <u>happened</u>. The
debate site is how he gets to bring this
up here.

                                           CUT TO:

50   **INT. DEBATE SITE - DAY**   50

                    SAM
Where's Leo?

                    JOSH
I'd still like to go over the Social
Security answer, we've gotta get it down
to 90 seconds.

                    C.J.
It's down to 90 seconds.

                    JOSH
It's not and they're gonna cut him off.

                    SAM
I put a stopwatch on him, when he just
speeds it up--

                    JOSH
When he speeds it up, he speeds it up,
when he doesn't it's 90 seconds, we need
to cut some words.

                    TOBY
Which words?

                    JOSH
Governor, what do you think?

But BARTLET's someplace else. He's feeling dizzy and he's
trying to will it away but it's getting slowly worse.

                    JOSH
Governor?

                    BARTLET
               (quietly)
No.

                    JOSH
Sir, we were just saying that the Social
Security answer--

                                      (CONTINUED)

50   CONTINUED:

          BARTLET
No.

          JOSH
It's a tight 90 seconds and--

          BARTLET
No, no, not now.

          JOSH
Well we've gotta do it now 'cause--

          SAM
Josh, I think there's something wrong.

          TOBY
Something's wrong.

          C.J.
Governor--

          BARTLET
No.

          JOSH
Sir--

And BARTLET says something that sounds like--

          BARTLET
Gabby.

          SAM
Do you wanna siddown?

          C.J.
Lemme get some water.

          BARTLET
Gabby.

          TOBY
He's saying get Abbey.

          JOSH
        (screaming to anyone)
Get Abbey!!

SAM and TOBY take BARTLET under each arm--

          SAM
Out of the way please.

(CONTINUED)

50   CONTINUED: (2)   50

                         TOBY
               C.J., no pictures, no pictures!

                                                          CUT TO:

51   **INT. ANTE ROOM - DAY**   51

                         JORDON
               He had an attack.

                         LEO
               No. It was a severe inner ear infection.

                                                          CUT TO:

51A   **INT. HOTEL SUITE - DAY**   51A

     LEO answers a ringing phone--

                         LEO
                    (into phone)
               Yeah.

                         JOSH
                    (through phone)
               Leo, the Governor's sick.

     The doorbell rings--

                         LEO
                    (into phone)
               Okay.

                         JOSH
                    (through phone)
               He collapsed, you gotta get down here.

     Doorbell--

                         LEO
                    (into phone)
               Okay.

                         GIBSON (OS)
               It's Gibson.

     LEO hangs up the phone--

                         LEO
               Okay.

     LEO goes to the door and opens it--

                                                    (CONTINUED)

51A   CONTINUED:

> GIBSON
> I forgot my briefcase.
>   (beat)
> You havin' a party?

> LEO
>   (pause)
> I have to get to the debate site. The
> Governor collapsed.

CUT TO:

51B   **INT. ANTE ROOM - DAY**   51B

> JORDON
>   (pause)
> I don't understand how you could have a
> drink. I don't understand, how after
> everything you worked for, how on that
> day of all days you could be so stupid.

> LEO
> That's because you think it has something
> to do with smart and stupid. You have any
> idea how many alcoholics are in Mensa?
> You think it's a lack of willpower?
> That's like thinking somebody with
> anorexia nervosa has an overdeveloped
> sense of vanity. My father was an
> alcoholic, his father was an alcoholic,
> so in my case--

> JORDON
> Ain't nothin' but a family thing?

> LEO
> That's right.

> JORDON
> Who knows?

> LEO
> Josh Lyman and the President.

> JORDON
> Why nobody else?

> LEO
> Because.

(CONTINUED)

51B   CONTINUED: 51B

                      JORDON
That's a little boy's answer.

                      LEO
I went to rehab. My friends embraced me
when I got out. You relapse and it's not
like that. Get away from me, that's what
it's like.

There's a knock on the door--

                    CONGRESSIONAL STAFFER
We're back in a minute.

                      JORDON
Thank you.
    (pause)
Just out of curiosity, why have you been
asking me to have a meal with you every
five minutes.

                      LEO
I like you. I've been trying to get it in
under the wire.

                      JORDON
    (pause)
You'll answer the questions simply and
directly. I don't wanna hear about Mensa.
That'll be my job beginning with the
first of about 683 press appearances
we're gonna have to make.

                      LEO
Okay.

                      JORDON
Let's go.

                      LEO
Okay.

                      JORDON
Yes, by the way.

                      LEO
Yes what?

                      JORDON
Yes, I'd like to have dinner with you
tonight.

(CONTINUED)

51B   CONTINUED: (2)   51B

                              LEO
                Okay.

        They walk out the door and we

                                                        CUT TO:

52   **INT. CLOAK ROOM - DAY**   52

        Where CLIFF, GIBSON and the CHAIRMAN are having it out.

                              CLIFF
                That's where you're going with this?

                              GIBSON
                Yeah.

                              CLIFF
                Just to embarrass the guy?

                              GIBSON
                Just?

                              CLIFF
                Leo McGarry's sobriety isn't the subject
                of these hearings, these hearings are to
                investigate if any rules, ethical or
                otherwise, were broken by Jed Bartlet
                while he was running for President.

                              GIBSON
                That's nice, but I live in the actual
                world where the object of these hearings
                is to win.

                              CLIFF
                No it's not.

                              GIBSON
                It's the object of the majority.

                              CLIFF
                Not while I'm the Majority Counsel it's
                not. This is *bush league*! This is why
                good people hate us, this, right here,
                this thing.
                              (MORE)

                                                    (CONTINUED)

52   CONTINUED: 52

> CLIFF (cont'd)
> This isn't what these hearings are about,
> he cannot <u>possibly</u> have been properly
> prepared by counsel for these questions
> nor should he <u>ever</u> have to answer them
> publicly and if you proceed with this
> line of questioning I will resign this
> Committee and wait in the tall grass for
> you, Congressman, 'cause you are killing
> the Party.

> GIBSON
> (pause--to the CHAIRMAN)
> Who the hell is this?

> CHAIRMAN
> He's a new Republican.

There's a long, tense silence before--

> CLIFF
> You don't have to make up your mind right
> now, Mr. Chairman.

> GIBSON
> Phil--

> CLIFF
> You don't have to make up your mind right
> now. Declare a recess until after the
> holidays, buy yourself two weeks.

> GIBSON
> And give him two weeks to circle the
> wagons, how do you think the Speaker's
> gonna feel about this to say nothing of
> the RNC?

> CHAIRMAN
> I need a minute.

CUT TO:

53   **INT. JOSH'S OFFICE - DAY   (FORMERLY HEARING ROOM)**   53

Where JOSH is watching TV as SAM comes in.

> SAM
> I tried everybody.

> JOSH
> It's all right.

(CONTINUED)

                         SAM
                    I tried everybody, it was just a tough
                    fit. And since I couldn't tell 'em what
                    it was about--

                         JOSH
                    They're back.

                         CHAIRMAN (ON TV)
                    Let's come to order.

                                                              CUT TO:

53A **INT. HEARING ROOM - DAY**   53A

                         CHAIRMAN
                      (pause)
                    Mr. Gibson, you can proceed with your
                    questioning.

          CLIFF doesn't believe it.

                         GIBSON
                      (beat)
                    Thank you, Mr. Chairman. Mr. McGarry, 30
                    October in St. Louis, Missouri, the day
                    Jed Bartlet was--

                         CHAIRMAN
                    No, I'm sorry. Mr. McGarry, it's been a
                    long day and unless Counsel has an
                    objection I'm gonna resume this after the
                    holidays.

                         LEO
                    What?

                         GIBSON
                    Mr. Chairman--

                         CHAIRMAN
                    Mr. Calley?

                         CLIFF
                    Mr. McGarry, that concludes our
                    questioning for today, we'll pick it up
                    here when the Chairman gavels these
                    hearings back to order.

                         LEO
                    I'm sorry?

                                                      (CONTINUED)

53A   CONTINUED: 53A

                         CHAIRMAN
              You're done for the day, sir. The House
              Reform and Government Oversight Committee
              stands in recess until January the fifth
              and the Chair wishes everyone a Merry
              Christmas.

The CHAIRMAN raps his gavel and everyone gets up--

                         LEO
              What the hell--

                         JORDON
              I don't know. We've got two weeks.

                         LEO
                   (pause)
              I really had to tell <u>you</u> the damn story.

                         JORDON
              Shut up, I'm going to dinner with you.

                         LEO
              Yeah. Listen, you wanna do it tomorrow
              night instead?

                         JORDON
              What's tomorrow night?

                         LEO
              It's Christmas Eve.

                         JORDON
                   (beat)
              Okay.

                         LEO
              Okay.

LEO's about to head out but catches CLIFF's eye. CLIFF stays
on him just long enough to show him nothing, then fades into
the crowd.

                                                    CUT TO:

54   **INT. WHITE HOUSE CORRIDOR - NIGHT**   54

The place is deserted. LEO comes down the hall and heads into--

55   **INT. LEO'S OFFICE - CONTINUOUS**   55

BARTLET's sitting at his desk.

                         BARTLET
          Well, well, well. Dodged a bullet.

                         LEO
          For the moment.

                         BARTLET
          Which is more than I can say for me at
          Rosslyn.

                         LEO
          Yeah.

                         BARTLET
          Did you get a date with her?

                         LEO
          None of your business. I just came back
          to catch up on some work. See how badly
          you screwed up this church thing in
          Tennessee.

                         BARTLET
          I <u>did</u> the church thing in Tennessee,
          okay, I did it without you.

                         LEO
          You mind if I make some calls, make sure
          Tennessee's still one of the states and
          stuff?

                         BARTLET
          So anyway, I have a Christmas present for
          you.

BARTLET hands him what looks like a giftwrapped picture frame.
LEO opens it. Mounted in a small frame is a crumpled up napkin
that says--

                  Bartlet for America

                         BARTLET
          Merry Christmas, Leo, that was awfully
          nice of you.

BARTLET walks out...

                                          (CONTINUED)

69.

55   CONTINUED: 55

> LEO
> Merry Christmas.

FADE TO BLACK

<u>END OF SHOW</u>

POSSE COMITATUS

"...*Aaaaand* CUT! Print that one."

"Yeah!" "Beautiful!" "Got it!"

Cheers and whistles and backslaps exploded on the roof of the ABC building in Times Square, one of three camera positions Alex Graves had set up for a shot of Bartlet's motorcade speeding toward 45th Street and the Booth Theatre, where Bartlet was to attend a fictional production of a fictional play called *The Wars of the Roses*.

The fact that it was well after midnight, raining and 45 degrees did nothing to dampen anyone's spirits, nor did the fact that shooting this night would continue until sunrise. And no one was surprised when, after the cheering subsided, Alex called out, "All right, let's do it one more time."

The single biggest reason for budget overages on the show is me, but I get a healthy assist in that department from directors, actors and crew members who insist on doin' it 'til they're satisfied.

We've shot 20 hour days, we've shot on Saturdays and Sundays. Actors have shot straight through the night in Washington, gone to the airport, flown to L.A. and come directly to the set and shot a four-page scene in which their only line is "Good morning, Mr. President."

A dream team.

Here's *Posse Comitatus*.

The West Wing

Posse Comitatus

GREEN REVISIONS: 05/10/02
YELLOW REVISIONS: 05/06/02
PINK REVISIONS: 05/06/02
BLUE REVISIONS: 05/06/02

THE WEST WING

"Posse Comitatus"

Written by
Aaron Sorkin

Directed by
Alex Graves

PRODUCTION #227 222
Episode Twenty-Two

JOHN WELLS PRODUCTIONS
in association with
WARNER BROS. TELEVISION
4000 Warner Blvd.
Burbank, CA 91522

Final Shooting Draft
May 3, 2002
Copyright © 2002
Warner Bros. Television
All Rights Reserved

THE WEST WING

"Posse Comitatus"

Script Revision History

DATE	COLOR	PAGES
05/06/02	BLUE PAGES	36,36A,37
05/06/02	PINK PAGES	SETS,50,51-53,56,56A,57, 57A,59,59A
05/06/02	YELLOW PAGES	37,47,47A,48,62
05/10/02	GREEN PAGES	TITLE PAGE

SET LIST

INTERIORS
WHITE HOUSE
    Bartlet's Bathroom
    Press Briefing
    Situation Room
    Communications Bullpen
    Roosevelt Room
    Mural Room
    Corridors
    Josh's Bullpen
    Bartlet's Study
    Oval Office
    Sam's Office
    Toby's Office
    Basement Meeting Room
    Mrs. Landingham's Office
    Josh's Office

DINER

FIDERER'S HOUSE

BROADWAY THEATRE
    Theatre
    Lower Lobby
    Upper Lobby
    VIP Room
    *
    Men's Lounge

KOREAN GROCERY

AMY'S LOFT

EXTERIORS
SUBURBAN MARYLAND STREET
    (FIDERER'S HOUSE) – DAY

BROADWAY THEATRE – EARLY
    EVENING (EST.)

SHUBERT ALLEY – EARLY EVENING

BROADWAY THEATRE – NIGHT

KOREAN GROCERY – NIGHT

AIR FIELD – NIGHT

FRONT STOOP – NIGHT *

TIMES SQUARE – NIGHT *

THE WEST WING

"Posse Comitatus"

CAST LIST

PRESIDENT JOSIAH BARTLET
LEO McGARRY
JOSH LYMAN
SAM SEABORN
TOBY ZIEGLER
C.J. CREGG
CHARLIE YOUNG
DONNA MOSS

ARTHUR
KATIE
STEVE
MARK
CHRIS
FITZWALLACE
STAHL
MCCANN
AMY GARDNER
SIMON DONOVAN
CAROL
DR. STANLEY KEYWORTH
NANCY
RON BUTTERFIELD

CIVILIAN #1	CANTWELL
MARINE OFFICER	LOBELL
CIVILIAN #2	AGENT
WAITRESS	AGENT #2
ANTHONY	BEDFORD
FISHER	REPORTER
BURNET	REPORTER #2
KEITH	KOREAN MAN
BRISTOL	YORK
DEBORAH FIDERER	ROBERT RITCHIE
ABDUL IBN SHAREEF	BOY
TRANSLATOR	COMPANY
SHAKER	
HOWELL	

"Posse Comitatus"

<u>TEASER</u>

FADE IN:

1   **INT. BARTLET'S BATHROOM - EARLY MORNING**   1

BARTLET's shaving. After a moment, he'll lazily start to sing
the chorus of a song he's looking forward to hearing tonight.
He's singing it half under his breath, but just loud enough so
that we can hear the words.

> BARTLET
> "*...And victorious in war, shall be made*
> *glorious in peace.*"
>   (beat)
> "*And victorious in war, shall be made*
> *glorious in peace.*"

BARTLET continues shaving but cuts himself at the top of his
throat.

> BARTLET
> Ah--dammit.

BARTLET grabs a hand towel but doesn't do anything with it.
He's looking at the small red line he's made on his throat and
the blood starting to trickle down. He looks at it,
expressionless, for an uncomfortably long moment before he
erases it with the hand towel and we

                                                  SMASH CUT TO:

MAIN TITLES

<u>END OF TEASER</u>

ACT ONE

FADE IN:

2   **INT. PRESS BRIEFING ROOM - DAY**   2

C.J.'s at the podium. She's in a great mood. Relaxed and
funny.

>   C.J.
> We're leaving exactly one hour later than
> we'd planned. At five o'clock he'll board
> Marine One for the trip to Andrews, where
> he'll board Air Force One for the trip to
> New York. We're just trying to be helpful
> 'cause we understand that a presidential
> motorcade rolling through midtown
> Manhattan at around six, six-thirty
> really helps keep things well-lubed up
> there. As a matter of fact we apologize
> to New Yorkers for the inconvenience but
> the delay was inevitable.
>   (laughing a little)
> I meant to say unavoidable. The delay was
> unavoidable. The President will make a
> short visit at City Hall and be in his
> seat at 6:59.

>   ARTHUR
> Why is it such an early curtain.

>   C.J.
> The play is 19 hours long. It's long,
> it's five and a half hours.

>   KATIE
> Do you have a nose count yet this
> morning?

>   C.J.
> On the welfare bill?

>   KATIE
> Yeah, I heard there was more movement
> last night.

>   C.J.
> Yeah, there's movement, it's close.

>   KATIE
> How close?

                                                    (CONTINUED)

2   CONTINUED:

                         C.J.
              Look at the color of Josh Lyman's hair.

She gets a laugh...

                         STEVE
              How much of at least your summer plans
              for the campaign depend on winning the
              vote.

                         C.J.
              I'd go beyond that, I'd say the future of
              the entire world depends on it.

Another laugh...

                         C.J.
              I don't want to scare anybody but I'd
              call your Congressman. Mark.

                         MARK
              Seriously, 50 dollars if you give me a
              straight answer. Are they gonna meet
              tonight.

                         C.J.
              The President and Governor Ritchie?

                         MARK
              Yes.

                         C.J.
              I don't know.

Everyone's laughing--

                         MARK
              Now I'm just gonna blow it on booze and
              women.

                         C.J.
              Hey I was once at a Broadway show and
              Peggy Fleming was there and we never met.
              Anything else? I'll see you in New York.

                         CHRIS
              Oh wait. You never told us why the delay?

                         C.J.
              I'm sorry?

                                            (CONTINUED)

2   CONTINUED: (2)   2

                              CHRIS
                    Why's the President leaving an hour
                    later.

                              C.J.
                    He scheduled a last minute meeting.

                              CHRIS
                    With who?

                              C.J.
                    Good question.

          C.J. flips a page in her notes and checks...

                              C.J.
                    Qumari Defense Minister Abdul Shareef.
                    Thank you.

                              ALL
                    Thank you/Thank you, C.J./etc.

                                                    CUT TO:

3   **INT. SITUATION ROOM - DAY**   3

          The small group that's been meeting as the "kill committee" is
          assembled as LEO walks in.

                              LEO
                    Where'd we get the wires crossed, how'd
                    the Pentagon put it on his schedule?

                              FITZWALLACE
                    We didn't get the wires crossed.

                              LEO
                    He's meeting with the guy, he's gonna be
                    in the Oval Office.

                              FITZWALLACE
                    He was always gonna do that.

                              LEO
                    It wasn't canceled?

                              FITZWALLACE
                    No way.

                              LEO
                    Fitz--

                                                    (CONTINUED)

CONTINUED:

> FITZWALLACE
> The White House cancels a meeting at the
> last minute he's gonna have somebody
> tasting his food for a month, I don't
> want him thinking.

> LEO
> And I don't want the President--all
> right.
> (beat)
> I was gonna say I don't want him putting
> a voice to the guy. I take my daughter to
> a seafood place, the first thing she does
> is name all the lobsters in the tank so I
> can't eat 'em.

BARTLET comes in.

> BARTLET
> Hello.

> ALL
> Good morning, sir/etc.

> STAHL
> Mr. President, we wanted to lay out some
> of the rules.

> BARTLET
> There are rules for these things?

> STAHL
> Yes sir. The first one being the National
> Security Act which says basically that
> only the President can trigger a covert
> action. This isn't a situation where we
> want you to know as little as possible,
> the law requires that you know
> everything.

> BARTLET
> Doesn't the law also require that I not
> assassinate someone?

> MCCANN
> Yes. Political assassination is banned by
> Executive Order. Two Executive Orders as
> a matter of fact.

> BARTLET
> I know, one of them was mine.

(CONTINUED)

3   CONTINUED: (2)   3

                    MCCANN
        You can get around the Executive Order,
        sir, if--

                    BARTLET
        --I ignore.

                    STAHL
        That's exactly right.

                    BARTLET
        I was kidding.

                    LEO
        The E.O. is law, but it was made up by
        the Executive, and the Executive can
        ignore it.

                    BARTLET
        I'm assuming that rule was written in an
        Executive Order someplace.

                    LEO
        There's also self-defense.

                    BARTLET
        Assume for a second that I say yes. How
        do we do it, Fitz walks up to him with a
        gun?

                    FITZWALLACE
        No, it can't be military.

                    BARTLET
        Why?

                    FITZWALLACE
        The Posse Comitatus Act of 1878 prohibits
        the military from civilian law
        enforcement. And it can't happen on
        American soil.

                    BARTLET
        The things we choose to care about.

                    CIVILIAN #1
        Mr. President, I should mention that if
        you give the order the law insists that
        you inform what we call the gang of
        eight. That's the Leadership on both
        parties in both Houses and the
        Chairpeople and ranking members of the
        two Intelligence Committees.

                                          (CONTINUED)

>   BARTLET
> If it can't happen here then why'd we
> care that Shareef was delivering himself?

>   FITZWALLACE
> He's flying back tonight on his
> Gulfstream. The pilot's gonna be one of
> our people. They'll experience a
> mechanical failure about 90 minutes into
> the flight and set down in a remote R.A.F
> airstrip in Bermuda, it's really not much
> more than a road in the grass.

>   BARTLET
> The British say yes?

>   FITZWALLACE
> Yes sir.

>   BARTLET
> How many over there know about this?

>   FITZWALLACE
> Three.

>   BARTLET
> And some people in Bermuda?

>   MARINE OFFICER
> Yes sir.

>   LEO
> This is as big as the club gets, all
> right?

Everyone agrees.

>   BARTLET
>   (getting up)
> Okay. Well. Surely this was the most
> absurd meeting I've ever sat in, and
> friends, that is saying something.

>   CIVILIAN #2
>   (stopping him)
> Sir, will you be exchanging gifts with
> Shareef when you meet this afternoon?

>   BARTLET
> Yeah, I imagine.

He takes out a pen--

(CONTINUED)

3   CONTINUED: (4)   3

                        CIVILIAN #2
            We'd like you to give him this.

BARTLET shakes his head and smiles...how'd he get into the
middle of an episode of "Get Smart"...

                        BARTLET
            What does the pen do, it squirts poison?

                        CIVILIAN #2
            It's got a small recording device in
            there. He'll probably throw it in the
            trash but you never know, you might get
            lucky, he sticks it in his breast pocket
            for the flight home.

It's really come to this...BARTLET tosses the pen back on the
table and starts out...

                        CIVILIAN #2
            Sir?

                        BARTLET
            We give 'em it boxed, tell 'em to put it
            in a box.

BARTLET exits and we

                                                              CUT TO:

4   **INT. DINER - DAY**   4

JOSH and AMY are giving their order to a WAITRESS.

                        AMY
            Can I get an egg white omelette and some
            toast that's badly burnt?

                        WAITRESS
            Yes.

                        JOSH
            Just coffee, thanks.

The WAITRESS exits.

                        JOSH
            That doesn't give you cancer?

                        AMY
            Burnt toast?

                                                         (CONTINUED)

4   CONTINUED: 4

                         JOSH
          Yeah.

                         AMY
          They're not sure, that's why I have the
          egg white omelette.

                         JOSH
          Welfare is a core issue with swing and
          independent voters. They use it as a
          barometer to measure a President's values
          on work and responsibility.

                         AMY
          Yeah.

                         JOSH
          We're gonna win the vote.

                         AMY
          We'll see.

                         JOSH
          We will but we're gonna. I've got a nine
          vote margin.

                         AMY
          I think you're gonna lose Burnet, Bristol
          and Keith.

                         JOSH
          They're on the fence.

                         AMY
          Yeah.

                         JOSH
          You understand we have to authorize
          welfare one way or another, you have to
          do it every six years.

                         AMY
               (pause)
          Have I done something to make you think
          I'm dumb?

                         JOSH
          Amy--

                         AMY
          Doesn't the fact that they have to
          reauthorize it mean you've got
          Republicans where you--

                                              (CONTINUED)

4   CONTINUED: (2)   4

                         JOSH
          We got an extra billion in child care.

                         AMY
          Which is great but the marriage
          incentives are terrible.

                         JOSH
          We don't like the marriage incentives
          either, don't be ridiculous, but
          independent voters--

                         AMY
          Would you please say white men instead of
          independent voters and if you're serious
          about making welfare a second chance and
          not a way of life then you have to give
          people job training.

                         JOSH
          Call off the hunt and I'll see to it that
          you guys can make up with the White
          House.

                         AMY
          Why?

                         JOSH
          'Cause we're gonna win.

                         AMY
          The food's here.

     The WAITRESS sets the food down as we

                                                      CUT TO:

5   **INT. BULLPEN - DAY**   5

     SIMON, in casual clothes, is talking to a 14 year-old boy
     named ANTHONY.

                         SIMON
          You know what you should do? You should
          bring your Mom a souvenir from the White
          House. Every day you should show your Mom
          some expression of love. A smile, 'You
          look pretty today, Mom', a good smack on
          the ass they like. You know why you give
          your mother an expression of love every
          day?

                                                  (CONTINUED)

5   CONTINUED:

                    ANTHONY
          'Cause she raised me.

                    SIMON
               (pause)
          Okay, sure. I was gonna say it just makes
          things easier.

                    ANTHONY
          So you're gonna be careful in New York,
          right?

                    SIMON
          I'm only going for a few hours.

                    ANTHONY
          I mean when the crazy guy shows up.

                    SIMON
          You don't think I can handle myself?

                    ANTHONY
          Well...

                    SIMON
          What?

                    ANTHONY
          You've got skills, I don't deny that. You
          can shoot and you're athletic.

                    SIMON
          But?

                    ANTHONY
          You're slow witted.

                    SIMON
          Let the beatings begin.

And SIMON starts smacking ANTHONY who's cracking up--

                    ANTHONY
          You're not very bright and the criminals
          sense this about you.

                    SIMON
          Get over here.

C.J. comes in--

                    C.J.
          Good morning.

                                        (CONTINUED)

5   CONTINUED: (2)   5

                    SIMON
          Good morning.

                         C.J.
          I thought you weren't on till this
          afternoon.

                    SIMON
          I'm not. I arranged this for my friend
          Anthony, here. Anthony, this is Miss
          Cregg.

                    ANTHONY
          Hi.

                    SIMON
          You think it'd be possible for Anthony to
          get a souvenir he can give his Mom.

                         C.J.
          Sure it is. Carol? That's really sweet,
          Anthony, doing something nice for your
          Mom.
                    (smacking SIMON on the arm)
          You should be like that.

                    SIMON
          Yes.

     CAROL comes in.

                         C.J.
          Can you set this gentleman up with a key
          chain, please.

                    CAROL
          Yep.

                         C.J.
          It's gonna have the Seal of the President
          on it and President Bartlet's signature.
          You can tell your Mom that you can't buy
          this in a souvenir shop, in fact you
          can't buy it anywhere 'cause it's against
          the law to sell the Seal of the
          President, you can only get it here.

                    ANTHONY
          Yeah, but if the cops stop me aren't they
          gonna think I stole it?

                                             (CONTINUED)

5   CONTINUED: (3)

                        C.J.
        If the cops stop you they're gonna think
        you're an important person.

                    SIMON
        Stop you for what?

                    ANTHONY
        Whatever.

                    SIMON
        Wait outside for a second, would you?

                    ANTHONY
        Yeah.

                        C.J.
        Nice meeting you.

ANTHONY exits.

                        C.J.
        Is he your nephew.

                    SIMON
        No, I'm a Big Brother. We've been
        together about three years.

                        C.J.
        Are you good at it?

                    SIMON
        I don't know. He says he wants to be a
        Big Brother when he gets older so I
        guess, you know...

                        C.J.
        Listen, I was thinking, there's really no
        reason for you to make the trip to New
        York.

                    SIMON
        Yeah?

                        C.J.
        I'm gonna be traveling with the President
        the whole time.

                    SIMON
        Can I say something?

                        C.J.
        Sure.

                                        (CONTINUED)

5   CONTINUED: (4)   5

                            SIMON
            I'm not allowed to date a protectee.

                            C.J.
            Who's trying to date you?

                            SIMON
            I'm not allowed to kiss a protectee.

                            C.J.
            Who's trying to kiss you?

                            SIMON
            You did.

                            C.J.
            No I didn't.

                            SIMON
            C.J., I'm trusted with a serious job.

                            C.J.
            Aren't you not allowed to call a
            protectee by their first name?

                            SIMON
              (pause)
            Yes ma'am. I'm gonna take Anthony home.

                            C.J.
            There's really no reason for you to come
            to New York.

                            SIMON
            I'll see you on the plane.

            SIMON exits.

                                        FADE TO BLACK.

                        END OF ACT ONE

ACT TWO

FADE IN:

INT. ROOSEVELT ROOM - DAY

Congressman FISHER is talking to SAM and TOBY.

> FISHER
> Welfare reform is a state issue, if you
> go ahead without the Governors you're
> asking for trouble.

> SAM
> You co-sponsored the bill.

> FISHER
> Yeah, I'm saying the Governors are the
> ones who have to make it work.

> SAM
> You know we've got the NGA and the RGA,
> right?

> FISHER
> I'm saying if you increase the work hours
> for example, what do the Governors do if
> there aren't enough jobs.

> SAM
> I don't even understand that.

> TOBY
> I don't think the Congressman's here as a
> co-sponsor of the bill, Sam, I think he's
> here as the leader of Florida's
> Republican delegation.

> FISHER
> The President should meet with Ritchie
> tonight.

> SAM
> That's not gonna happen.

> FISHER
> They should walk in the door together and
> they should--

> SAM
> Walk in the door together?

(CONTINUED)

6   CONTINUED: 6

                              TOBY
               It's a Catholic fundraiser, Ted, it's not
               a network debate.

                              FISHER
               They should walk in the door together,
               they should go in a room and talk and
               then they should watch the play and there
               are five Congressmen who'd be interested
               in the outcome of that meeting.

                              SAM
               We get the votes if the President meets
               with Ritchie.

                              FISHER
               Yes.

                              SAM
               We already had yours.

                              FISHER
               You get four more.

                              TOBY
               Ted, the President enters the room with
               his wife and the President of China, he
               doesn't do it with the Governor of
               Florida.

                                                        CUT TO:

7   **INT. MURAL ROOM - DAY**   7

     JOSH is consulting with three Congressmen.

                              BURNET
               Can I ask how you guys are taking in a
               Broadway show during a vote like this?

                              JOSH
               That was a scheduling error.

                              BURNET
               It was.

                              JOSH
               Nonetheless--

                              KEITH
               I've got a primary.

                                                        (CONTINUED)

7   CONTINUED:

                    JOSH
          I know.

                    KEITH
          I'm spending money already.

                    JOSH
          We can help you raise money.

                    KEITH
          So can Amy Gardner.

                    JOSH
          Look, this isn't a bad bill, we're
          fixing--

                    KEITH
          How are the women--

                    JOSH
          --ten things that were wrong with
          welfare. Transportation subsidies--

                    KEITH
          How are the women supposed to train for
          life after welfare when they're required
          to work 38 hours a week?

                    BRISTOL
          Forget the work requirement, it's the
          marriage incentives, I can't stomach
          that. But setting aside the policy, it's
          bad politics, you're pissing off our base
          late Spring of an even numbered year.

                    JOSH
          Hey Jamie, you wanna talk about bad
          politics, how 'bout getting yanked to the
          left when we need to swing center.

                    BRISTOL
          I can't run without women.

                    JOSH
          All right, these are three 'no' votes,
          right?

                    BURNET
          Yeah.

                    JOSH
          Okay, the President's gonna call you.

                                        (CONTINUED)

7   CONTINUED: (2)   7

> BRISTOL
> Do you know when?

> JOSH
> No. Sometime during the first
> intermission, I don't know.

JOSH exits into--

8   **INT. CORRIDOR - CONTINUOUS**   8

--where TOBY comes along.

> JOSH
> What'd Fisher want?

> TOBY
> We get four new votes if the President
> meets with Ritchie, tell me you don't
> need four votes.

> JOSH
> I need every vote.
> (pause)
> Don't do it.

> TOBY
> You're sure, 'cause it's bad, but not as
> bad as--

> JOSH
> Yeah, no don't do it, I can get it done.

> TOBY
> Good.

TOBY heads off as DONNA comes along--

> JOSH
> Burnet, Bristol and Keith, move 'em to
> 'no'.

> DONNA
> Definite 'no'?

> JOSH
> Yeah, but put 'em under 'leaning no',
> maybe it'll make us feel better.

                                                        CUT TO:

9   **EXT. SUBURBAN MARYLAND STREET - DAY**   9

A well-used Honda Civic pulls up to a modest house and CHARLIE
hops out. He goes up the walk, checking an address he has
scribbled down, and rings the doorbell.

A woman in a business suit answers. She's DEBORAH FIDERER, an
extremely bright and capable woman who's spent way too much
time alone in the last few years.

                    CHARLIE
Mrs. DiLaguardia.

                    FIDERER
Yes.

                    CHARLIE
It's Charlie. I think there's trouble
with your phone line, we kept getting
disconnected. I hope you don't mind, I
just drove on out.

                    FIDERER
No, yeah, we weren't getting
disconnected, I was hanging up.

                    CHARLIE
      (beat)
Why?

                    FIDERER
I wasn't interested in the job.

                    CHARLIE
Why didn't you just say so.

                    FIDERER
You would've asked me why.

                    CHARLIE
Yeah.

                    FIDERER
My way was faster.

                    CHARLIE
Why aren't you interested?

And the door closes. CHARLIE waits a moment, then rings the
doorbell again. The door opens--

                                    (CONTINUED)

9   CONTINUED: 9

                              FIDERER
                    So you have my address, what other
                    corners of my personal life have you
                    rooted out?

                              CHARLIE
                         (pause)
                    You <u>worked</u> at the White House, we know
                    where you live!

                              FIDERER
                    I'll bet you do.

                              CHARLIE
                    May I come inside for one minute?

                              FIDERER
                    You're not allowed to park there.

                              CHARLIE
                    Yes I am.

                              FIDERER
                    All right.

          CHARLIE walks into--

10   **INT. FIDERER'S HOUSE - CONTINUOUS**   10

                              CHARLIE
                    Mrs. DiLaGuardia--

                              FIDERER
                    I'm not married to Mr. DiLaGuardia
                    anymore, my name's Debbie Fiderer.

                              CHARLIE
                    Fidler?

                              FIDERER
                    Fiderer.

                              CHARLIE
                    Ms. Fiderer, you've worked as Executive
                    Assistant to Terrance Hunt, Managing
                    Editor of Gannet News, Jack Kent Cooke,
                    former owner of the Washington Redskins,
                    Jordan Williams, founding partner at
                    Cutler, Williams, Rossi, and the White
                    House Office of Presidential Personnel
                    and I'd like you to come meet with the
                    President today to discuss filling
                    Delores Landingham's job.

                                              (CONTINUED)

> FIDERER
>
> No.

> CHARLIE
>
> Why?

> FIDERER
>
> This is so much worse than the phone call
> would've been.

> CHARLIE
>
> Why?

> FIDERER
>
> Because I don't work for anyone, Charlie.
> I'm my own boss. I set my sail...
>> (not knowing the end of the
>> expression but fully
>> committing to it anyway)
>
> ...and then I go that particular
> direction.

> CHARLIE
>
> You do.

> FIDERER
>
> Yeah.

> CHARLIE
>
> How's the sailing been?

> FIDERER
>
> I beg your pardon?

> CHARLIE
>
> How's business?

> FIDERER
>
> I'll admit I got off to a rocky start.

> CHARLIE
>
> What'd you try?

> FIDERER
>
> Gambling.

> CHARLIE
>
> Didn't work out?

> FIDERER
>
> No, but all that's changed.

(CONTINUED)

10   CONTINUED: (2)   10

                         CHARLIE
                'Cause now you're...

                         FIDERER
                An alpaca farmer.

                         CHARLIE
                    (pause)
                Are you serious?

                         FIDERER
                It's the world's finest livestock
                investment, Charlie.

                         CHARLIE
                You're talkin' about those sheep they
                show on late-night TV?

                         FIDERER
                Well they're alpacas and if you knew that
                the textiles made from their fiber are
                coveted by the best fashion houses.

                         CHARLIE
                You swallowed a brochure?!

                         FIDERER
                I've got two of the Huacaya variety.

                         CHARLIE
                You were Executive to the head of the US
                Olympic Organizing Committee, were you
                not?

                         FIDERER
                Yes.

                         CHARLIE
                I'm sending a car for you in 90 minutes.

CHARLIE starts for the door but FIDERER stops him with--

                         FIDERER
                I was fired from the White House,
                Charlie.

                         CHARLIE
                I know you were.

And he heads out as we

                                              CUT TO:

11   **INT. BULLPEN - DAY**   11

DONNA's at her desk eating french fries and drinking a coke as
SIMON comes in, having changed into a suit.

>   DONNA
>   Hey, Simon.

>   SIMON
>   How you doin', Donna.

>   DONNA
>   When are you guys leaving?

>   SIMON
>   Well we're going down early, that's why
>   I'm here.

>   DONNA
>   She ran across to OEOB, she should be
>   back in a minute.

>   SIMON
>   Thanks.

>   DONNA
>   You want some french fries?

>   SIMON
>   We have a nutritionist that's put me on a
>   low cholesterol diet.

>   DONNA
>   What does it consist of?

>   SIMON
>   Being hungry all the time.

DONNA smiles...

>   SIMON
>   (pause)
>   So.
>   (pause)
>   C.J. Cregg.

DONNA nearly spits out her coke at how clumsy that was...

>   SIMON
>   Never mind.

>   DONNA
>   Sorry.

                                              (CONTINUED)

11   CONTINUED: 11

                    SIMON
          Don't worry about it.

                    DONNA
          No, talk to me.

                    SIMON
          There's a vote tonight.

                    DONNA
          No, really, you just caught me off guard.

                    SIMON
          Tell me about the vote.

                    DONNA
          It's a big vote, I'm sorry.

                    SIMON
          And Josh is in charge.

                    DONNA
          Yeah.

                    SIMON
          Is that a big deal for him?

                    DONNA
          Josh gets put in charge of anything that
          absolutely, positively has to get done.

                    SIMON
          Does he have political aspirations
          himself?

                    DONNA
          No.

                    SIMON
          Why not?

                    DONNA
          Josh doesn't want to be the guy. Josh
          wants to be the guy the guy counts on.

                    SIMON
          You like talking about him.

                    DONNA
          Yeah.
              (pause)
          So.
                    (MORE)

                                              (CONTINUED)

11   CONTINUED: (2)   11

                              DONNA (cont'd)
                       (pause)
                  C.J. Cregg.

                              SIMON
                  Shut up.

                              DONNA
                  Okay.

                                                          CUT TO:

12   **INT. BARTLET'S STUDY - DAY**   12

      BARTLET's in session with STANLEY...

                              BARTLET
                  It's the Wars of the Roses, all the
                  Henrys, and Richards too for that matter.

                              STANLEY
                  In some kind of condensed form.

                              BARTLET
                  Yeah.

                              STANLEY
                  'Cause you'd be there for a few weeks,
                  right, if--

                              BARTLET
                  Yeah. There's also singing.

                              STANLEY
                  It's a musical?

                              BARTLET
                  No, but they're gonna sing from time to
                  time. And one of the songs is a song I
                  love.
                       (pause)
                  ...and I can't think of the name of it
                  now but it's an Edwardian...
                       (beat)
                  ...it always reminds me of, it makes me
                  think of college. Like I don't know, like
                  they should be singing it in the dining
                  hall at Christ College in Cambridge. The
                  chorus is "And victorious in war shall be
                  made glorious in peace." I was just
                  singing it this morning.

                              STANLEY
                  How've you been sleeping?

                                                     (CONTINUED)

12   CONTINUED:

                    BARTLET
        Good. Lemme ask you something. Is there a
        crime, which if it weren't illegal you
        would do it.

                    STANLEY
            (pause)
        I'd park anywhere I want.

                    BARTLET
        Right, but you wouldn't rob a bank.

                    STANLEY
        No.

                    BARTLET
        Connecticut had a law prohibiting the use
        of contraceptives. It was written out of
        rage against adultery. But in the age of
        AIDS don't Connecticut residents do more
        for the general welfare by flagrantly
        breaking the law?

                    STANLEY
        There was a law against contraceptives?

                    BARTLET
        Yeah.

                    STANLEY
        Can I ask, sir, how someone used to get
        caught?

                    BARTLET
            (frustrated)
        Stanley--

                    STANLEY
        What's on your mind, Mr. President?

                    BARTLET
        I can't tell you.

                    STANLEY
        Yeah, but you can.

                    BARTLET
        No I really can't, it's high security to
        say nothing of--

                                                    (CONTINUED)

12   CONTINUED: (2)   12

          BARTLET smiles for a second...this is starting to get
          ludicrous...

                              STANLEY
                    To say nothing of what?

                              BARTLET
                    If I tell you that I intend to commit a
                    crime you're required by law to report
                    it. I have a pretty strange meeting
                    coming up, I'm gonna go. Good seeing you.

          BARTLET walks out and we

                                                      FADE TO BLACK.

                         <u>END OF ACT TWO</u>

ACT THREE

FADE IN:

13   **INT. THE OVAL OFFICE - DAY**   13

We're hearing a man speak in Arabic and seeing that he's
holding in his hands a blue pen box bearing the Seal of the
President.

                    SHAREEF
               (in Arabic)
          ...and that the friendship established
          long ago between the United States and
          the Nation of Qumar is based on frankness
          and serves the interest of both the
          American and Qumari people.

BARTLET is having a two minute courtesy meeting with SHAREEF,
with a U.S. translator standing between them. Two BODYGUARDS
are standing nearby. LEO and FITZWALLACE are off to the side.

The TRANSLATOR translates as--

                    LEO
               (quietly to FITZWALLACE)
          This is surreal.

                    FITZWALLACE
          He's doing well.

                    BARTLET
               (re: the BODYGUARDS)
          Who are these men?

                    FITZWALLACE
          Not any more.

                    TRANSLATOR
               (in Arabic)
          Who are these men?

                    SHAREEF
               (in Arabic)
          Bodyguards.

                    TRANSLATOR
               (in English)
          Bodyguards.

                    BARTLET
          Okay.

                                              (CONTINUED)

13   CONTINUED:

                        SHAREEF
          (in Arabic)
I would like to personally congratulate
you, Mr. President, on the renewal of
your ten year lease on the air base in
Tiaret.

                      TRANSLATOR
          (in English)
I would like to personally congratulate
you, Mr. President, on the renewal of
your ten year lease on the air base in
Tiaret.

                      BARTLET
Yeah, I'm feeling particularly proud of
that today.

                      TRANSLATOR
          (in Arabic)
Yes I'm feeling particularly proud of
that today.

                      BARTLET
We're happy that you visited us, Mr.
Defense Minister, you're welcome here
anytime, and please send the best wishes
of the President of the United States to
the Royal Sultan.

This gets translated and SHAREEF smiles and extends his hand
but his hand isn't met. It's an awkward moment as BARTLET just
stands there.

                      BARTLET
Not in the Oval Office.

                      TRANSLATOR
          (pause)
Sir?

                      BARTLET
          (without taking his eyes off
           SHAREEF)
Tell him I have a rash on my hand. Make
sure you apologize.

                      TRANSLATOR
The President apologizes but he has a
rash on his hand.

                      (CONTINUED)

13   CONTINUED: (2)   13

                         SHAREEF
                       (in Arabic)
                    Good bye, then.

                              BARTLET
                    Yeah.

SHAREEF and the BODYGUARDS exit.

                              BARTLET
                         (to the TRANSLATOR)
                    Thanks.

                         TRANSLATOR
                    Yes sir.

The translator exits. BARTLET lazily holds up the gift he was
given.

                              BARTLET
                    It's a hand-carved incense burner. Gypsum
                    and sandalwood.

He tosses it to FITZWALLACE and heads out. FITZWALLACE and LEO
stand there a moment before--

                         LEO
                    We have to do this other thing now.

They head out of the room in a different direction and we

                                              CUT TO:

14   **INT. SAM'S OFFICE - DAY**   14

He's not taking his eyes off his reading material as he picks
up a sandwich that's on his desk. Just as he gets the sandwich
to his mouth, a rubber ball hits the window.

He puts the sandwich down.

Another rubber ball.

He gets up and walks into--

15   **INT. TOBY'S OFFICE - CONTINUOUS**   15

TOBY throws a ball at the window.

                         SAM
                    What's up?

                                              (CONTINUED)

                         TOBY
            A.P. called with a quote from Kevin Kahn.
            "Governor Ritchie looks forward to
            meeting with the President tonight so he
            can talk about the Federal Government's
            plan for the Everglades which would tax
            sugar farmers into unemployment."

                         SAM
            It wouldn't.

                         TOBY
            Yeah, but now he's got another 'What's
            Bartlet hiding from us today' spot.

                         SAM
            Call A.P.--what about this--call A.P. and
            tell 'em that Governor Ritchie is
            mistaken and that he's not on the
            President's schedule. And go further, say
            the President would love to meet with
            Ritchie but he's gonna be busy tonight
            passing a vote--

                         TOBY
            --that's being hung up by the Florida
            delegation.
                 (calling)
            Josh!

    JOSH was out into hallway. TOBY runs out into--

16   **INT. BULLPEN/CORRIDOR - CONTINUOUS**   16

                         JOSH
            Yeah.

                         TOBY
            In response to a tactical leak from Kevin
            Kahn I'm gonna let A.P. know that
            Florida's messing with the welfare vote,
            you're all right with that?

                         JOSH
                 (pause)
            Yeah.

                         TOBY
            I'm asking 'cause if we lose the vote
            then we've just said that he's the one
            who brought us down.

                                                (CONTINUED)

16   CONTINUED: 16

                              JOSH
                    Yeah.

                              TOBY
                    You're all right with this.

                              JOSH
                    Yeah.

TOBY heads off and we

                                                                    CUT TO:

17   **INT. BASEMENT MEETING ROOM - DAY**   17

It's very secure. Eight men sit at a table reading a document
that's been put in front of their chairs.

LEO and FITZWALLACE walk in.

                              LEO
                    Good morning. After being presented with
                    overwhelming evidence provided by foreign
                    and domestic intelligence agencies, the
                    President has requested the intelligence
                    finding you have in your hands right now.
                    That finding has been prepared and signed
                    off by the Directors of the NSA and
                    Central Intelligence.

                              FITZWALLACE
                    It was subsequently submitted for review
                    and approval by the National Security
                    Advisor, the Secretaries of State and
                    Defense, the Attorney General, White
                    House Counsel and finally myself and I
                    submit it to you for notification.

                              SHAKER
                    How are you getting around 11905.

                              LEO
                    The President's rescinding his own
                    Executive Order.

                              HOWELL
                    He's on US soil right now, why can't the
                    FBI act on this?

                              LEO
                    The FBI's role is investigatory, they're
                    not allowed to engage in a police action.

                                                              (CONTINUED)

17   CONTINUED: 17

                              CANTWELL
                    And the military?

                              LOBELL
                    Posse Comitatus, you're killing Shareef?

                              LEO
                    I don't know.

                              LOBELL
                    What does that mean?

                              SHAKER
                    Leo, when does the President give the
                    green light?

                              LEO
                    At the last possible minute. Consider
                    yourselves notified. Thank you. I have
                    theatre tickets.

          LEO and FITZWALLACE get up and we

                                                          CUT TO:

18   **INT. MRS. LANDINGHAM'S OFFICE - DAY**   18

          CHARLIE's working as MISS FIDERER comes in. She's wearing a
          different business suit.

                              FIDERER
                    Hello.

                              CHARLIE
                    Good, I was worried you were gonna be
                    late.

                              FIDERER
                    No.

                              CHARLIE
                    You want some water or something?

                              FIDERER
                    No thanks.

                              CHARLIE
                    Have you met him before?

                              FIDERER
                    We shook hands for a second before a
                    group picture.

                                                      (CONTINUED)

18   CONTINUED: 18

                         CHARLIE
                 You'll be fine.

                         FIDERER
                 Yeah.

                         CHARLIE
                 You seem a little better than you were
                 before.

                         FIDERER
                 Well I took a pill.

                         CHARLIE
                 Why?

                         FIDERER
                 I was a little nervous about coming back
                 to the White House.

                         CHARLIE
                 You took a pill?

                         FIDERER
                 I took a couple.

NANCY comes out of the Oval Office--

                         NANCY
                 She can go in now.

                         CHARLIE
                    (pause)
                 Okay.

FIDERER follows CHARLIE into--

19   **INT. THE OVAL OFFICE - CONTINUOUS**   19

BARTLET is distracted with some things for the beginning of
this.

                         CHARLIE
                 Mr. President, this is Deborah Fiderer.
                 I'll be right outside.

CHARLIE exits.

                         BARTLET
                 It's Fiderer?

                         FIDERER
                 Fideler. Fiderer. It's Fiderer.

                                                        (CONTINUED)

19   CONTINUED:

> BARTLET
> I saw your resume, we don't need to talk
> about that. What've you been doing
> recently?

> FIDERER
> I'm an alpaca farmer.

> BARTLET
> (pause)
> Like the sweaters?

> FIDERER
> Before they're sweaters.

> BARTLET
> (pause)
> Mm-hm. And before that?

> FIDERER
> Craps and blackjack.

> BARTLET
> You were a professional gambler.

> FIDERER
> I like the way that sounds.

> BARTLET
> Whereabout?

> FIDERER
> Bally's mostly.

> BARTLET
> Okay. Why'd you leave the White House?

> FIDERER
> Well, Mr. President, you wanna talk about
> gettin' screwed with your pants on.

> BARTLET
> (calling)
> Charlie!

> FIDERER
> Yeah, I guess I got pretty well doinked.

CHARLIE's come in--

> CHARLIE
> Yes sir.

(CONTINUED)

19   CONTINUED: (2)

> BARTLET
> Could I have a minute?

> CHARLIE
> Yes sir.

> BARTLET
> (to MRS. FIDERER)
> Would you mind waiting outside just a
> moment?

> FIDERER
> Not at all, sir.

FIDERER exits.

> BARTLET
> Is this a joke?
> (beat)
> If it's a joke it's both funny and well
> executed. But I think you and I both know
> that it's not. I sent you out to replace
> Delores Landingham, and that's what you
> came home with.

> CHARLIE
> Was she--

> BARTLET
> She's an alpaca farmer who needed two
> tries to get her own name.

> CHARLIE
> Well sir, maybe--

> BARTLET
> Don't worry about it, I'm gonna put the
> personnel office on it. I've gotta go
> change for New York.

> CHARLIE
> Thank you, Mr. President.

BARTLET heads out the portico--

CHARLIE heads back into--

20   **INT. MRS. LANDINGHAM'S OFFICE - CONTINUOUS**   20

> CHARLIE
> Okay. Okay, that was my fault. I didn't
> properly prepare you for the meeting.
> That was bad staff work.
> (MORE)

(CONTINUED)

20   CONTINUED: 20

                              CHARLIE (cont'd)
                    Before your next job interview with the
                    President, I'm gonna remind you that you
                    probably don't wanna be stoned.

                              FIDERER
                    There's gonna be a second interview?

                              CHARLIE
                    There's gonna be as many as it takes,
                    we're gonna get this right.

                              FIDERER
                    Well lemme back you up for a second, have
                    we done the first one yet?

                              CHARLIE
                    I'm calling a cab now.

                              FIDERER
                    What ever happened to the Swingle
                    Singers?

                              CHARLIE
                         (dialing)
                    I don't know.

                                                              CUT TO:

21   **EXT./EST. BROADWAY THEATRE - EARLY EVENING**   21

       All kinds of security, police barricades, lights, uniformed
       police and plain clothes Secret Service are making this
       section of the theatre district the safest place on Earth.

22   **INT. THEATRE - EARLY EVENING**   22

       BUTTERFIELD and SIMON are standing with a group of AGENTS in
       the orchestra with a blue print spread out over some seats.

                              BUTTERFIELD
                    The secure exits are indicated in red.
                    The site agents are standing post.

                              AGENT
                    Yes sir.

                              BUTTERFIELD
                    And the UD?

                              AGENT #2
                    Yeah.

                              BUTTERFIELD
                    They can bring the dogs in. Thank you.

                                                              (CONTINUED)

22   CONTINUED: 22

The group breaks up.

                    BUTTERFIELD
          Simon.

                    SIMON
          Yes sir.

                    BUTTERFIELD
          We've got a lead, I think I'm gonna have
          news for you in a few minutes.

                    SIMON
          Is that right?

                    BUTTERFIELD
          Yeah.

                    SIMON
          Thank you.

SIMON continues into--

23   **INT. THEATRE LOBBY - CONTINUOUS**   23

--which is a sea of business. He looks around but doesn't see
C.J. and we

                                                   CUT TO:

24   **EXT. SHUBERT ALLEY - EARLY EVENING**   24

C.J.'s standing outside, getting some air. SIMON comes out the
theatre door.

                    SIMON
          I asked you to wait with an agent.

                    C.J.
          I wanted to get some air.

                    SIMON
          And that's fine, but I asked you to wait
          with an agent.

                    C.J.
          Simon--

                    SIMON
          You can say to the agent, I'd like to go
          outside and get some air, and he'll go
          with you.

                                              (CONTINUED)

24   CONTINUED: 24

                              C.J.
          --I'm standing in the middle of the
          President's security detail. What do you
          think is gonna happen to me?

                              SIMON
                         (shouting)
          I don't know what's gonna happen to you!
          If I did, this'd be easy!

                              C.J.
          Maybe if we didn't shout so much.

                              SIMON
          You know what? I've spent my adult life
          protecting people and you're the first
          person who's got me seriously thinking
          about switching sides.

                              C.J.
          Well I'm sorry you feel that way, I think
          I've been a treat.

                              SIMON
          Yes you have. A little Easter treat. *Just
          for me!*

                              C.J.
          You seem a little riled.

                              SIMON
          From the first day you acted like this
          was all my fault when that's a pretty
          tough case to make.

                              C.J.
          I don't think any of it's your fault and
          I appreciate everything you've done.

                              SIMON
          I gotta say there are times when it seems
          like you like me.

                              C.J.
          I do like you.

                              SIMON
          And then you just walk off to stick it to
          me and, forget the personalities, it's
          just _stupid_!

                              C.J.
          I said I do like you.

                                              (CONTINUED)

24   CONTINUED: (2)   24

> SIMON
> I meant the other way.

> C.J.
> So did I, I tried to kiss you.

> SIMON
> You said you didn't.

> C.J.
> *I was lying, you idiot!*

> SIMON
> (pause)
> All right, I'm switching sides now.

> C.J.
> I was embarrassed, I fumbled it.

> SIMON
> You <u>didn't</u>, I <u>told</u> you, I'm not allowed--

> C.J.
> That sounded like an excuse.

> SIMON
> *It's not!* Somebody's threatening to kill
> you, I can't be--I watched you for three
> seconds trying on dresses at Barney's and
> the *guy showed up*, I can't be--

> C.J.
> You watched me at Barney's?

SIMON's cell phone rings. He just stares at C.J. in blank
disbelief.

> SIMON
> (pause)
> You're like the girl in Drivers Ed. who
> won't watch the prom night movie 'cause
> it's gross and so ends up missing an
> important lesson about drinking and
> driving.

> C.J.
> (pause)
> What in God's name are you talking about.

SIMON answers his phone--

(CONTINUED)

24   CONTINUED: (3)

                          SIMON
                     (into phone)
               Simon Donovan.

                          C.J.
               You're saying I need to take my
               protection more seriously? 'Cause, Simon,
               this is happening to me. I think I take
               the situation plenty seriously but I have
               to live my life, and maybe sometimes--

                          SIMON
                     (calmly)
               I have a phone to my ear, what's that
               mean to you.

                          C.J.
               I shouldn't be talking.

                          SIMON
                     (into phone)
               Yes sir, thank you.
                     (SIMON hangs up)
               They've got him.

                          C.J.
                     (beat)
               What do you mean?

                          SIMON
               We have him in custody, it's him.
                     (into his sleeve)
               10-50, it's Donovan, they got my guy.

          From over on Shubert Alley we can hear the clapping and
          whistles of a couple of dozen AGENTS.

                          C.J.
               They have him?

                          SIMON
               They stopped his train in Trenton.

                          C.J.
               Where was he going?

                          SIMON
               Here. He wasn't gonna do anything to you.

                          C.J.
               This is over.

                                        (CONTINUED)

24   CONTINUED: (4)

                          SIMON
                There's paperwork.

                          C.J.
                I meant for me.

                          SIMON
                Yeah.

                          C.J.
                Thank you.

                          SIMON
                You're welcome.

                          C.J.
                Seriously.

C.J. hugs him, then kisses him on the cheek a few times, and
that turns into kissing him on the lips for a moment.

                          C.J.
                Thanks.
                     (pause)
                So I'm free.

                          SIMON
                You can drive your car, walk in a crowd,
                eat a grapefruit, do what you want.

                          C.J.
                How 'bout a drink?

                          SIMON
                Sure, you can drink.

                          C.J.
                     (pause)
                Can you meet me after the play?

                          SIMON
                Yes.

We HEAR the sirens from the Presidential motorcade
approaching--

                          C.J.
                Good.

                          SIMON
                Where?

                                                        (CONTINUED)

24   CONTINUED: (5)

                          C.J.
                   Anywhere you want.

                          SIMON
                   How 'bout right here?

C.J. smiles--

                          C.J.
                   I have to go to work.

SIMON heads off. C.J. goes to join the motorcade which has
pulled around the corner and pulled up to the cheers of
onlookers.

                                             FADE TO BLACK.

                   <u>END OF ACT THREE</u>

ACT FOUR

From the BLACK we HEAR--

                    BEDFORD (VO)
            Hung be the heavens with black, yield day
            to night!

                                          CUT TO:

25   **INT. THEATRE - NIGHT**   25

We hear a stately march as the lights come up on the hearse of
Henry V, lying in state. The NOBILITY OF ENGLAND enter behind
the coffin, their standards and banners unfurling overhead.

                    BEDFORD
            Comets, importing change of time and
            states, brandish your crystal tresses in
            the sky, and with them scourge the bad
            revolting stars that have consented unto
            Henry's death.

BARTLET's sitting in the front row of the mezzanine, along
with several dignitaries including Catholic clergy. TOBY and
C.J. are scattered further back.

                    BEDFORD
            King Henry the Fifth, too famous to live
            long! Virtue he had, deserving to
            command; He ne'er lift up his hand but
            conquered.

SAM steps in from the upper lobby with his cell phone and taps
TOBY on the shoulder. TOBY follows him out into--

26   **INT. UPPER LOBBY - CONTINUOUS**   26

                    SAM
            He went to the Yankee game.

                    TOBY
               (pause)
            Ritchie?

                    SAM
             Yes.

                    TOBY
             He's at the Yankee game right now?

                                      (CONTINUED)

26 CONTINUED:

                    SAM
Local news covered it. He said this was
how ordinary Americans got their
entertainment.

                    TOBY
              (pause)
I've been to 441 baseball games at Yankee
Stadium, there's not a single person
there who's ordinary.

                    SAM
I know.

                    TOBY
You makin' fun of the Yankees?

                    SAM
No.

                    TOBY
Now?

                    SAM
I'm not.

                    TOBY
They went to the Yankee game.

                    SAM
He's coming at intermission.

                    TOBY
Well I'm not sure that suits me.

                    SAM
I know what you mean.

                    TOBY
Making an entrance after the President,
that's just not how we play bridge. It's
not, how we say, cricket.

                    SAM
Okay, but you're starting to freak me out
a <u>little</u> bit.

                    TOBY
Talk to me.

                    SAM
How many people are at the game?

                                          (CONTINUED)

195

26   CONTINUED: (2)

                  TOBY
It's a good game, about 40,000 probably.

                  SAM
There was an incumbent President who was
facing a primary challenge. On the day of
the primary his staff sent his motorcade
into a district that was heavily favored
by his opponent in order to tie up
traffic. Now I would like to make it
plain that I would never do anything to
tamper with an <u>election</u>, but--

TOBY puts his hand on SAM's head...and cheek and face...like a
blind man feeling what a person looks like except here it's
affection...

                  TOBY
I'm so proud of you.

                  SAM
You're really very much freaking me out.

                                CUT TO:

27   **INT. JOSH'S OFFICE - NIGHT**   27

He's at his desk as DONNA comes in--

                  DONNA
It's Toby on 1.

                  JOSH
           (picking up the phone)
Hey.

                          INTERCUT WITH:

28   **INT. UPPER LOBBY - SAME TIME**   28

TOBY's on his cell phone.

                  TOBY
Hey listen, I'm gonna send the motorcade
up the Major Deegan, is that okay with
you?

                  JOSH
Why?

                          (CONTINUED)

28   CONTINUED:

                    TOBY
                 (to SAM)
            Hey Josh has a good point, we should
            think of a reason.

                    JOSH
            Why don't you guys get back to me.

                    TOBY
            How's it going?

                    JOSH
            They'll start voting in about a half
            hour.

                    TOBY
            You bringing in Brenda?

                    JOSH
            Yeah.

                    TOBY
            I didn't hear you.

                    JOSH
            Yeah, I'm bringing in Brenda. We're gonna
            make her chairman of the Platform
            Committee.

                    TOBY
            Hey, did I put too much pressure on you
            with the vote?

                    JOSH
            No.

                    TOBY
            With the Ritchie meeting and the AP
            quote?

                    JOSH
            No.

                    TOBY
            And I understand the President jumped up
            and down on you pretty hard last week.

                    JOSH
            It's over Toby. We won.

                    TOBY
                 (pause)
            Amy's incredibly employable, Josh.

                                    (CONTINUED)

28   CONTINUED: (2)

                        JOSH
                    (laughing a little)
            All right.

                        TOBY
            All right.

                                                              CUT TO:

29   **INT. JOSH'S OFFICE - CONTINUOUS**   29

He hangs up the phone. Sits back.

                        JOSH
                    (lazily)
            Donna, Donna, Donna...
                    (spoken just as lazily)
            I had a girl...and Donna was her name.
                    (again)
            Donna, Donna...Donna McDoo.

All this was in vain effort to get Donna to come into the
office without raising his voice. He gave it time, it didn't
work...

                        JOSH
                    (shouting)
            Donna!

After a moment, DONNA ambles into the doorway slowly...

                        DONNA
            I wanted to see what else you had.

JOSH smiles...

                        DONNA
            You did all right, okay.

                        JOSH
            I bought her boss.

                        DONNA
            Yeah that's how you had to win this one.
            You think her job's really in jeopardy?

                        JOSH
            No, she'll lose it for sure.
                    (beat)
            Anyway, good job, I'll see you tomorrow.

                        DONNA
            You're not sticking around for the vote?

                                              (CONTINUED)

29   CONTINUED: 29

                              JOSH
                    We won by eight.

          JOSH is out the door and we

                                                              CUT TO:

30   **EXT. THEATRE - NIGHT**   30

          The intermission crowd is spilling out onto the sidewalk. The
          crowd behind the barricades flashes pictures. SAM and TOBY are
          working a cluster of reporters.

                              REPORTER
                    Toby.

                              TOBY
                    Yeah.

                              REPORTER
                    Governor Ritchie's stuck in traffic and
                    won't get here till the middle of the
                    second act.

                              TOBY
                    He shoulda taken the Cross Bronx to the
                    west side.

                              REPORTER #2
                    Sam?

                              SAM
                    I don't know, but I wanna tell you some
                    good facts. 1.8 million dollars raised
                    for Catholic charities thanks to all the
                    people who...who made it here tonight.
                    While we're talking the House is passing
                    the President's welfare reform bill and
                    he appreciates all the Governors who
                    worked the vote.

                              TOBY
                    Yeah, and the Yankees are about to snap a
                    twelve game winning streak, thanks a lot.

                              SAM
                    What Toby means to say is that if 90% of
                    success is showing up, we're just happy
                    there's someone standing up for the other
                    ten.

          TOBY and SAM head off--

                                                              (CONTINUED)

30   CONTINUED: 30

                         TOBY
              I love the theatre.

                          SAM
              I know what you mean.

                                              CUT TO:

31   **INT. VIP ROOM - NIGHT**   31

      BARTLET is done talking quietly with a few people and comes
      over to CHARLIE who's standing on the side.

                        BARTLET
              What's goin' on?

                        CHARLIE
              Nothing, sir. I'll be arranging a second
              meeting with Deborah Fiderer when we get
              back to town.

                        BARTLET
              From this afternoon?

                        CHARLIE
              Yes sir.

                        BARTLET
                 (pause)
              Are you pledging a fraternity or
              something? 'Cause this'd be a good one.

                        CHARLIE
              Sir--

                        BARTLET
              What is it with you and this woman?

                        CHARLIE
              She hired me. That's why she was fired.

      BARTLET shakes his head as he exits and we

                                              CUT TO:

32   **OMITTED**   32

33   **EXT. KOREAN GROCERY - NIGHT**   33

      SIMON's coming down the street and stops when he gets to the
      grocery. He pulls a cellophane-wrapped rose out of the display
      in front and walks into--

34   **INT. KOREAN GROCERY - CONTINUOUS**   34

SIMON's in too good a mood to notice, otherwise he'd think it
was strange that there was only one other customer in the
place. A MAN squeezing vegetables. SIMON goes up to the
counter and picks up a Milky War bar and speaks to the KOREAN
owner--

                    SIMON
        Do you happen to know if a Milky Way bar
        has red meat in it?
            (beat)
        I'm sorry, I'm kidding, I'm gonna buy
        this and the flower.

The KOREAN MAN is acting strangely. His voice isn't much above
a hush and he's not making any sense. He doesn't gesticulate
at all or make any eye contact...

                  KOREAN MAN
        No...No, we don't have that.

SIMON's holding them both in his hand...

                    SIMON
            (pause)
        No, I mean I'm gonna buy this, how much
        is it?

                  KOREAN MAN
        No, it's okay.

                    SIMON
        No, how much is it?

                  KOREAN MAN
        You can go.

SIMON doesn't understand the strange behavior...and then he
sees it. The cash register drawer is open.

SIMON looks at the KOREAN, a faint, warm smile on his face
that says, trust me, I've got you.

                    SIMON
            (whispering)
        It's all right. Why don't you get down
        behind the counter now.

And SIMON pulls out his gun as he turns to face the MAN
squeezing the vegetables--

                                    (CONTINUED)

34   CONTINUED: 34

                              SIMON
                    Don't move at all, I'm a Federal Officer.
                    Don't reach, I'm Secret Service, you know
                    you'll never get there. Put your hands in
                    the air, that's it, you're doin' great
                    it's okay. I want you to lie down face
                    first on the floor, let's go, keep it up,
                    you're doin' great.

The MAN is lying on the floor and SIMON pulls the gun out of
the back of the MAN's pants and pulls off his own necktie.
During the following he'll use the tie for handcuffs and make
a sailor's quality knot in eight seconds.

                              SIMON
                    You shouldn't be down on yourself. A
                    Secret Service Agent walking into the
                    middle of an armed robbery, that's just
                    bad luck, that's not gonna happen again.
                    Maybe I'm just feelin' good today but
                    when you get out I'd definitely give it
                    another shot, I think you owe it to
                    yourself. Lie still, okay.
                         (into sleeve)
                    This is Donovan, I need the NYPD at a
                    Korean Grocery on 8th Avenue between 44th
                    and 45th.
                         (to the KOREAN MAN)
                    Sir, I hate to be a problem customer, but
                    if I don't get a Milky Way bar pretty
                    soon--

BAM! BAM!

Two shots ring out and SIMON falls to the floor.

Everything seems to go silent. Then we HEAR the lonely guitar
from Jeff Buckley's cover of *Hallelujah*.

As the music plays, we see fragments of the man who just shot
SIMON in the back untying his partner and hustling him out the
door.

Then, MOS, the KOREAN MAN comes out from behind the camera and
runs out onto the sidewalk to get help.

                              SONG
                    "I heard there was secret chord that
                    David played and it pleased the Lord, but
                    you don't really care for music do
                    you..."

                                                            (CONTINUED)

34   CONTINUED: (2)   34

The KOREAN man is starting to attract a crowd as he shouts for
help in both Korean and English. People start to come into the
grocery and kneel down next to SIMON, putting a coat on top,
getting blood on themselves--

> SONG
> *"Well it goes like this, the fourth, the*
> *fifth, the minor fall and the major lift,*
> *it's a baffled king composing*
> *hallelujah..."*

And now we see the squad cars from SIMON's radio call and
police officers jumping out and people on the sidewalk
pointing and shouting--

> SONG
> *"Hallelujah, Hallelujah, Hallelujah,*
> *Hallelujah..."*

The song continues as we

                                                      CUT TO:

35   **INT. THEATRE - NIGHT**   35

The song continues as we watch Henry VI, Part Three, Act I,
Scene 4. C.J.'s eating up the play with a spoon...

> SONG
> *"Well her faith was strong but you needed*
> *proof. You saw her bathing on the roof.*
> *Her beauty in the moonlight overthrew*
> *you."*

> YORK
> And every drop cries vengeance for his
> death, 'gainst thee, fell Clifford, and
> thee, false Frenchwoman.

BUTTERFIELD comes in the door in back and makes his way down
the few steps to C.J. and taps her on the shoulder. The song
continues as C.J. follows BUTTERFIELD out into--

36   **INT. UPPER LOBBY - CONTINUOUS**   36

> BUTTERFIELD
> Something terrible has happened.

And the song continues as we

                                                      CUT TO:

36A   **EXT. KOREAN GROCERY - NIGHT**   36A

A crowd's gathered and klieg lights set up as police are
cordoning off the crime scene and paramedics take a sheet-
covered body out on a stretcher. The KOREAN MAN is talking to
two detectives and we

                                      CUT TO:

36B   **INT. UPPER LOBBY - NIGHT**   36B

> C.J.
> Somebody's made a mistake. He was just
> going to the field office--

> BUTTERFIELD
> No--

> C.J.
> Yeah, for the paperwork on--

> BUTTERFIELD
> C.J.--

And C.J. loses her legs as BUTTERFIELD helps her and we

                                        CUT TO:

37   **INT. AMY'S LOFT - NIGHT**   37

The song continues as we join JOSH and AMY in mid-argument--

> JOSH
> What'd you _think_ I was gonna do?

> AMY
> I thought you were gonna do this.

> JOSH
> And?

> AMY
> And I didn't think it was gonna work.

And we

                                        CUT TO:

37A   **INT. FIDERER'S HOUSE - NIGHT**   37A

FIDERER's sitting alone with not a lot of lights on. She capped off the last three years of her life by punting a meeting with the President of the United States and the song continues

> SONG
> *"There was a time when you let me know,*
> *What's really going on below, But now you*
> *never show that to me do ya..."*

                               CUT TO:

37B   **EXT. FRONT STOOP - NIGHT**   37B

In a poor section of D.C. and ANTHONY is sitting out front, holding a key chain in his hand and we

                               CUT TO:

37C   **INT. AMY'S LOFT - NIGHT**   37C

> JOSH
> Are you fired?

> AMY
> I'm resigning on Monday.

> JOSH
> You have to?

> AMY
> I had an entire policy initiative
> reversed in an hour.

And the song continues as we

                               CUT TO:

37D   **EXT. KOREAN GROCERY - NIGHT**   37D

The crime scene's grown and TOBY, SAM and BUTTERFIELD look on. Spectators. And we

                               CUT TO:

37E   **EXT. TIMES SQUARE - NIGHT**   37E

C.J. sits alone and we

                               CUT TO:

37F   **INT. AMY'S LOFT - NIGHT**   37F

                    AMY
          Weren't you offered a chance to get the
          votes you needed by setting up a meeting
          with Ritchie.

                    JOSH
          I'm not a dating service.

                    AMY
          What is wrong with you?!

                    JOSH
          Every serious member of this party is
          gonna unite behind the President and I'm
          not kidding around.

                    AMY
          And I think serious Democrats should be
          thinking about leading and not following.

                    JOSH
          How's it goin' so far?

The phone RINGS...

                    AMY
          As a matter of fact it's going all right
          and I'd do it again.

                    JOSH
          That's what's scaring the hell out of me.

                    AMY
          Good, it's about time.

                    JOSH
          You can't win the White House while the
          middle class thinks you disdain work and
          responsibility.

                    AMY
          I would hope not, and I congratulate you
          for punishing poor women as a symbol of
          the strength of mainstream values.

AMY picks up the phone--

                    JOSH
          That's not what we did.

                                            (CONTINUED)

37F   CONTINUED: 37F

                         AMY
                    (into phone)
               Hello.

                         JOSH
               Do you not consider it relevant that it
               would be worse with Rob Ritchie in the
               White House? Why isn't that part of the
               equation?

          AMY covers the phone with her hand...

                         AMY
               Honey, Simon Donovan was shot and killed.

          JOSH looks at her for a moment, then gets up and takes the
          phone...

                         JOSH
                    (into phone)
               C.J.?

                                                            CUT TO:

38   **INT. UPPER LOBBY - NIGHT**   38

          BARTLET is waiting alone but he's well guarded. After a moment
          LEO comes out...

          They'll speak very quietly which'll mask some of the emotion
          in what they're saying--

                         BARTLET
                    (quietly)
               Civilians get trials.

                         LEO
               I'd argue he's not a civilian, so would
               the Attorney General.

                         BARTLET
               They're gonna find out it's us. We can
               make it look like the plane went down but
               they're gonna find out it's us and I'm
               gonna be running for re-election while
               I'm fighting a war with Qumar.

                         LEO
               That's why you want to say no?

                         BARTLET
               I want him tried.

                                                         (CONTINUED)

                              LEO
            That can't happen.

                              BARTLET
            I understand.

                              LEO
            I was talking this morning about how
            Mallory names all the lobsters in the
            tank.

                              BARTLET
            Yeah.

                              LEO
            Would it be helpful if I brought you a
            list of names of Shareef's victims?

                              BARTLET
            What do you want from me?

                              LEO
            Who was the monk who wrote "I don't
            always know the right thing to do, Lord,
            but I think the fact that I want to
            please you pleases you?"
                  (beat)
            You have two minutes, sir.

                              BARTLET
            This isn't a matter of religion.

                              LEO
            Yes sir.

                              BARTLET
            I recognize that there's evil in the
            world.

                              LEO
            What is your objection exactly, sir?

                              BARTLET
            Doesn't this mean we join the league of
            ordinary nations?

                              LEO
            That's your objection? I'm not gonna have
            any trouble saying the Pledge of
            Allegiance tomorrow.

                              BARTLET
            That's not my objection.

                                              (CONTINUED)

38   CONTINUED: (2)   38

                              LEO
              Sir--

                              BARTLET
              It's just wrong. It's absolutely wrong.

                              LEO
              I know. But you have to do it anyway.

                              BARTLET
              Why?

                              LEO
              'Cause you won.

BARTLET thinks...exhales...

                              BARTLET
              Take 'em.

LEO opens his cell phone and walks into a corner. BARTLET puts
his hands in his pockets and walks toward a sign that reads
MEN'S LOUNGE, DOWNSTAIRS as we

                                                            CUT TO:

39   **INT. MEN'S LOUNGE - NIGHT**   39

Comfortable furniture. BARTLET lights a cigarette and sits in
a chair. After a moment he looks across the room and sees that
an elderly usher is peering at him from behind an entrance
way.

                              BARTLET
                      (re: the cigarette)
              Caught me.

BARTLET goes back to thinking his thoughts when he hears--

                              RITCHIE (OS)
              Mr. President.

                              BARTLET
              Governor.

RITCHIE's just come out of the men's room.

                              RITCHIE
              Are you enjoying the play.

                              BARTLET
              I am, how 'bout you?

                                                        (CONTINUED)

                              RITCHIE
                    We just got here. We were at the Yankee
                    game, we got hung up in traffic.

                              BARTLET
                    Yeah I know. Listen, politics aside and I
                    don't want to make a big deal out of it,
                    but you probably insulted the church and
                    you can head it off at the pass if you
                    speak to the Cardinal tonight.

                              RITCHIE
                    Well I didn't mean to insult anybody--

                              BARTLET
                    No.

                              RITCHIE
                    It's a baseball game, it's how ordinary
                    Americans--

                              BARTLET
                         (understanding)
                    Yeah.
                         (beat)
                    No, I don't understand that, the center
                    fielder for the Yankees is an
                    accomplished classical guitarist. People
                    who like baseball can't like books?

                              RITCHIE
                    Are you taking this personally?

                              BARTLET
                    No, something horrible happened about an
                    hour ago. C.J. Cregg was getting threats
                    so we put an agent on her. He's a good
                    guy, he was on my detail for a while, he
                    was in Rosslyn. He walked into the middle
                    of an armed robbery and was shot and
                    killed after detaining one of the
                    suspects.

                              RITCHIE
                         (pause)
                    Crime.
                         (beat)
                    Boy, I don't know.

          BARTLET takes this in. He's heard the stories but this is the
          first conversation he's had with the man.

                                                            (CONTINUED)

39   CONTINUED: (2)

> BARTLET
> We should have a great debate, Rob. We
> owe it to everyone. When I was running as
> a Governor I didn't know anything, I made
> them start Bartlet College in my dining
> room. Two hours every morning on foreign
> affairs and the military. You can do
> that.

> RITCHIE
> How many different ways do you think
> you're gonna find to call me dumb?

> BARTLET
> I wasn't, Rob. But you've turned being
> unengaged into a zen-like thing, and you
> shouldn't enjoy it so much is all. And if
> it appears at times as if I don't like
> you, that's the only reason why.

> RITCHIE
> You're what my friends call a superior
> sonofabitch. You're an academic elitist
> and a snob. You're Hollywood. You're
> weak, you're liberal and you can't be
> trusted. And if it appears from time to
> time as if I don't like you, those are
> just a few of the many reasons why.

We HEAR the MUSICAL FANFARE of *The Patriotic Song* come from
the stage. BARTLET listens and smiles...

> BARTLET
> They're playing my song.

BARTLET puts out his cigarette and goes to the door...

> BARTLET
> In the future, if you're wondering,
> "Crime. Boy. I don't know" was when I
> decided to kick your ass.

BARTLET heads out as we

                                                            CUT TO:

40   **INT. THEATRE - NIGHT**   40

A BOY has begun singing what is the FINALE.

                                                        (CONTINUED)

40   CONTINUED: 40

                              BOY
                  "England arise, join in the chorus. There
                  is a bright new song you should be
                  singing..."

BARTLET comes in the back of the theatre as the BOY is joined
by the full company...

                              COMPANY
                  "See each one do what he can to further
                  God's almighty plan..."

The singing continues as we

                                                        CUT TO:

41   **EXT. AIR FIELD - NIGHT**   41

Through the dark haze we can see the flashing strobe lights of
a Gulfstream jet taxiing in. In the distance we see ground
crew MECHANICS rolling in on flat vehicles and we

                                                        CUT TO:

42   **INT. THEATRE - SAME TIME**   42

The COMPANY continues...

                              COMPANY
                  "...with Prosperity and industry forever
                  hand in hand..."

                                                        CUT TO:

43   **EXT. AIR FIELD - NIGHT**   43

A pair of hands flips open a toolbox on one of the vehicles.
Someone reaches in and gets a speed handle. Some else reaches
in and gets bearing separators, another hand reaches in and
gets a Sig Sauer .357 with a silencer, and another, and
another, and another and we

                                                        CUT TO:

44   **INT. THEATRE - NIGHT**   44

The COMPANY continues...BARTLET's enjoying this...and we

                                                        CUT TO:

45   **INT. SITUATION ROOM - NIGHT**   45

FITZWALLACE waits alone and

                                                        CUT TO:

46   **EXT. AIR FIELD - NIGHT**   46

The two BODYGUARDS step out of the plane, followed by SHAREEF,
followed by the PILOT and we

                                                        CUT TO:

47   **INT. THEATRE - NIGHT**   47

The COMPANY continues...

                                                        CUT TO:

48   **EXT. AIR FIELD - NIGHT**   48

And the guns come out of the MECHANIC's coveralls as SHAREEF
and the BODYGUARDS get two bullets apiece. One of the flat
vehicles swings around and they start jumping on, except for
one who's fumbling around inside SHAREEF's coat. Even though
we can't hear anything, we can see that his friends are
motioning for him to hurry it up. Finally he pulls out what he
was looking for. A fountain pen. He hops on the already moving
vehicle as another MECHANIC flips open a cell phone and we

                                                        CUT TO:

49   **INT. SITUATION ROOM - NIGHT**   49

FITZWALLACE picks up the phone, listens, and then hits a
number on another phone as we

                                                        CUT TO:

50   **INT. UPPER LOBBY - NIGHT**   50

LEO flips open his phone and listens as we

                                                        CUT TO:

51   **INT. THEATRE - NIGHT**   51

BARTLET's still standing at the back of the mezzanine
listening and watching. BARTLET looks over at the shaft of
light that's been made by LEO opening the door. LEO looks over
at him. There are people who've killed people and people who
haven't and BARTLET'll never be in the second group again.

                                                        (CONTINUED)

51   CONTINUED: 51

The music becomes thunderous. Swelling and chaotic. Voices and
brass and climbing Edwardian harmonic phrases...BARTLET mouths
lazily along with the words...

                    COMPANY
          "And victorious in war shall be made
          glorious in peace. And victorious in war
          shall be made glorious in peace."

                                        BLACK OUT.

                    <u>END OF SEASON III</u>

THE
WEST WING

Alex up late with a scene from *Commencement*

Dulé and his brand new F-14 Tomcat

Chris Misiano directs a scene from *20 Hours in America*. It's a low-pressure job where no one's ever looking over your shoulder.

Getting it right: Brad, John, Allison and Alex

Brad and NiCole Robinson say hi to a visiting Boy Scout troop between scenes.

Chris leads a production meeting.

Brad runs lines with Janel and dialogue coach Hilary Griffiths.

Tommy with some final words before a shot

Most likely Allison and Tim Davis Reed are laughing at me, not with me.

Lunch, once a year, catered by our friends at Legal Seafood

Allison's birthday

Brad and Richard wait to do a scene from *College Kids*

Tommy and the Whiffenpoofs

Alex with Josh and Martin at Georgetown University

SEASON FOUR

The relationship between a journeyman director and a TV series is an unusual one in that the director's a visitor. They come in for prep, photography and one pass at editing before the episode is handed over to the executive producers. Oftentimes, on a long-running show, the cast knows more about an episode that's being made than the director does, and that makes for a strange, sometimes strained relationship.

It's not "all right there on the page" as I would like to believe, and what is right there on the page needs to be realized.

The West Wing, I think, is a more director-sensitive show than most. If you don't get it, you can't do it and even if you do get it you probably can't do it. It's not for beginners and it's not for hacks. For one thing, you're going to have to gain the trust of Richard Schiff, and right there alone you're gonna earn your $32,077 paycheck.

Which is what Alex Graves did when, during our first season, he was slotted in for Episode 10, which turned out to be *In Excelsis Deo*, a show in which Richard's Toby crosses paths with a dead, homeless, Korean War veteran. Alex would go on to direct *Galileo*, *The Mid-Terms* and *17 People*.

Chris Misiano's first show was *Mr. Willis of Ohio* (also a Richard winner-over) and then directed *Celestial Navigation*, *Bartlet's Third State of the Union*, *The War at Home* and *The Fall's Gonna Kill You*.

Alex and Chris were beloved and deserved to be. At the end of the second season, Tommy, John and I offered them permanent jobs on the show as producing directors. Along with Tommy, they would be directing the lion's share of the season's episodes, but also working on prep, post and photography with the journeymen. Other than the departure of Tommy and myself, which would come two years later, this was the most significant personnel move made on the show.

But another significant move came in the writers' suite before the start of Season 4, which was that I'd put together the writing staff I'd wanted since the start of *Sports Night*.

It was a no-brainer that Kevin and I would hold on to our two top people, Paul Redford and Eli Attie, in fact we'd bolt them to their desks.

Paul, a former *Harvard Lampoon* editor and a family man whose only apparent fault is that he steeps his tea by hand, raises the IQ of any room he walks into. He'd been on the *Sports Night* staff the first season and *The West Wing* since after the pilot. He was Kevin's second-in-command and had just been promoted to producer.

Eli Attie, also a Harvard grad (as well as, coincidentally, a graduate of my mother's fourth grade class at P.S. 40 in Manhattan) looks like Harry Potter. A rock-and-roll connoisseur (he contributes a music column to the *Washington Post*), Eli worked for David Dinkins, then Majority Leader Richard Gephardt, then Minority Leader Richard Gephardt, then Clinton, and then Al Gore's ill-fated run at a promotion. Eli made a big impact immediately, was promoted as quickly as was seemly, and was relied upon daily.

And with Eli duplicating much of the knowledge and experience of the part-time consultants, Kevin and I were able to free up money in the budget to hire more permanent staff. We'd keep Dee Dee Myers, who'd been with the show from the beginning, and Gene Sperling, Clinton's chief economic advisor, and thank the others.

There was speculation in the newspapers that we'd "fired the Republicans!" which I suppose we had (though Pat Caddell, a former McGovern, Carter, Jerry Brown aide who'd been with us until the reorganization of the staff would tell you we also fired the Democrat.)

The truth is that the contribution of the consultants had nothing to do with their political affiliations. You could read a memo about the Press Briefing Room from Dee Dee and then one from Marlin Fitzwater, gain a great deal from both and have no idea which one worked for President Reagan and which one worked for President Clinton. Frank Luntz was on staff to help with issues of polling, not Republican polling. Peggy Noonan would talk to me about what life was like in the speechwriting shop.

So with Paul, Eli, Dee Dee and Gene, Kevin and I started the staffing process and were lucky to find:

—David Gerken, of Orange County and Princeton, who's beaten the #1 and #2 ranked doubles players on the ATP Tour and worked for former Senate Majority Leader George Mitchell. Senator Mitchell called to make the recommendation himself.

—Michael Oates Palmer, stepson of political Merlin Bob Shrum was following in his step father's footsteps when Warren Beatty told me to hire him as a writer.

—Billy Sind, who went to Cornell I suppose because he couldn't get into Syracuse and who has an incredibly entertaining distaste for things that are illogical. Larry David called and said "Hire Billy Sind" and so I did.

—Mark Goffman, who after getting his Masters from the Kennedy School of Government at Harvard, was hired by the U.S. Army to plan hypothetical wars they couldn't win. The universe of women Mark hasn't dated grows smaller every day.

—Paula Yoo, a 14-year-old boy in the body of a beautiful Asian woman. She wrote for *People* magazine after Yale and would become the inspiration for every *Star Trek* and Internet joke made on the show.

—Debora Cahn, out of Columbia, was a writers assistant on the short-lived NBC half-hour *Inside Schwartz* when Kevin and I read her spec script and decided we wouldn't tell anyone at *Inside Schwartz* about her.

—David Handelman, with whom I'd graduated in 1979 from Scarsdale High School. David was editor of our yearbook, then editor of *The Harvard Crimson*. After college, it didn't take him long to become a senior editor at *Rolling Stone* and then *Vogue*. He'd co-written a *Sports Night* with me and following his separation from *New Yorker* editor Susan Morrison I was able to convince him to come to California and work with us.

The entry-level position on our writing staff is Writers Assistant, which is a terrible job that pays worse. After that comes Researcher, also a terrible job, but at least it's not so much about coffee and spelling anymore. Overqualified people do these jobs because what they want is the next promotion, which is to Staff Writer where your career begins.

Lauren Schmidt had interned for us right after college in Ohio, then was promoted to Production Assistant, then Writers Assistant for the second and third seasons before being promoted to Researcher. Melissa Myers and Stephen Hootstein (Dartmouth and Penn) were our new Writers Assistants.

We started the second week in June and by the third week in June I was the happiest I'd ever been coming to work in the morning.

It was a year later now and it seemed like time had done its thing, the show didn't feel so out of place to me. I wanted to start out with a two-hour episode and I wanted it to be a romp.

Kris Engskov, a Personal Aide to Bill Clinton told Dulé Hill that from time to time, the presidential motorcade will accidentally leave someone behind in the middle of nowhere and from that point you're on your own. Dulé had passed what Kris had said on to me a few years earlier. That would be one of the things going on in the opener.

We also, for the first time, already knew something about what was going to happen this season. There was going to be an election. And since the audience already knew who was going to win, we were going to have to dramatize something else. I decided it would be *Intellect in American Leadership: Virtue or Vice.*

Three weeks before the first day of shooting I began the actual writing and while I was far from finished, the massive pre-production work was well underway.

(Lew Wells, Alex, Chris, especially Tommy, they'd all grown very used to starting their work before I'd finished mine.)

> LEW
>
> Can you tell me anything about Act 3? Anything at all you can give me a heads up on?

> ME
>
> We're gonna need a rural train platform.

> LEW
>
> No problem.

> ME
>
> And a train.

LEW

Okay.

ME

And the train's gonna have to pull out of the station and I mean exactly on cue or a joke isn't gonna work right.

LEW

A train with comic timing. Got it.

Toby, Josh and Donna, having missed the motorcade at a campaign stop in Indiana are trying to get home and it would take them 20 hours, their progress being diverted by a soy diesel car that runs out of diesel, an obscure time zone shift that covers one county (true), and a train that's going in the wrong direction.

Chris was directing and he and the location scouts found the perfect Indiana locations in Pennsylvania. The casting was going well and with 48 hours to spare before the first table read, I delivered *20 Hours in America*, the Season Four opener, to the writers assistants, who spent the next three hours correcting my spelling and adding shot numbers for the UPM (Unit Production Manager) before overseeing collating of 200 copies, which got loaded into the back seats of the $1100 Hondas driven by the PAs, and delivered to the front doors of the cast, crew, Warner Bros. staff and Peter Roth, NBC staff and Jeff Zucker, John and Tommy.

With the script in the hands of the writers assistants, I took the staff out for margaritas at Burbank's El Torito Bar and Grill and told them how optimistic I was about the season to come. I went home (after a year at the Four Seasons, I'd rented a house in the Hollywood Hills above the Chateau Marmont Hotel, ordered the crispy, spicy beef from Twin Dragons and walked out back to take in the panoramic view of the L.A. night which was the calling card of the house. The hiatus had passed mercifully without incident. Last year was over. And 48 hours early.

And the phone rang.

ROB LOWE

Hey man, it's Rob.

ME

Your timing is perfect, I just delivered.

ROB

Lemme tell you what's going on.

ME

Is everything all right?

ROB

Well you tell me. My agents went back to Warner Bros. to renegotiate and they won't, they won't have the conversation. Now I've been a good soldier the last year, I haven't said anything, but enough is enough. I'm sorry to involve you in this, you know I love you, but I won't be at the table read.

Okay. All right. This'll get worked out, I assured him.

Rob skipped the table read and a publicity shoot but was coaxed into showing up for shooting via a sternly worded letter to his lawyer from the Warner Bros. Legal Department. Shooting on *20 Hours in America* was going well. Better than well. In return for a job well done, Tommy had given Alex the Season Three finale and Chris the Season Four opener. Directors get as nervous as anyone before they start and Alex and Chris get more nervous than most so the night before Chris started I'd called him to calm him down.

"This is the most important episode we've ever done," I said, "and the future of the show pretty much depends on your doing a good job."

"I hate your breathing guts," he responded.

As shooting began on the opener, the staff and I started work on the second episode. I took time out from having no ideas to step over to the set and watch a camera rehearsal of a scene between Rob and Kim Webster, the actress playing a recurring White House aide named Ginger. After we'd gotten the shot, I walked Rob out to his trailer to ask him if progress was being made on his salary situation.

ROB

No. They won't discuss it. Tommy says I should wait until after Warners re-ups their deal with NBC.

>   ME
> Tommy's right.

>   ROB
> This is bullshit. I'll tell you what else. It's only a matter of
> time before the press gets hold of this.

Really. How would that happen?

I went back to the writers suite and told them not to be nervous but
chances are in the next couple of days you're gonna be reading about
Rob threatening to quit the show.

I called Peter Roth.

>   PETER
> Please, Aaron, let Business Affairs handle this.

But things were clearly moving to DefCon level. Rob's represented by
powerful, proud people who'd put a threat on the table and there was
no way they were taking it off without something in return. So three
days later, ignoring Peter's admonition, I was back in Rob's trailer.

>   ROB
> You know what? If they'd just come back with
> anything...*anything*...a lousy feature development deal,
> then at least—

>   ME
> You'd be all right? With a rider? A feature deal?

>   ROB
> Hell yeah.

>   ME
> I'm calling Peter now.

Looking back, I'm amazed Peter let me work for him as long as he
did.

>   ME
> A development deal from the feature department. I think
> it'll do it. In fact he just told me it would.

Long pause...breathing...thinking about other fields he could've
chosen to go into...

> PETER
>
> (pause)
>
> All right.

> ME
>
> All right?

> PETER
>
> All right.

And I hung up the phone, strut into the writers conference room and announced that lunch from the Mandarin was on me today. Why? Because I am Henry Clay. I am the Great Compromiser.

The phone rang at my house that night. It was Peter.

> PETER
>
> Well they said they'll take the feature deal, but they still want more money.

> ME
>
> Really.

> PETER
>
> Yeah.

> ME
>
> That wasn't my understanding in Rob's trailer.

> PETER
>
> Yeah.

I decided this would be a good time to take Peter's advice and stay out of it.

Two months later, on the third Wednesday in September, Julia and I hosted our annual premiere party at our house (now Julia's house) for the cast, crew and staff. A half-dozen big screen TVs were mounted in the backyard and as the sun set we dined on hot dogs, hamburgers, fried chicken, macaroni and cheese and beer and martinis. At 8:55, Allison, Janel and Lily Tomlin unveiled our third Best Drama Emmy, which we'd won the previous Sunday, and five minutes later our season began.

Here's *20 Hours in America*.

The West Wing

20 Hours in America

Parts I & II

YELLOW REVISIONS:	08/23/02
PINK REVISIONS:	07/19/02
BLUE REVISIONS:	07/17/02

THE WEST WING

"20 Hours in America"

Part I

Written by
Aaron Sorkin

Directed by
Christopher Misiano

PRODUCTION #175-301
Episode One

JOHN WELLS PRODUCTIONS
in association with
WARNER BROS. TELEVISION
4000 Warner Blvd.
Burbank, CA 91522

Final Shooting Script
July 12, 2002
Copyright © 2002
Warner Bros. Television
All Rights Reserved

THE WEST WING

"20 Hours in America"

Part I

Script Revision History

DATE	COLOR	PAGES
07/17/02	BLUE PAGES	SETS,6,10,16,17,19-20, 21,22,28,44,50,52,58-59, 61,62,65
07/19/02	PINK PAGES	SETS,18,22,23
08/23/02	YELLOW	PAGES 8,9,10

SET LIST

INTERIORS
WHITE HOUSE
    Leo's Office
    Corridors
    Situation Room
    Communications Bullpen
    Lobby
    Roosevelt Room
    Oval Office

NAVAL WARFARE CENTER CRANE *
    Catacombs
    Stage
    Backstage

TRUCK
    Cab
    Bed

AIR FORCE ONE
    Press Cabin
    Bartlet's Office
    Senior Staff Cabin
    Main Cabin

GAS STATION

SAM'S BEDROOM

ROADSIDE DINER

EXTERIORS
FARM/CAMPAIGN AREA – DAY

SOYBEAN FIELDS – DAY

COUNTRY ROAD – DAY

GAS STATION – DAY

ROADSIDE DINER – DAY

THE WEST WING

"20 Hours in America"

Part I

CAST LIST

PRESIDENT JOSIAH BARTLET
LEO McGARRY
JOSH LYMAN
SAM SEABORN
TOBY ZIEGLER
C.J. CREGG
CHARLIE YOUNG
DONNA MOSS

MARGARET
FITZWALLACE
GINGER
BRUNO GIANELLI
NANCY
MARK
KATIE
ED
LARRY
CAROL

CATHY	MANAGER
VOLUNTEER	TYLER
WOMAN	KIKI
OFFICER	FRIEND #1
CIVILIAN	FRIEND #2
CIVILIAN #2	MARY HARRISON
CIVILIAN #3	PILOT (V.O.)
CIVILIAN #4	STAFFER
AIDE	FIONA
SPEAKER	MAN
CAP	EARL
CHOIR	BRYCE
DRIVER	PETER LIEN
MRS. WALKER	

YELLOW REVISIONS: 08/23/02
PINK REVISIONS: 07/19/02
BLUE REVISIONS: 07/17/02

THE WEST WING

"20 Hours in America"

Part II

Written by
Aaron Sorkin

Directed by
Christopher Misiano

PRODUCTION #175-302
Episode One – Part II

JOHN WELLS PRODUCTIONS
in association with
WARNER BROS. TELEVISION
4000 Warner Blvd.
Burbank, CA 91522

Final Shooting Script
July 12, 2002
Copyright © 2002
Warner Bros. Television
All Rights Reserved

"20 Hours in America"

Part II

Script Revision History

DATE	COLOR	PAGES
07/17/02	BLUE PAGES	CAST,SETS,74,77,82,83, 85,86-88,91,91A,92-93, 98,110,111,112,113,115, 116,117,118,122,123-124, 125
07/19/02	PINK PAGES	74,112,114,115,117
08/23/02	YELLOW PAGES	CAST,111

SET LIST

INTERIORS
WHITE HOUSE
    Mrs. Landingham's Office
    Mural Room
    Sam's Office
    Oval Office
    *
    Situation Room
    Corridors
    Lobby
    Residence Vestibule
    Bartlet's Bedroom
    Press Briefing Room
    Margaret's Office
    Leo's Office
    *
    Josh's Bullpen
    Communications Bullpen
TRAIN STATION
TRAIN

MARRIOTT
    Front Area
    Bar
BALLROOM
VAN

EXTERIORS
COUNTRY ROAD – DAY
AIRPORT MARRIOTT – DUSK
    (EST.)
PORTICO – EARLY MORNING
PARKWAY – EARLY MORNING
ROADSIDE – EARLY MORNING

THE WEST WING

"20 Hours in America"

Part II

CAST LIST

PRESIDENT JOSIAH BARTLET
LEO McGARRY
JOSH LYMAN
SAM SEABORN
TOBY ZIEGLER
C.J. CREGG
CHARLIE YOUNG
DONNA MOSS
ABIGAIL BARTLET
DEBORAH FIDERER

GINGER
BRUNO GIANELLI
LARRY
NANCY MCNALLY
FITZWALLACE
NANCY
ARTHUR *
MARK
KATIE
MARGARET
ANTHONY
MALLORY

FEMALE REPORTER (V.O./ON TV)
MURIEL KEITH
PHOTOGRAPHER
CONDUCTOR
TYLER
SENATOR #1
SENATOR #2
LACEY
MCKITTRIDGE
BUTLER
DESKMAN
MAN
BARTENDER
DRIVER

"20 Hours in America"

<u>TEASER</u>

From the BLACK we HEAR

A big round of APPLAUSE and CHEERS. BARTLET's just hit one
from three point range and the crowd loves it.

> BARTLET (OS)
> You know the story about--

But it's no use, 'cause the cheers have turned into a loud
chant of "FOUR MORE YEARS."

We HEAR BARTLET laughing a little--

> BARTLET (OS)
> There's a guy back there holding a sign
> that says "Eight More Years." Don't get
> me wrong, I like your thinkin', but I've
> probably tested the Constitution about as
> far as Abbey's gonna allow me to for a
> little while.

And the crowd goes crazy when Abbey's mentioned.

TITLE:
> **A10:25 –   President concluded campaign
>   event. Motorcade departed
>   for Unionville.**

> BARTLET (OS)
> You know the story about the guy whose
> car gets stuck in a muddy hole.

FADE IN:

1   **EXT. FARM/CAMPAIGN AREA – DAY**   1

And we know immediately we're at a big time campaign event. A
huge crowd, a stage full of Indiana Democrats, giant press
coverage, bunting, Bartlet for America, Indiana's Bartlet
Country, Re-Elect the President and maybe we even see a guy
holding a sign with the "Four" crossed out that now reads
"Eight More Years."

(CONTINUED)

1   CONTINUED:

> BARTLET
> A farmer comes along and says he'll pull
> the car out of the hole but he's gonna
> have to charge fifty bucks 'cause this is
> the tenth time he's had to pull it out of
> the mud today. The driver says, "God,
> when do you have time to plough your
> land? At night?" The farmer says, "No,
> no, nighttime's when I fill the hole with
> water." We need to find energy
> alternatives, we're getting our cue,
> we're getting it right now. The
> Republicans are busy. They're trying to
> convince us that they care about new
> energy and that they're not in the vest
> pockets of big oil and that's a tough
> sell, I don't envy them 'cause their only
> hope is that we don't notice that they're
> the ones who are filling the hole with
> water every night and I think Americans
> are smarter than that I think we noticed.

APPLAUSE. BARTLET continues as C.J. comes over to DONNA.

> C.J.
> Where are Josh and Toby?

> DONNA
> They're in the soybean fields talking to
> Cathy.

> C.J.
> Cathy...?

> DONNA
> The daughter, but I like saying that Toby
> and Josh are in the soybean fields.

> C.J.
> He's wrapping up and we're getting right
> in the car, we're already late for
> Unionville.

> DONNA
> I'll get 'em from the soybean fields.

> C.J.
> Thanks.

DONNA heads off--

(CONTINUED)

1   CONTINUED: (2)

>   BARTLET
>   This isn't a time for people whose
>   doomsday scenario is a little less at the
>   pump for Texaco and Shell. This isn't a
>   time for people who say there aren't any
>   energy alternatives just because they
>   can't think of any. This is a time for
>   American heroes and we reach for the
>   stars.

And off the huge APPLAUSE we

                                                    CUT TO:

2   **EXT. THE SOYBEAN FIELDS - DAY**   2

CATHY, the daughter of the man who owns the farm, is giving a
tour to JOSH and TOBY. CATHY may look like a farmer's daughter
but she's got a Masters in Agribusiness. She has a
relationship with JOSH through work in the Indiana Democratic
party. A little less so with TOBY, who's walking a few steps
behind them. Every once in a while, off in the distance, we
can HEAR the crowd reacting to BARTLET.

>   CATHY
>   (quietly to JOSH)
>   He seems a little tense.

>   JOSH
>   Yeah.

>   CATHY
>   Why?

>   JOSH
>   'Cause the President's speaking.

>   CATHY
>   (to TOBY)
>   Why aren't you there?

>   TOBY
>   It's tough to explain.

>   JOSH
>   No it's not.

>   TOBY
>   Ssh.

TOBY's stopped. He's listening for something we can't hear.

                                            (CONTINUED)

                         TOBY
          Okay.

And he keeps walking.

                         JOSH
          The President has his blood pressure
          taken every morning. On higher blood
          pressure days, Toby's not allowed to be
          in the President's sight line while he's
          speaking.

                         CATHY
          Why?

                         TOBY
               (to no one)
          Stepped on it.

                         JOSH
          He has trouble concealing his
          displeasure.

                         TOBY
          Stepped on it and he knows it too.

                         CATHY
          Look--

                         JOSH
          What do I say to people who ask why we
          subsidize farmers when we don't subsidize
          plumbers.

                         CATHY
          The Government *shouldn't* subsidize
          farmers.

                         JOSH
          No?

                         CATHY
          No problem, it actually leaves people
          with <u>two</u> alternatives. They can make the
          decision to never be hungry.

                         JOSH
          Or?

                         CATHY
          They can pay $7 for a potato.

(CONTINUED)

2   CONTINUED: (2)   2

                         JOSH
          Okay.

                         CATHY
          This is two-hundred acres of soy fields,
          it nets my family $30 an acre, which is
          $6000 a year.

                         TOBY
          Ssh.

Waits.

                         TOBY
          Okay.

And he continues--

                         CATHY
          Toby--

                         TOBY
          I worked with the Conference Committee to
          increase payment limits for small farmers
          and we'd have done it too but no one
          could agree what small meant.

DONNA is hurrying to join them in the field.

                         DONNA
                    (calling)
          Josh!

                         JOSH
          I think we've gotta head back.

                         DONNA
          He's wrapping up.

                         JOSH
                    (to CATHY)
          Walk us to the car?

                         CATHY
          Yeah.
                    (to TOBY)
          You seem pissed that I brought it up?

                         TOBY
          No, we're just talkin'.

                         DONNA
          We've really gotta go now.

                                        (CONTINUED)

2   CONTINUED: (3)   2

                         JOSH
              Donna's a little nervous. A couple of
              weeks ago some guys got left behind by
              the motorcade in Kentucky.

                         DONNA
              It was in Tennessee and they were never
              heard from again.

                         JOSH
              They took a cab.

They start back--

                         CATHY
              Look--

                         JOSH
              I think the real point is that whatever
              Toby and the Conference Committee,
              whatever definition they came up with
              would've just created more business for
              the lawyers of the big farm corporations.
              I wish we could have had more time to
              talk, but--

                         CATHY
              There's no way you guys could stay a
              little and meet some people? Maybe catch
              up with the campaign at the next stop?

                         JOSH
              Nah, we've got one more stump in
              Unionville then we get on the plane. It's
              a full schedule at the office.

                         CATHY
              We've got some voters here, Josh, did you
              forget?

                         JOSH
              No.

                         TOBY
              They're voting for Ritchie.

                         CATHY
              What?

                                                      (CONTINUED)

CONTINUED: (4)

                         TOBY
          Indiana's voting for Ritchie. If there
          was someone less competent on the ballot
          than Ritchie, that's who Indiana would be
          voting for.

                         CATHY
          Why'd you come out here?

                         TOBY
          When somebody can give me an answer to
          that question I'll let you know.

                         JOSH
          Toby--

                         CATHY
          Listen, write off Indiana but don't write
          off the small farmers, it's getting bad
          out here, it is bad out here.

                         JOSH
          We paid farmers 67 billion over the last
          three years.

                         CATHY
                 (she's cooked)
          Oh God.

                                                    CUT TO:

3   **EXT. CAMPAIGN AREA - DAY**   3

Some local workers are just beginning to dismantle the
equipment on the stage as JOSH, TOBY, DONNA and CATHY come
around from behind the house and walk onto the stage.

                         JOSH
                 (quietly to TOBY)
          You wanna lighten up a little?

                         TOBY
          I am lightened up, this is me lightened
          up, you're saying lighter?

                         JOSH
          Yeah.

                         TOBY
          Okay.

                                            (CONTINUED)

3   CONTINUED: 3

                          CATHY
               Josh, the 67 billion has bought this
               country the least expensive food and the
               greatest variety of it in the world.
               Surely that's gotta--

                          DONNA
               Hang on.

                          CATHY
               That's gotta register with people who--

                          JOSH
               No she's right, where'd it go?

                          TOBY
               Where the hell did it go?

                          JOSH
               Where's the motorcade?
                    (then, calling to a local
                     volunteer who's covered with
                     buttons)
               Hey. Excuse me. Where's the motorcade?

                          VOLUNTEER
               It's out there.

And the VOLUNTEER is pointing in the distance where a kick of
dirt and dust reveals the flashing lights as the motorcade
exits the farm.

                          JOSH
                    (screaming)
               HEY!!!

                          VOLUNTEER
               You guys need a button? Bartlet for
               America?

                                        SMASH CUT TO:

MAIN TITLES

                          END OF TEASER

ACT ONE

FADE IN:

4   **EXT. FARM/CAMPAIGN AREA - DAY**   4

The dismantling continues as the large crowd begins
dispersing. DONNA's trying to listen to her cell phone over
the noise, JOSH is stomping around and TOBY's looking lost.

                    JOSH
          All right, Donna, listen--

DONNA puts her hand up to say she's on the phone--

                    JOSH
          You gotta get the trailer car.

                    DONNA
          Hang on--

                    JOSH
          Call Campaign Scheduling and Advance and
          tell 'em--

                    DONNA
          Hang on--

                    JOSH
          You gotta hang up with whoever you're
          talking to and call Campaign Scheduling
          and Advance and tell 'em--

And DONNA simply stares at JOSH...

                    JOSH
               (pause)
          Unless you're already talking to Campaign
          Scheduling and Advance.

                    DONNA
               (into phone)
          Thank you.
               (to JOSH)
          There's no trailer car today.

                    JOSH
          Really.

                    DONNA
          Yeah.

                                              (CONTINUED)

4   CONTINUED: 4

                        JOSH
          Good budget cut, good item.
              (calling)
          Cathy, where's the closet cab?

                        CATHY
          About 110 miles as the crow flies.

                        JOSH
              (beat)
          All right.

                        DONNA
              (to CATHY)
          What's the best way for me to get these
          guys to Unionville?

                        CATHY
          We'll take you.

                        JOSH
          Really?

                        CATHY
          It'll gimme a chance to show you the soy
          diesel car.

                        JOSH
              (beat)
          Okay. This car, it can--

                        CATHY
          It's a regular car.

                        JOSH
              (calling)
          Toby!

                        CATHY
          It's actually Cap's car, he's gonna come
          along. Meet us in back of the house.

                        JOSH
          Thank you, very much.
              (to DONNA)
          Who's Cap?

                        DONNA
          I don't know.

                        JOSH
              (calling)
          Toby!

                                             (CONTINUED)

4   CONTINUED: (2)

                        TOBY
             Yeah.

                        JOSH
             We got a ride.

TOBY can't help himself so he stops an elderly WOMAN.

                        TOBY
             Excuse me.

                        WOMAN
             Yes.

                        TOBY
             You heard the speech, right?

                        WOMAN
             Oh yes.

                        TOBY
             The section on HMOs, did he land it?

                        WOMAN
             I'm sorry?

                        TOBY
             He didn't land it, did he.

                        WOMAN
             I thought he was very good.

                        TOBY
             The muddy hole joke?

                        JOSH
             Toby!

                        TOBY
             Okay, thank you.

                        JOSH
             Let's go.

                        DONNA
             Never heard from again, Josh.

And the three of them head off as we

                                                    CUT TO:

5   **INT. LEO'S OFFICE - DAY**   5

LEO's on his way out to a meeting, but he's stopped in front
of the TV monitor to watch the stock ticker go by. MARGARET
comes in--

                    MARGARET
          They're on their way to Unionville.

                    LEO
          Is the First Lady still in Madison?

                    MARGARET
          I'm pretty sure, I'll check.

They're heading out the door and into--

6   **INT. CORRIDOR - CONTINUOUS**   6

                    LEO
          Tell me again when the President's back?

                    MARGARET
          3:00 wheels down.

                    LEO
          What's his first.

                    MARGARET
          The Treasurer of the United States, not
          to be confused with Treasury Secretary.

                    LEO
          The Treasurer of the United States deals
          with the color of money, what's the
          meeting about?

                    MARGARET
               (checking her notes)
          Color currency.

                    LEO
          Push it. And push his meeting on health
          and fitness. I want the Trade Rep and as
          many of the economic advisors as we can
          at the 3:30.

                    MARGARET
          Speaking of health and fitness--

                    LEO
          Oh merciful God--

                                        (CONTINUED)

6   CONTINUED: 6

                         MARGARET
               What'd you have for--

                         LEO
               I had half a grapefruit.

                         MARGARET
               Really?

                         LEO
               You think I'm lying?

                         MARGARET
               No.

                         LEO
               Okay.

                         MARGARET
               Yes.

                         LEO
               I'll be in the Sit Room for a minute. I'd
               like him when he's done at the site.

                                                          CUT TO:

7   **INT. SITUATION ROOM - DAY**   7

People are gathering around the table for a quick meeting as
LEO comes in--

                         LEO
               Good morning.

                         ALL
               Morning/Hey/Good morning/etc.

                         LEO
               The Dow's down 260.

                         OFFICER
               Is it gonna rebound?

                         LEO
               What do I know? Could somebody get me
               half a grapefruit, I've got Jack LaLanne
               working for me this week. Let's go around
               the table for the quicksheet.

                         FITZWALLACE
               A small force of North Korean soldiers
               may stage an incursion into the DMZ.

                                                          (CONTINUED)

>   LEO
> That's a reaction to the President's trip
> to Seoul, right?

>   FITZWALLACE
> Yeah.

>   LEO
> Okay, South America.

>   CIVILIAN
> General Garcia has declared himself in
> rebellion against Carlos Velasco.

>   LEO
> Is Velasco's government in danger or is
> this just another crazy general with
> guns?
>   (beat)
> No offense, Fitz.

>   FITZWALLACE
> Yeah.

>   CIVILIAN
> The Venezuela Desk still says wait'll
> Garcia calls for the elections.

>   LEO
> Okay, Africa.

>   CIVILIAN #2
> The government of Mozambique is
> requesting a peacekeeping force to help
> distribute grain.

>   LEO
> A peacekeeping force to distribute grain.

>   CIVILIAN #2
> Yes sir.

>   LEO
> Middle East.

>   CIVILIAN #3
> Nothing really. We've got a communique
> from the new Ambassador.

>   LEO
> To where?

                                                    (CONTINUED)

> CIVILIAN #3
> I'm sorry, Qumar.

> LEO
> (quick beat)
> About what?

> CIVILIAN #3
> Well a month ago they re-opened the
> investigation into Shareef's missing
> plane.

> LEO
> They find anything?

> CIVILIAN #3
> I don't know, but the Emergency Locator
> Transmitter never went off, so--

> LEO
> Yeah.

> FITZWALLACE
> (to CIVILIAN #3)
> We'll assemble all the military rescue
> efforts and feed 'em into State. They can
> give the Ambassador and the Sultan
> another report.

> LEO
> Yeah. All right, Eastern Europe.

And we watch LEO and FITZWALLACE avoid eye contact with each
other as the next speaker begins--

> CIVILIAN #4 (OS)
> Warsaw transit workers are threatening to
> go on strike.

> CIVILIAN #2 (OS)
> Why?

> CIVILIAN #4 (OS)
> They haven't been paid in four months.

CUT TO:

8   **INT. COMMUNICATIONS BULLPEN - DAY**   8

GINGER's at her desk as SAM comes in in jeans and a
sweatshirt.

(CONTINUED)

8   CONTINUED:

> GINGER
> Whoa, whoa, you're not supposed to be
> here.

> SAM
> Yeah, I just wanted to check with--

> GINGER
> The orders were very strict.

LEO's passing in the corridor--

> LEO
> Hey!

> SAM
> I just--

> LEO
> Go home.

> SAM
> I am.

> LEO
> You haven't had a day off since the
> Convention, you've been up the past two
> nights and I don't want a zombie.

> SAM
> Right.

> LEO
> The energy book is done, the Mid-West
> poll is out, pawn off the surrogate
> movements and get a few hours sleep.

> SAM
> I just came in to check the Southern
> Governors, somebody's gotta be watching
> the politics.

> LEO
> Somebody is, it's the White House Office
> of Political Affairs.

> SAM
> Where is he?

> LEO
> He's about to go on at Ft. Bristol.

(CONTINUED)

> SAM
> You know the Dow's down 270.

> LEO
> Go to sleep.

> SAM
> I'm not fightin' with you.

                                        DISSOLVE TO BLACK:

TITLE:

> A11:15 -   **President arrived at Naval Warfare Center Crane and began his remarks.**
>
> P12:55 -   **Motorcade proceeded to Reynolds Air Force Base. President boarded AF-1.**
>
> P12:57 -   **Wheels up.**

FADE IN:

9   **INT. NAVAL WARFARE CENTER CRANE/CATACOMBS - DAY**   9

BARTLET's entourage is making its way through underground corridors. Off in the distance we can HEAR a warm-up act getting the crowd ready.

> BRUNO
> He should remind 'em about the military pay raise.

> C.J.
> He won't.

> BRUNO
> He should.

> C.J.
> He won't.

> BRUNO
> Of course not. We're adding a hundred outpatient clinics to the VA hospitals, is he gonna mention--

> C.J.
> No.

                                                    (CONTINUED)

9   CONTINUED: 9

                    BRUNO
Of course not. Military housing upgrades?

A FEMALE AIDE is taking a cellphone to BRUNO--

                    AIDE
Bruno?

                    BRUNO
He should say we don't give these people
anything, they *earn* it.
     (into phone)
Yeah.

C.J. catches up to BARTLET--

                    C.J.
Gehrman-Driscoll announced before
the bell it was filing for bankruptcy and
an hour later Jennings-Pratt and DWA--

                    BARTLET
They had exposure in the fund?

                    C.J.
Yeah.

                    BARTLET
I'm amazed it's only down 270.

                    C.J.
It's early.

                    BARTLET
That's what you want to say to me?

                    BRUNO
     (catching up)
Mr. President--

                    BARTLET
Driscoll announced it was filing and
Jennings and DWA are in the fund.

                    BRUNO
Pay raises, military housing, outpatient
clinics.

                    BARTLET
It's against the law to campaign on a
military base.

                             (CONTINUED)

9   CONTINUED: (2)   9

                         BRUNO
              Yes technically.

                         BARTLET
              No legally.

                         BRUNO
              Sir--

                         BARTLET
              These guys are DRF-1, they're Division
              Ready, they can be deployed in two hours.

                         BRUNO
              Yes sir, I didn't realize.

                         BARTLET
              A duffle bag, an M-16 and they're on a C-
              5 going wherever I send 'em and that's
              when their wives are told. I don't want
              to screw around with 'em.

                         BRUNO
              I didn't realize they were division-
              ready.

                         BARTLET
              Yeah.

                         BRUNO
              You could always wink and--I'm kidding
              that's a joke. I kid because I love.

     And they've reached the opening of the stage with perfect
     timing because now we HEAR--

                         SPEAKER (OS)
              So gentlemen and ladies, the President of
              the United States.

     And BARTLET walks out onto--

10   **OMITTED**   10

11   **OMITTED (INCORPORATED INTO SCENE 9)**   11

12   **INT. NAVAL WARFARE CENTER CRANE/STAGE - CONTINUOUS**   12

     --where he's greeted by a standing ovation from several
     hundred SOLDIERS.

                                                    (CONTINUED)

12   CONTINUED: 12

                              BARTLET
                    Good morning, we haven't met, I'm your
                    Commander in Chief.

Laughter.

                              BARTLET
                    This is the greatest fighting force in
                    the history of the world and I'm a big
                    part of that and I want to tell you why.
                    There's a D.O.D. regulation that says
                    uniformed officers aren't allowed to
                    publicly criticize the President and I
                    feel that the new levels of restraint
                    that I personally inspire in your
                    superiors in Washington...

And BARTLET gets a huge laugh followed by APPLAUSE as we

                                                    CUT TO:

13   **EXT. COUNTRY ROAD - DAY**   13

A pick-up truck's breezing down the road. DONNA and CATHY are
sitting up front. TOBY and JOSH are riding in the truck bed
with CAP.

                              CAP
                    It's just a regular diesel engine, no
                    retrofitting. The glow plugs heat up the
                    fuel but from there the soy diesel just
                    keeps exploding on itself like any
                    engine.

                              JOSH
                    You did it yourself?

                              CAP
                    It's easy.

                              TOBY
                    He's out there right now, he started.

                              JOSH
                    We really need to get this guy to
                    Unionville, he's gonna wig.

                              TOBY
                    He's out there.

                              JOSH
                    Take your mind off it, think about the
                    lovely Cathy.
                              (MORE)

                                                    (CONTINUED)

13   CONTINUED: 13

                              JOSH (cont'd)
              Farmer's daughter with a Masters Degree?
              Wholesome but maybe not too wholesome? I
              think she liked you too.

                              TOBY
              He's out there.

                              JOSH
                   (to CAP)
              How do you know Cathy?

                              CAP
              She's my girlfriend.

                              JOSH
                   (pause)
              That's great, she's really nice.
                   (beat)
              Is that corn out there?

                              CAP
              No.

                              JOSH
              What is it?

                              CAP
              Trees.

                              JOSH
              Okay.

                                                              CUT TO:

14   **INT. NAVAL WARFARE CENTER CRANE/AUDITORIUM - DAY**   14

       BARTLET's still at the podium...

                              BARTLET
              So what'll I remember, what'll I tell my
              grandchildren? I'll tell them that I
              stood on the Great Wall of China and that
              I stood in the well of the U.S. House of
              Representatives. I'll tell them I sat
              with Kings and Cardinals and made an
              appointment to the Supreme Court. And
              I'll tell them that for a few minutes one
              morning in September I got to be in a
              room with the men and women of the 39th
              Airborne. God bless you and your families
              and may He continue to shed His
              magnificent grace upon the United States
              of America.

                                                           (CONTINUED)

14   CONTINUED: 14

And the place breaks into a huge standing ovation as a 14 man
military choir sings *Glory, Glory Hallelujah*. It's a
triumphant moment as BARTLET now makes his way through the
crowd on stage to shake as many hands as possible and the
hands that he's shaking are the only ones not clapping.

An AIDE comes up to CHARLIE--

                    AIDE (NANCY)
              (over the noise)
          Charlie.

                    CHARLIE
          Yeah.

                    AIDE (NANCY)
          I've got Leo McGarry for the President.

                    CHARLIE
              (taking the phone)
          Thanks. C.J.--

                    C.J.
          Hey, I need to talk to you about
          something.

                    CHARLIE
          In a minute, okay, I've got Leo for the
          President.

C.J. waits until she's got eye contact with BARTLET then
subtly motions for him to step backstage and we

                                                    CUT TO:

15   INT. LEO'S OFFICE - SAME TIME   15

As MARGARET comes in--

                    MARGARET
          You've got the President.

                    LEO
              (hitting the speaker phone)
          Good morning, sir.

                                                    INTERCUT WITH:

16   INT. AUDITORIUM/BACKSTAGE - SAME TIME   16

                    BARTLET
          How's it goin'?

                                                    (CONTINUED)

16   CONTINUED:

               LEO
You tell me.

               BARTLET
It feels good.

               LEO
You know about the Dow?

               BARTLET
Jennings-Pratt was in the fund?

               LEO
Yeah.

               BARTLET
It'll rebound.

               LEO
Yeah.

               BARTLET
No kidding, it feels good out here.

               LEO
Good.

               BARTLET
What are you doing?

               LEO
I'm gonna meet with Fitzwallace for a
minute.

               BARTLET
About what?

               LEO
Nothing.

               BARTLET
You don't meet with Fitzwallace about
nothing.

               LEO
Just something from the quicksheet
briefing.

               BARTLET
What?

               LEO
Nothing.

                     (CONTINUED)

16   CONTINUED: (2)

> BARTLET
> Leo--

> LEO
> Qumar's reopened the investigation.

There's a long silence...

> LEO
> Mr. President?

> BARTLET
> Yeah all right, well we're coming home
> now.

> LEO
> Yes sir.

And BARTLET hands off the phone. He watches the choir sing...

> CHOIR
> *...His truth is marching on...*

FADE TO BLACK:

<u>END OF ACT ONE</u>

ACT TWO

FADE IN:

17   **EXT. COUNTRY ROAD - DAY**   17

As the pick-up truck drives along.

18   **INT. TRUCK - DAY**   18

> DONNA
> You're sure we're not taking you away
> from something you need to be doing?

> CATHY
> No actually this is on the way to my job.

> DONNA
> You have a second job?

> CATHY
> I work as a claims adjustor.

> DONNA
> That's unusual isn't it?

> CATHY
> It has benefits.

> DONNA
> You get to meet people.

> CATHY
> No I meant job benefits. Health
> insurance.

> DONNA
> It covers your father?

> CATHY
> Yeah.

> DONNA
> Good.

The truck starts to sputter a little...

> CATHY
> Uh-oh...

> DONNA
> What is it?

(CONTINUED)

18   CONTINUED:

                          CATHY
               Oh no, you guys are gonna kill me.

                          DONNA
               Is it outa gas?

CATHY nods her head...

                          CATHY
               There's a gas station about 1000 yards
               down the road.

                                              CUT TO:

19   **INT. TRUCK BED - DAY**   19

                          JOSH
               Why are we slowing down?

                          CAP
               Uh-oh.

                          JOSH
               Are we outa gas?

                          CAP
               Diesel.

                          JOSH
               Are we out of it?

The truck stops and CATHY and DONNA hop out.

                          CATHY
               We're outa gas.

                          CAP
               Diesel.

                          TOBY
               Nobody cares.

                          DONNA
               Cathy says there's a gas station about
               1000 yards down the road.

                          CAP
               They don't have diesel.

                          TOBY
               They don't have diesel.

                                         (CONTINUED)

>   JOSH
>   (to CAP)
>   Did we run out of gas because I called
>   her wholesome but not too wholesome.
>
>   CAP
>   I can't make a car run out of gas.
>
>   JOSH
>   I don't know, you can make glow plugs
>   explode stuff.
>
>   DONNA
>   Where's the closest diesel?
>
>   CAP
>   About ten miles.
>
>   DONNA
>   All right, can I suggest this. We've
>   missed Unionville. We've got a little
>   over an hour till the plane leaves and we
>   can make it if we call a volunteer and
>   have them pick us up at the gas station.
>   (to CATHY)
>   You guys can have the tow truck meet you
>   there.
>
>   CATHY
>   Oh we're not calling a tow truck, it's
>   just outa gas.
>
>   CAP
>   Diesel.
>
>   JOSH
>   What are you gonna do?
>
>   CATHY
>   We'll hitch back to the farm and pick
>   some up.
>
>   JOSH
>   Somebody's gonna pick you up out here?

And at that moment CAP casually raises his hand to a passing
car, which stops.

>   DRIVER
>   Guys run out of diesel?
>
>   CAP
>   Yeah.

                                                    (CONTINUED)

28.

19   CONTINUED: (2)   19

                              DRIVER
                    Need a lift back to the farm?

                              CAP
                    Thanks.

                              CATHY
                    Sy, these guys work for Bartlet.

                              JOSH
                    How you doin'.

                              DRIVER
                    Didn't vote for him the first time, don't
                    plan to the second time.

                              CATHY
                    Have a good trip back. And remember some
                    of the stuff I said, okay?

                              JOSH
                    All right, thanks a lot for your help.

CAP and CATHY get in the car and the car drives off. JOSH
turns to DONNA, who's on her cell.

                              JOSH
                    Call the State office and have 'em send a
                    local volunteer. Tell 'em we don't have
                    any time to you're doing it already,
                    right?

                              DONNA
                    Yeah.

                              JOSH
                    Okay.

JOSH goes to TOBY...

                              JOSH
                    This is fun, we're roughing it.

TOBY stares at him...

                              JOSH
                    It's fun.

                                                        CUT TO:

20   **INT. LEO'S OFFICE - DAY**   20

LEO's watching the stock ticker again as MARGARET comes in.

                                                    (CONTINUED)

                    MARGARET
          The Chairman's here.

                    LEO
          Thanks.

                    MARGARET
          Do you have any idea why there were women
          with aprons and rolling pins at Mrs.
          Bartlet's Madison event this morning?

                    LEO
          I'm sorry?

                    MARGARET
          A friend of mine just called me from
          Madison to say that she'd gone to see
          Mrs. Bartlet and there were about 20
          women in back wearing aprons and holding
          rolling pins.

                    LEO
          I don't know, maybe they were making
          pies.

                    MARGARET
          Yeah. Doesn't sound quite right though,
          does it.

                    LEO
          Send him in.

MARGARET steps out and FITZWALLACE comes in and closes the
door. They keep their voices down a bit.

                    FITZWALLACE
          The tracks are covered.

                    LEO
          Yeah?

                    FITZWALLACE
          We did a legitimate SAR with the UK and
          Royal Qumari Guard, this was a plane that
          went down in the Bermuda Triangle plain
          and simple.

                    LEO
          And that really happens.

                    FITZWALLACE
          What do you mean?

                                                        (CONTINUED)

                              LEO
          The Bermuda Triangle.

                              FITZWALLACE
          Does it really happen?

                              LEO
          I thought maybe it was like Toscanini
          landing in a corn field.

                              FITZWALLACE
          Planes, boats, about 200 of them
          including five Navy Avenger Bombers and
          the rescue plane that went in after them.

                              LEO
          Is there a chance they're gonna find the
          plane?

                              FITZWALLACE
          We dismantled the ELT and left the plane
          in 27 pieces, scattered among other
          wrecks, hidden in underwater landslides
          and limestone cliffs, and if they find
          the plane there's still no evidence of
          anything being anything. These were SEALS
          and these were Special Ops and these guys
          know what they're doing.

                              LEO
          Okay.
              (beat)
          Let's obviously stay in touch during the
          day.

                              FITZWALLACE
          Yeah.

                              LEO
          Just out of curiosity, what do you think
          would happen?

                              FITZWALLACE
          I don't know what would happen to you and
          me, but I'm pretty sure the President
          would be invited to see the inside of the
          Hague.

                              LEO
          Yeah, well, they can invite all they
          want, he ain't goin'.

(CONTINUED)

20   CONTINUED: (3)   20

                              FITZWALLACE
                   Perhaps this would be a good time for you
                   to reconsider your position on an
                   International War Crimes tribunal?

                              LEO
                   Perhaps this would be a good time for you
                   to--

                              FITZWALLACE
                   --get out of your office?

                              LEO
                   Yeah.

                              FITZWALLACE
                   Talk to you later.

                              LEO
                   Thank you.

                                        DISSOLVE TO BLACK:

        TITLE:

                   P1:20 - President met with Mrs. Walker

                   P1:40 - President met with Mrs. Harrison.

        FADE IN:

21   **INT. AIR FORCE ONE/PRESS CABIN - DAY**   21

        C.J. is strolling through...

                              C.J.
                   We've got a new addition to our running
                   list of things Robert Ritchie's not.
                   Speaking this morning at the Philadelphia
                   Financial Council, the Governor said,
                   "I'm no scientist but I know a thing or
                   two about physics." So for the week, you
                   can add scientist to doctor, mind reader
                   and Chinese.

                              MARK
                   C.J., do you have any idea why there were
                   women at the First Lady's rally this
                   morning who were dressed in aprons and
                   rolling pins?

                              C.J.
                   They were dressed in rolling pins?

                                        (CONTINUED)

21   CONTINUED:

> **MARK**
> They were holding them I guess, this is
> from the Milwaukee Sentinel.

> **C.J.**
> I don't know. Find out, though, would
> you.

> **KATIE**
> Is the President coming back for
> questions.

> **C.J.**
> He's gonna try, but he's gotta spend some
> time in his office interviewing secretary
> candidates. It's barbecue for lunch, I'll
> see you later.

CUT TO:

22   **INT. AIR FORCE ONE/BARTLET'S OFFICE - DAY**   22

ED and LARRY are standing with BARTLET.

> **LARRY**
> As of ten minutes ago, it's down another
> 90, that's almost 400 for the day.

> **BARTLET**
> It's still mostly transportation and
> technology?

> **LARRY**
> And energy.

> **BARTLET**
> Listen, I don't make a statement yet.

> **LARRY**
> No.

> **BARTLET**
> If the President's so concerned he's
> gotta make a statement--

> **ED**
> Yeah.

> **BARTLET**
> But have Josh and Toby weigh in at some
> point, okay?

(CONTINUED)

22   CONTINUED: 22

                              ED
                    Yes sir.

                              BARTLET
                    Okay.

                              ED/LARRY
                    Thank you, sir/Thank you, Mr. President.

ED and LARRY exit as CHARLIE pops his head in--

                              CHARLIE
                    Sir.

                              BARTLET
                    Yeah.

BARTLET's about to interview a Landingham replacement and his
heart's not really in it. He's not overtly rude but he's not
overtly warm either.

                              CHARLIE
                    Sir, this is Meredith Walker.

                              BARTLET
                    Come on in.

MRS. WALKER steps in and CHARLIE closes the door behind her.

                              BARTLET
                    Nice to meet you.

                              WALKER
                    Likewise, Mr. President.

                              BARTLET
                    It's crazy, I know, but sometimes the
                    schedule gets so tight that we have to
                    schedule meetings on the plane. So we ask
                    you to fly with us and we hit you on the
                    way back.

                              WALKER
                    Yes sir.

                              BARTLET
                    Were you impressed by the plane?

                              WALKER
                    It's an airplane, sir, I'm not very
                    easily impressed.

                                                        (CONTINUED)

                    BARTLET
          It's got an apartment and an operating
          room.

                    WALKER
          Yes sir.

                    BARTLET
          Okay, well you've met with Donald
          McKittridge, he directs the Office of
          Presidential Personnel.

                    WALKER
          Yes.

                    BARTLET
          You've had a moment to meet with Charlie
          Young?

                    WALKER
          Yes.

                    BARTLET
          He probably mentioned that this was a job
          where you need to be able to hold a lot
          of dates and names and numbers in your
          head.

                    WALKER
          Yes.

                    BARTLET
          You were told what the pay scale is?

                    WALKER
          Yes.

                    BARTLET
          And some of the perks.

                    WALKER
          Like what?

                    BARTLET
          Well for instance we have our own 747 and
          it's flown by an Air Force general.

                    WALKER
          Yes.

                                                    (CONTINUED)

22   CONTINUED: (3)   22

                                  BARTLET
                    Okay, let's talk about your last job.

                                                              CUT TO:

23   **INT. GAS STATION - DAY**   23

The MANAGER is behind the counter doing some work. Through the
window we see JOSH, TOBY and DONNA show up. JOSH heads inside.

                                  MANAGER
                    Good morning.

                                  JOSH
                    Good morning. We're stranded and waiting
                    for a ride. You mind if we wait here?

                                  MANAGER
                    How'd you get stranded?

                                  JOSH
                    Well we work for the President actually
                    and he was campaigning nearby this
                    morning--

                                  MANAGER
                    Oh yeah.

                                  JOSH
                    Anyway, we got left behind by the
                    motorcade and then our ride ran out of
                    diesel and so--

                                  MANAGER
                    Didn't vote for him the first time, don't
                    plan on voting for him the second time.

                                  JOSH
                    Okay, well we'll just wait outside if
                    that's all right.

                                  MANAGER
                    I don't like loitering.

                                  JOSH
                    Well we'll just be a few minutes I'm
                    sure.

The MANAGER does a "suit yourself" shrug and JOSH goes out to--

24   **EXT. GAS STATION - CONTINUOUS**   24

--where he joins DONNA and TOBY.

                                                       (CONTINUED)

24   CONTINUED:

                              JOSH
               Can we just call ahead and make sure the
               plane's still gonna be there when we get
               there.

                              DONNA
               It's gonna be there.

                              JOSH
               Can we call ahead?

                              DONNA
               I've been calling, I can't get anyone's
               cell. They're in a bad calling area.

                              JOSH
               Keep trying.

                              DONNA
               Yeah.

JOSH picks a rock up off the ground and whips it across the
road at an empty oil drum that's turned on its side. The rock
rattles inside the drum for a strike.

                              JOSH
                           (to TOBY)
               You see that?

TOBY picks up a rock and whips it across the road. Perfect
strike.

                              JOSH
               First guy to miss?

                              TOBY
               What's the bet?

                              JOSH
               First guy to miss has to shave his beard.

                              TOBY
               For the rest of the day, the first guy to
               miss, anytime he says his name, has to
               follow it with "I work at the White
               House."

                              JOSH
               Okay, but I don't think you've met our
               current host. Here we go.

JOSH whips a rock. Strike. TOBY whips a rock. Strike. This
continues as they talk.

                                              (CONTINUED)

                    TOBY
        You didn't say if you thought it was a
        good event this morning.

                    JOSH
        Well I didn't see the President speak
        this morning.

                    TOBY
        I know.

                    JOSH
        I was out there talking to Cathy, I was
        asked to.

                    TOBY
        Yeah.

                    JOSH
        I was.

                    TOBY
        But you read the remarks.

                    JOSH
        Yeah.

                    TOBY
        What was your problem?

                    JOSH
        You know what, Toby, I don't want this to
        be a high blood pressure day for me
        either.

TOBY looks at him, whips the rock and it clanks off the side.

                                    FADE TO BLACK:

                    END OF ACT TWO

<u>ACT THREE</u>

FADE IN:

25 **EXT. COUNTRY ROAD - DAY**   25

An open Jeep is coming down the road. TOBY and JOSH are in
back, DONNA's riding up front with the driver, TYLER, who's
started his senior year in high school.

> DONNA
> It's great that you're volunteering,
> Tyler. You're not even old enough to vote
> yet and here you are working for a
> campaign, that's great.

> TYLER
> They give us school credit.

> DONNA
> Well good for your school.

> TYLER
> I mean that's not the only reason I did
> it or anything.

> DONNA
> You like the President?

> TYLER
> Yeah, I think he's okay, I mean most of
> my friends are for Ritchie. Not that
> they're that political or anything I
> guess but their parents are for Ritchie
> so you know I guess...

> DONNA
> Yeah.

They ride in silence for a while...

> DONNA
> This is beautiful countryside.

> JOSH
> "He pretends there are no energy
> alternatives 'cause he can't think of
> any" that wasn't in the staff copy
> yesterday how did it make it in today?
> "He pretends there are no energy
> alternatives 'cause he can't think of
> any."

(CONTINUED)

> TOBY
> *They*. They can't think of any.

> JOSH
> We were touring flood damage in Missouri
> last Thursday, four times the President
> said "emergency management's complex."

> TOBY
> It _is_ complex.

> JOSH
> What does that matter to people who just
> lost their house?! Finding a place for
> their kids to sleep tonight is complex!

> TOBY
> Thanks, 'cause I was having a tough time
> prioritizing that one.

> JOSH
> Sustainable growth in Michigan, new
> economy in Ohio, information technology
> in Pennsylvania, that's what you talk
> about in September, and that's what we've
> mapped out for a year, and you and Bruno
> and the President are calling audibles.

> TOBY
> 'Cause we're coming to the line and we're
> seeing a hairdo from Florida in pass
> coverage and so that's where we want to
> put the ball, what's your concern?

> JOSH
> I have any number of concerns, not the
> least of which is we'll lose.

> TOBY
> I don't think so.

> JOSH
> When did we decide to make this about
> being the smartest kid in the class, what
> meeting did I miss?

> TYLER
> I have to pull over for a minute.

> DONNA
> Why?

(CONTINUED)

>   TOBY
>   Lemme tell you something--what did he
>   say?

>   TYLER
>   This'll just take a minute.
>   (shouting)
>   Kiki!

Here's what's happened: KIKI and her two friends have just
passed the Jeep on their bicycles. KIKI and TYLER went out
most of junior year but apparently that's over now and TYLER
hasn't quite adjusted to it.

>   TOBY
>   What the hell--

>   TYLER
>   You don't return phone calls anymore.

>   KIKI
>   I return some.

>   TYLER
>   Thanks a lot.

>   KIKI
>   We have to get back to school.

>   TYLER
>   What about the stuff I sent to your
>   house?

>   KIKI
>   Yeah, could you stop sending stuff to my
>   house, it's kinda creepy.

>   TYLER
>   Yeah, you know what, sue me I guess,
>   'cause I love you. Place me under arrest,
>   Kiki, let's everybody do that, let's
>   everybody get a writ of injustice, lock
>   me up and throw the book.

>   JOSH
>   Tyler?

>   TYLER
>   Just a second, Mr. Lyman.

                                                    (CONTINUED)

25   CONTINUED: (3)   25

                              KIKI
               You can't be creepy stalking guy, you're
               not that guy, Tyler, you're better than
               that.

                              DONNA
                    (to JOSH and TOBY)
               Not that much better.

                              JOSH
               Would you get in there.

                              FRIEND #1
               You have to move <u>on</u>, Tyler, you have to
               live in the <u>now</u>, you're totally stressing
               her.

                              DONNA
                    (calling)
               Excuse me.

     DONNA's hopped out of the Jeep, followed by TOBY and JOSH.

                              KIKI
               Yeah?

                              DONNA
               I'm so sorry to interfere in what's
               obviously a private moment between the
               two of you...and her two friends. We came
               in this morning for--

                              FRIEND #2
               We know who you are, we're not rednecks.

                              DONNA
               Okay, well I'm Donna Moss and this is my
               boss.

                              JOSH
               Josh Lyman.

                              TOBY
               Toby Ziegler.

                              DONNA
               Anyway, we're very crunched for time--

     But JOSH has shot TOBY a look to remind him that--

                              TOBY
               I work at the White House.

                                                   (CONTINUED)

                     FRIEND #2
          Wow, humongous whoop.

                     JOSH
          Hey come on, he's Communications
          Director, it's a decent sized whoop.

                     FRIEND #1
          How many unborn babies did you guys kill
          today?

                     JOSH
          Whoa, whoa, whoa, hey, hey, hey, *danger*
          Will Robinson. Tyler, no foolin' around,
          we've got 15 minutes to get to a plane
          that's three miles from here. That plane
          I swear to God is taking off at one
          o'clock.

                     TYLER
          It's taking off at one.

                     JOSH
          Yes it is.

                     KIKI
          Are you guys stupid or something. It's
          1:45 right now.

                     JOSH
          It's 12:45.

The three girls look knowingly at each other and smile a
little...

                     KIKI
          Not here it's not.

                     DONNA
             (pause)
          Oh my God, she's right.

                     TYLER
             (quietly to JOSH)
          See we crossed over from Unionville into
          Dearborn County which doesn't observe
          Daylight Savings Time.

                     FRIEND #1
          I think it's the other way around,
          genius.

                                        (CONTINUED)

> TYLER
> Hey what did I ever do to you?

> DONNA
> It says on the schedule all times are
> local, this is why I couldn't get anyone
> on their cell.

> JOSH
> Wait, wait, no, you're no...we changed
> time zones?
>   (to TOBY)
> We changed--
>   (back to TYLER)
> We changed time zones?

> TYLER
> It's a common mistake.

> JOSH
> *NOT FOR THE U.S. GOVERNMENT!*

> TOBY
> *WHAT KINDA SHMUCKASS SYSTEM--*

And now JOSH and TOBY simply go to the zoo. In the foreground,
DONNA will be speaking reasonably to kids, while in the
background, JOSH and TOBY are tromping all over the road and
into the field on the other side. Just walking around in
disorganized circles, muttering and shouting and gesticulating
to no one in particular, walking out of the frame and back in
again...

> DONNA
> Okay, so this is a whole new thing now.
> My guys are gonna need to walk it off a
> little before they can re-group. Kiki,
> you and your friends get back to school.
> Tyler, you and I are gonna come up with a
> plan to get us to a commercial airport.

> TYLER
> Okay.
>   (beat)
> How long are *they* gonna be?

> DONNA
> 'Couple of more minutes.

> TYLER
> Okay.

                                                            CUT TO:

26   **INT. AIR FORCE ONE/SENIOR STAFF CABIN - DAY**   26

C.J.'s staring out the window a little lost in thought as
CHARLIE comes into the cabin.

                    CHARLIE
          C.J.?

                    C.J.
          Yeah.

                    CHARLIE
          You wanted to talk to me?

                    C.J.
          I'm sorry?

                    CHARLIE
          You said back at the base that you wanted
          to talk to me.

                    C.J.
          Oh yeah. Listen, I wanted to ask you
          something. Simon was a Big Brother to a
          kid named Anthony Marcus.

                    CHARLIE
          I met him a couple of times.

                    C.J.
          I've been trying to spend a little time
          with him but he's not wild about me.

                    CHARLIE
          He's associating you with Simon's death,
          I did that for a while with some of the
          cops my mom worked with.

                    C.J.
          Yeah, well he was arrested for stealing a
          car. He stole his homeroom teacher's car,
          drove it around for a few hours and left
          it in front of a strip club. You could
          chalk it up to a stupid prank except
          Anthony had a string of shoplifting
          incidents before Simon came along so the
          A.D.A. sees it as an escalating problem,
          which is--

                    CHARLIE
          --graduating from a misdemeanor to a
          felony.

                                        (CONTINUED)

> C.J.
> Right, and she's pushing juvenile
> detention. I've spoken to her and if a
> White House staffer will play a role in
> his life, she's willing to re-consider.

> CHARLIE
> (pause)
> God, C.J....

> C.J.
> I know.

> CHARLIE
> I just got Deanna off to school.

> C.J.
> I know.

> CHARLIE
> And with the campaign now the days are
> even longer and I didn't think that was
> possible.

> C.J.
> I know, it was a long shot.

> CHARLIE
> I just don't think I'm the right guy for
> the job.

MARK sticks his head into the cabin--

> MARK
> C.J.

> C.J.
> Yeah.

> CHARLIE
> I'm sorry.

> MARK
> I've got an answer on the rolling pins.

> C.J.
> (getting up)
> Okay.
> (to CHARLIE)
> I shouldn't have asked you.

> CHARLIE
> I'm glad you did. Listen.

(CONTINUED)

26   CONTINUED: (2)   26

                              C.J.
                    Yeah.

                              CHARLIE
                    You're not just gonna ask the people who
                    look like me, right, 'cause a Big
                    Brother's a Big Brother, it doesn't
                    matter if--

C.J. smiles and holds up her hand to stop CHARLIE from
talking.

                              C.J.
                         (beat)
                    Sam's next.

C.J. disappears with MARK as we

                                                           CUT TO:

27   **INT. SAM'S BEDROOM - DAY**   27

SAM's asleep in his bed when the phone rings. The machine
answers it--

                              SAM'S VOICE (VO)
                    Hi, it's Sam. I'm sleeping for a few
                    hours right now so you can leave a
                    message, or if you really need me, just
                    shout into the machine and I'll wake up.

                              JOSH (VO)
                         (shouting)
                    SAM!!!!

SAM's awake now. He lunges for the phone but miscalculates the
distance and sends the whole thing flying. He tries to pull it
back by the cord and crashes the lamp to the floor.

                                                     INTERCUT WITH:

28   **EXT. COUNTRY ROAD - SAME TIME**   28

JOSH is standing next to the Jeep and through the cell phone,
which he's holding away from his ear now, we can HEAR the
continued crashes and clanks and bangs of SAM's attempt to
talk on the phone. We HEAR him saying--

                              SAM (VO)
                    It's all right. Hang on. No problem.

                                                      (CONTINUED)

                         JOSH
                    (to the others)
               It'll just be a second.

                         SAM
                    (finally--into phone)
               Hi. Sorry.

                         JOSH
               No, I'm sorry, buddy, I know you're
               supposed to be sleeping today.

                         SAM
               It's no problem, what's goin' on?

                         JOSH
               I'm with Toby and Donna and we're
               stranded somewhere in Indiana.

                         SAM
               You got left behind by the motorcade?

                         JOSH
               Yeah, and then we ran out of gas and then
               there was a time zone foul up and also we
               were waylaid by some mean schoolgirls.
               Alpha girls, you know what I'm sayin'?

                         DONNA
               Josh?

                         JOSH
                    (to DONNA)
               They were.

                         SAM
               So what are you doing now?

                         JOSH
               We're getting a lift to the Connersville
               Metro which is gonna take us to
               Indianapolis where we're gonna get a
               flight to either Dulles, BWI or
               LaGuardia.

                         SAM
               Hey if you want me to take your call
               sheet and I can farm out a few memos.

                         JOSH
               I actually need you to do more than that,
               Sam. I need you to staff the President.

                                             (CONTINUED)

28   CONTINUED: (2)

There's a long silence...

                    JOSH
          He's got one of those days.

                    SAM
               (pause)
          I don't know what it is you do in there.

                    JOSH
          Yeah you do. Anything ceremonial,
          security related or personal you leave
          the room. As it gets later in the day
          he's gonna start to talk to you. You're
          gonna tell him how the meeting he just
          had with his Council of Economic Advisors
          relates to the meeting he had with the
          Agriculture Secretary relates to his
          intelligence briefing relates to the
          environment relates to jobs relates to
          education relates to the campaign. You're
          his wide angle lens.

                    SAM
          There are gonna be any number of areas in
          which I can't give him expert advice.

                    JOSH
          Welcome to the club, partner, we've got
          jackets.

                    SAM
          All right, I'm not gonna let you down.

                    JOSH
          You never do.

SAM hangs up the phone.

                    SAM
               (to himself)
          Get dressed now.

                                        CUT TO:

29   **EXT. COUNTRY ROAD - SAME TIME**   29

     JOSH clicks the cell phone shut and stands there a moment,
     thinking to himself that Wally Pipp was probably a nice guy
     too.

     Then--

                                        (CONTINUED)

29 CONTINUED: 29

                         JOSH
              Let's get to the train station.

JOSH and DONNA climb into the Jeep. TYLER looks at TOBY, says
to him man-to-man...

                         TYLER
              You ever love so much it hurts? Like
              physically hurts?

                         TOBY
                   (pause)
              Get in the car.

                         TYLER
              Yeah.

                                                          CUT TO:

30 **INT. AIR FORCE ONE/BARTLET'S OFFICE - DAY**   30

BARTLET's in the middle of interviewing MARY HARRISON. He's in
the same mood he was in for the woman who wasn't easily
impressed.

                         BARTLET
              There's a tremendous amount of
              information you'll need to keep track of--
              dates, numbers and names--things I'm not
              very good with.

                         HARRISON
              That's unusual, isn't it?

                         BARTLET
              What's that?

                         HARRISON
              A man of your intellect not being good
              with names and numbers. Especially an
              economist of your stature.

                         BARTLET
              It's not intellect, it's memory, it's a
              different gift. A wonderful one, I've
              never had it.

                         HARRISON
              There are exercises you can do.

                                                    (CONTINUED)

> BARTLET
> (smiling)
> Well...okay, I'll try to find the time,
> but let's get back to you. What would you
> say was the most challenging part of
> working for the Ambassador to France?

> HARRISON
> The pliable relationship the French have
> with time.

> BARTLET
> Hm.

> HARRISON
> Yes sir?

> BARTLET
> I make fun of the French as much as
> anybody and I don't even know what that
> meant.

> HARRISON
> It means--

> BARTLET
> No that's okay, I think you're terrific
> and I appreciate your coming in and
> talking to us.

> HARRISON
> Thank you, sir, I'll look forward to
> hearing from your office.

> BARTLET
> Thanks again.

CHARLIE's already opened the door from the outside--

> CHARLIE
> (to HARRISON)
> I'll be right with you.

HARRISON has exited--

> CHARLIE
> (to BARTLET)
> Can you see Bruno?

> BARTLET
> Yeah.

BRUNO steps in--

(CONTINUED)

30   CONTINUED: (2)

                          BARTLET
              Hey.

                          BRUNO
              You want some good news, Mr. President?

                          BARTLET
              Please, the market's down 425 points.

                          BRUNO
              Well I think it's gonna rally but even if
              it doesn't this one isn't attributable to--

                          BARTLET
              I know.

                          BRUNO
              I'm saying--

                          BARTLET
              425 points represents billions of dollars
              which aren't there anymore heading into
              the fourth quarter which is Christmas.

                          BRUNO
                   (pause)
              Well I think it's gonna rally.

                          BARTLET
              What's your good news?

                          BRUNO
              We've held or made slight gains in almost
              all the polls. ABC/*Washington Post*,
              Bartlet 50, Ritchie 44--I'm all right
              referring to you colloquially?

BARTLET smiles and lets out a short laugh, BRUNO smiles. These
two are going through a war together and there's a lot of
respect.

                          BRUNO
              CBS/*New York Times*, Bartlet 50, Ritchie
              43. NBC/*Wall Street Journal*, Bartlet 49,
              Ritchie 43.

                          BARTLET
              You said almost all.

                          BRUNO
              CNN/*USA Today*/Gallup. Bartlet 46, Ritchie
              45.

                                                        (CONTINUED)

30   CONTINUED: (3)   30

                    BARTLET
          Why does Gallup have it a one point race?

                    BRUNO
               (beat)
          It's 'cause--

                    BARTLET
          It's 'cause they're polling likely voters
          and not registered voters. That's why
          they're getting the same numbers we do.

                    BRUNO
          Wait'll the debates. Election's in six
          weeks, Mr. President. The world was
          created in a lot less time.

                    BARTLET
          Well one day I'll buy you a beer, you'll
          tell us all how you did it.

                    BRUNO
          Thank you, sir.

     BRUNO exits into--

31   **INT. MAIN CABIN - CONTINUOUS**   31

     --where C.J.'s coming along.

                    C.J.
          Bruno.

                    BRUNO
          Yeah.

     C.J. leads BRUNO to a more private place.

                    C.J.
          Yesterday the First Lady appeared on K-
          CAL which is a local LA station. She was
          asked about the suspension of her medical
          license and she said something like "I'm
          just a wife and mother."

                    BRUNO
          And that has been interpreted in some
          circles as *merely* a wife and mother?

                                                      (CONTINUED)

31   CONTINUED:

                    C.J.
                (looking at notes)
        This is Flint Aldridge, a Southern
        Baptist radio host: "This is another sign
        that Abbey Bartlet is a liberal, elitist
        feminist."

                    BRUNO
        Elitist, feminist, you can't do that to
        the English language.

                    C.J.
        And this is from Janet Ritchie.

                    BRUNO
        Janet Ritchie went on the record?

                    C.J.
        "Being a wife and mother are the most
        rewarding roles I've ever played. I think
        Abbey Bartlet and I have two different
        ambitions."

                    BRUNO
        Hey, she won 50 dollars, said the magic
        word, right there. Ambition. Phylis
        Schlafly and Ann Coulter are gonna have a
        square dance.

                    C.J.
        Anyway, it's waiting for us down on the
        ground.

                    BRUNO
        Then let's stay up here and have drinks.

                    PILOT (VO)
        Good afternoon, ladies and gentlemen,
        from the flight deck this is General
        Baker. I've begun our descent into
        Andrews Air Force Base and I'm gonna ask
        those who are so inclined to take their
        seats and fasten their seatbelts.

                    BRUNO
        Janet Ritchie really went on the record?

                    C.J.
        Yeah.

                                        (CONTINUED)

31   CONTINUED: (2)   31

                BRUNO
            (walking away)
      I love it when the women get involved.

We stay on C.J., then--

                                    FADE TO BLACK:

                    <u>END OF ACT THREE</u>

<u>ACT FOUR</u>

TITLE:

>   **P3:30 - President met with Secretary**
>   **Bryce. Joined by Messrs.**
>   **Wendel, Lee, Aldee and**
>   **Stanislous and Ms. Wissinger.**
>
>   **P3:35 - President met with Mr. Lien.**
>   **Joined by Mr. McGarry.**
>
>   **P3:45 - Photo-op with Mr. Keith.**
>   **(Re-scheduled)**

FADE IN:

32 **INT. WEST WING LOBBY - DAY**   32

GINGER is waiting with some briefing material. SAM comes in--

                    GINGER
          The first two are easy.

                    SAM
          It's Bryce?

                    GINGER
          He just wants to talk about why the
          Department didn't participate more in--

                    SAM
          Okay.

                    GINGER
          Then it's Peter Lien and a photo-op.

                    SAM
          What's the photo-op?

                    GINGER
          It's a man who's shaken the hand of every
          President since Herbert Hoover.

                    SAM
          All right, do we have some sort of
          condensed...Reader's Digest index
          of...well, all human knowledge?

                    GINGER
          We usually just use Margaret.

                                            (CONTINUED)

32   CONTINUED: 32

                              SAM
               Okay, well we should talk about that but
               we'll do it another time.

They walk into--

33   **INT. CORRIDOR - CONTINUOUS**   33

                              GINGER
               Yeah.

                              SAM
               Soon though. Why don't you get me my
               notes from this morning's speech in
               Bloomfield.

                              GINGER
               I've got 'em out.

BRUNO comes along--

                              SAM
               Hey--were there women with aprons and
               rolling pins at a rally in Madison,
               Wisconsin this morning?

                              BRUNO
               Yeah.

                              SAM
               Why?

                              BRUNO
               Abbey Bartlet's a lesbian.

BRUNO walks into--

34   **INT. ROOSEVELT ROOM - CONTINUOUS**   34

--where an impromptu meeting's about to get underway.

                              C.J.
               What the hell does *that* mean, I love it
               when the women get involved?

                              BRUNO
                         (to a STAFFER)
               She's talking to me, right?

                              C.J.
               Abbey--

                                                        (CONTINUED)

34   CONTINUED:

                         BRUNO
          I'm not talking about Abbey and Janet
          Ritchie, I'm talking about the women, the
          voters. Continuing their unbroken streak,
          the biggest nonsense issue in the
          campaign will belong to the women. Does
          Abbey Bartlet love her children. Next
          week, Grandpa. Friend or foe.

                         C.J.
          This is not a woman's issue, this is a
          dumb woman's issue.

                         BRUNO
          I think anybody who's got a five point
          majority and still doesn't control the
          agenda might be spending a little too
          much time reading about how to get a man
          over his fear of commitment.

                         C.J.
          Remind me to mention that to the
          population of South Africa.

                         BRUNO
          You know what? In the scheme of things?
          Took 'em about five minutes.

                         C.J.
          Can we start?

                         BRUNO
          Yeah.

Everybody sits. Assistants flip open notebooks. C.J. turns to
BRUNO--

                         C.J.
          Several of the men I've dated haven't yet
          gotten over their fear of frogs.

                         BRUNO
          Okay.

                         STAFFER
          Has anybody seen tape on this?

                         C.J.
          I still haven't.

                         CAROL
          We're getting it.

                                             (CONTINUED)

34 CONTINUED: (2)   34

                         BRUNO
            She was asked about her license, she said
            right now I'm just a wife and a mother.

                         STAFFER
            Option 1 is we make a joke out of it.

                         BRUNO
            We *make* a joke out of it? What would we
            have to *do* to it to--

                         C.J.
            Yeah, the rolling pins took care of that.

                         BRUNO
            It is prêt-à-porter.

                         C.J.
                  (to CAROL)
            Remind me to get Josh in on this. Option
            2?

                                                   CUT TO:

35 **EXT. ROADSIDE DINER - DAY**   35

    TOBY, JOSH, DONNA and TYLER are getting out of the jeep and
    walking up to the restaurant.

                         JOSH
            Today's Monday.

                         DONNA
            Yeah, why?

                         JOSH
            I don't know, it was just something I
            said. All right, ten minutes, we get the
            stuff to go.

                         TOBY
            Tyler.

                         TYLER
            Yes sir.

                         TOBY
            What's a Hoosier?

                         TYLER
            A Hoosier's someone from Indiana.

                                              (CONTINUED)

35 CONTINUED: 35

Not quite the answer TOBY was looking for, but okay. They head
inside as DONNA pops some change into a newspaper box.

                                                              CUT TO:

36 **INT. DINER - DAY**   36

JOSH and TYLER take a seat at the table and they'll be joined
in a minute by DONNA. TOBY heads to the counter, which is
attended by a 60-ish black woman named FIONA.

                          TOBY
              Good afternoon.

                          FIONA
              Yes.

                          TOBY
              We'd like some food to go.

                          FIONA
              What would you like?

                          TOBY
              What's good?

                          FIONA
              Everything.

                          TOBY
              What's your specialty?

                          FIONA
              Taking someone's order and giving it to
              them.

                          TOBY
              Okay.

                          FIONA
              I saw you drive up, you people gonna
              cause trouble.

                          TOBY
              I swear not on purpose.

                          FIONA
              Every time he comes around here there's
              trouble. I don't want leaflets in my
              place, you handing out leaflets?

                          TOBY
              No we just want the food.

                                                    (CONTINUED)

> FIONA
> What do you need?

> TOBY
> (pause)
> You wouldn't say that there's some sort
> of...local delicacy that--

> FIONA
> I'm getting my husband.

And FIONA disappears into the kitchen. There's a TV up on
brackets in the corner and it's showing a daytime soap right
now. TOBY looks down at the only other customer sitting at the
counter, a man who maybe grew corn a long time ago.

> TOBY
> Excuse me.

The MAN looks at him.

> TOBY
> Would you mind terribly if I changed the
> channel to CNN for just a minute? I've
> been a little out of touch today and I'd
> like to check in with what's been going
> on.

> MAN
> Earl and Fiona don't get cable TV. Three
> channels are enough.
> (pause)
> The picture's fuzzy today. I think
> there's gonna be weather.

EARL comes out from the kitchen. He's a pretty big guy but
he's carrying a baseball bat anyway.

> EARL
> What the hell, boy?

> TOBY
> I was just asking what's good.

> EARL
> Yeah?

> TOBY
> We'll take four cheeseburgers.

> EARL
> The dry rub is good.

(CONTINUED)

>   TOBY
> Dry rub?

>   EARL
> You dry rub beef with spices for a day or
> two. Sauce is a myth.

>   TOBY
> Okay, Fiona, this is exactly what I was
> talking about.

>   FIONA
> *Shut up.*

>   TOBY
> We'll take it to go.

>   EARL
> She's been in a bad mood for...well about
> 45 years now I guess.

TOBY smiles at him as he gets off his stool and heads over to
the table.

>   DONNA
> Out in the parking lot, when you said
> it's Monday, I flashed on the song. A few
> days ago someone told me that a girl shot
> up her school one morning and when they
> asked her why she said, "I don't like
> Mondays" and that's where the song comes
> from.

>   JOSH
> Yeah.

>   DONNA
> You knew that?

>   JOSH
> Yeah.

>   DONNA
> That that's where the song comes from?

>   JOSH
> Yeah.

>   DONNA
> *I'm sorry about the time zones!*

                                          (CONTINUED)

                         JOSH
                      (to TOBY)
              Why is it we cite Ritchie's advisors by
              name? The Milton Friedman economic plan.
              The Leonard Tynan education plan?

                         TOBY
              I give credit where credit is due.

                         JOSH
              It's our way of calling him a puppet,
              right?

                         TOBY
              Josh, he cites 'em more than we do. Which
              is his way of saying I want to be
              President the same way you want a cold
              beer.

                         JOSH
              No, it's his way of saying I think it's
              great that Bartlet's a Nobel Prize
              winner, when I'm elected I'm gonna hire
              me some of those.

                         TOBY
              No, *no*, that *should* be what he's saying.
              What he's saying is Eastern education
              isn't for real men but don't worry, I'll
              have Jews for the money stuff.
                      (to DONNA)
              Would you mind calling C.J. for me?

                         JOSH
              That line in the convention speech,
              "challenges too great for a Potemkin
              presidency?"

                         TOBY
              It is true.

                         JOSH
              Most people *weren't* the smartest kid in
              the class. Most people didn't like the
              smartest kid in the class.

                         TOBY
              Yeah?

                         JOSH
                      (beat)
              I don't care how subliminal it is. This
              can't be a national therapy session.

                                              (CONTINUED)

36   CONTINUED: (4)   36

                            DONNA
                    (holding out the cell)
                C.J.

But TOBY looks at JOSH a moment longer...

                            TOBY
                Thank you.
                    (into phone)
                Hello.

                                      INTERCUT WITH:

37   **INT. CORRIDOR - SAME TIME**   37

C.J.'s standing outside the Roosevelt Room while her meeting
continues.

                            C.J.
                Hey, before I forget, if you see Josh,
                could you ask him to stop by my office?

TOBY thinks about this a moment...then casually places the
phone down on the table.

                            C.J.
                    (pause)
                Toby?

                            JOSH
                What.

                            TOBY
                She'd like you to stop by her office.

                            C.J.
                Toby, you there?

JOSH picks up the phone...

                          JOSH
                C.J., it's me. Did you happen to *notice*
                we weren't on the plane?

                          C.J.
                You weren't on the plane?

                          JOSH
                We missed the plane.

                          C.J.
                What happened between Unionville and the
                plane?

                                    (CONTINUED)

37   CONTINUED: 37

                              JOSH
              We missed Unionville, we missed the
              motorcade.

                              C.J.
                   (pause)
              Bummer.

                              JOSH
              Yeah.

                              FIONA
                   (shouting)
              Dry rub's up!

                              C.J.
              I <u>love</u> dry rub. They take the meat and--

      JOSH snaps the phone closed and tosses it to DONNA as we

                                                         CUT TO:

38   **INT. OVAL OFFICE - DAY**   38

      SAM is standing alone. After a moment, BARTLET comes in from
      the portico with a newspaper in his hand.

                              SAM
              Good morning, Mr. President.

                              BARTLET
              Seth Weinberger's assistant has come
              forward with the information that he was
              having an affair with a colleague. And a
              newspaper has printed it.

                              SAM
              What was the assistant's thing?

                              BARTLET
              You tell me. He'd already stepped down
              over OSHA it's been two months, this is
              an assistant getting her name in the
              paper. And it's unbelievably hurtful to
              his wife, I don't understand it. I don't
              understand the paper printing it either,
              but that's another day, this is terrible.

                              SAM
              Yes sir.

      CHARLIE steps in--

                                                         (CONTINUED)

> CHARLIE
> Secretary Bryce.

> BARTLET
> Good.

> SAM
> Is there a place you'd like me to stand
> or sit?

> BARTLET
> Hm?

BRYCE has come in along with an AIDE, and at the same time,
several STAFFERS have come in from the corridor door and one
from Leo's office. Oval Office hours have just begun.

> BRYCE
> Mr. President.

> BARTLET
> Mitch, come on in.
>   (turning back)
> Just rock and roll, Sam.

> LARRY
>   (quietly)
> Josh likes to stand over there.

> SAM
> Thanks.

> BRYCE
> I wanted to mention first of all, Mr.
> President, that I think you could seek
> Commerce's input on--or I'm not gonna
> tell you what to seek--lemme say that --

> SAM
> Actually, Mr. Secretary, if you're
> talking about the stump speech, and
> energy in particular, that's not the
> President's fault, that's mine. I was
> just looking at my notes from this
> morning's--

> BARTLET
> We have your input, you're talking about
> the exemption.

(CONTINUED)

> BRYCE
> It's sheer lunacy to suggest that America take unilateral steps while exempting 80 percent of the world's nations from the same obligations.

> BARTLET
> Developing nations and I think what's lunacy is a nation of SUVs telling a nation of bicycles that they have to change the way they live before we'll agree to do something about greenhouse emissions.

> BRYCE
> Among our economic competitors, there's the principle of fairness.

> BARTLET
> Well in international law there's a principle called differentiated responsibilities. *WE'RE THE ONES MAKING THE GREENHOUSE GAS!*

And the White House STAFFERS try not to, but they crack up at BARTLET's outburst of frustration. A couple of them clap.

> ED
> 47 seconds, who had 47 seconds?

> BRYCE
>   (pause)
> You're losing the support of the business community.

> BARTLET
> Mr. Secretary, it's not your job to tell me whose support I'm losing. We have people who do that. It's your job to tell me whose support you just got for me.

> BRYCE
> Yes sir.

> BARTLET
> Okay.

> BRYCE
> Thank you, Mr. President.

CHARLIE's opened the door from the outside--

(CONTINUED)

38   CONTINUED: (3)   38

                         BARTLET
          Ed.

                         LARRY
          Well I'm Larry, sir, but--

                         BARTLET
          Whatever. Seth Weinberger's old assistant--

                         LARRY
          I saw that.

                         BARTLET
          I don't think a lot of blind loyalty but
          I think a lot less of blind betrayal.

                         LARRY
          That's why I haven't gotten married yet,
          sir.

                         BARTLET
          Yeah, that's probably why.

CHARLIE steps in--

                         CHARLIE
          Congressman Lien.

                         BARTLET
          Could somebody get Leo for me please.
          Peter, you hear that, he called you
          Congressman.

PETER LIEN has come in. He's a 34 year old Vietnamese-
American. He maybe has a slight Texas drawl.

                         LIEN
          Yes sir.

                         BARTLET
          You think when your folks got you out in
          '74 they imagined they were taking you to
          a place that'd be willing to make you a
          Congressman?

                         LIEN
          As a matter of fact, sir, I think that's
          exactly what they imagined.

                         BARTLET
          Me too. How's fishing?

                                                        (CONTINUED)

> LIEN
> It's been a good season.

> BARTLET
> You catch any marlin?

> LIEN
> Marlin's a game fish, sir, not a lot of
> people eat them.

> BARTLET
> Takes a fisherman to catch one though,
> right?

> LIEN
> Oh yeah.

> BARTLET
> 'Kay, I'm just sayin'.

LEO's come in--

> LEO
> Good afternoon, Mr. President.

> BARTLET
> Leo, meet Congressman Peter Lien, Texas
> 22nd. Peter, this is Leo McGarry, U.S.
> Air Force, 144th Fighter Wing.

> LEO
> Pleased to meet you, Congressman.

> BARTLET
> Peter's family fishes in Galveston Bay
> but they don't catch marlin. It's a sore
> spot and he doesn't like to talk about
> it. Peter's 34 years old.

> LEO
> I'm sorry, it's been two months and we
> haven't been able to get you up here
> until now.

> LIEN
> No, please, it's a busy time. If there's
> any help I can give you in Texas.

(CONTINUED)

                        BARTLET
              Ordinarily I'd tell you that Jim Coor was
              a good public servant and you've got big
              shoes to fill and he was and you do but
              obviously you have a bigger symbolic
              responsibility than that.

                        LIEN
              Yes sir.

                        BARTLET
              But your biggest responsibility isn't
              symbolic, right?

                        LIEN
              Yes sir.

                        BARTLET
              What is it?

                        LIEN
              It's to my district, my country and the
              Congress of the United States.

                        BARTLET
              Welcome my friend to the show that never
              ends.

A quick spray of flashes as the American President and the
Vietnamese Congressman shake hands.

                        LIEN
              Thank you, Mr. President.

LIEN exits. BARTLET stands there a moment...

                        BARTLET
                   (to LEO)
              Isn't that a helluva thing?
                   (beat)
              What's next?

                                          FADE TO BLACK:

                        END OF ACT FOUR

ACT FIVE

FADE IN:

39   **INT. MRS. LANDINGHAM'S OFFICE - DAY**   39

We HEAR a sustained bell and a gavel coming down three times.
CNN is showing a live picture of the close of trading on the
stock exchange.

> FEMALE REPORTER (VO FROM TV)
> And that ends this day of trading, the
> Dow dropping 685 points, the seventh
> largest percentage drop in history and
> the largest point total ever. The bad
> news hit before the opening bell when--

BARTLET is watching this with a few STAFFERS...

> FEMALE REPORTER (VO FROM TV)
> The Gehrman-Driscoll Fund, the largest
> hedge fund in the U.S. announced it was
> filing for bankruptcy and that was
> followed by investment banking
> powerhouses Jennings-Pratt and DWA
> revealing they had significant exposure
> in the--

> BARTLET
> Yeah it's a proud day for Alfred Nobel.

> CHARLIE
> Mr. President?

> BARTLET
> (to SAM)
> When do you think I say something?

> SAM
> If Japan doesn't step up.

> BARTLET
> (pause--then to CHARLIE)
> Tell me again?

> CHARLIE
> Keith. Muriel Keith.

CHARLIE and BARTLET head into--

40   **INT. MURAL ROOM - CONTINUOUS**   40

--where MURIEL KEITH, a man in his late 80's is waiting with a
couple of INTERNS and a White House PHOTOGRAPHER.

                    BARTLET
        Mr. Keith?

                    KEITH
        Mr. President.

                    BARTLET
        I told my granddaughter I was meeting you
        and I asked what question she wanted me
        to ask you and she said to ask you of all
        the presidents you've met, who was your
        favorite and I assured her that it would
        be me.

                    KEITH
        No, no. Mr. Truman. He was a good man.

                    BARTLET
             (pause)
        Okay. Well. I was just kidding
        but...sure, Truman, if you like that
        kinda thing.

                    PHOTOGRAPHER
        Gentlemen, I'll be ready in just one
        minute, I'm sorry.

                    BARTLET
        How old were you when you met President
        Hoover?

                    KEITH
        Nine years old, it was my birthday.
        October the 23rd, nineteen hundred and
        twenty-nine.

                    BARTLET
        The 23rd?

                    KEITH
        Yes sir.
             (pause)
        Something unusual about that?

                    BARTLET
        No.
             (pause)
        No.
                    (MORE)

                                        (CONTINUED)

40   CONTINUED:

                    BARTLET (cont'd)
        (beat)
It's just...it's...you shook hands with
him and then the next day the Great
Depression started.

                    KEITH
Yes sir.

                    BARTLET
Okay.
        (pause)
The stock market took a stumble today.
You know, we'll call it...well a little
bigger than a pre-rally decline. If you
watch the news or read a newspaper
or...really are alive in any way you're
gonna hear about it in the next couple of
hours. I'm not worried, though, 'cause
Tokyo opens at 7pm Eastern, and Tokyo's
gonna be my mother's milk tonight. It's
in the bag.

                    PHOTOGRAPHER
Okay, gentlemen, right this way. On the
count of three. One--

                    BARTLET
No.

                    PHOTOGRAPHER
I'm sorry?

                    BARTLET
I'm sorry. Sorry. Could I--just have one
second. Charlie?

CHARLIE and BARTLET huddle in a corner of the room and speak
very softly...

                    BARTLET
        (pause)
How you doin'?

                    CHARLIE
Fine, thank you.

                    BARTLET
There's a lot of science in economics to
be sure, but like a lot of things, a lot
depends on the user. I need the Nikkei
Index to do what I need it to do tonight
and I've got Hoover's good luck charm
over here.
        (MORE)

(CONTINUED)

                    BARTLET (cont'd)
        But now while I'm talking I feel like
        it's ridiculous that someone like me
        would consider canceling a photo-op
        'cause--

                    CHARLIE
        I can't believe you're considering doing
        it, sir.

                    BARTLET
        I'm not, it was momentary--

                    CHARLIE
        No, I mean I can't believe you're
        considering doing it.

                    BARTLET
        Really?

                    CHARLIE
        Tokyo opens in three hours, you're gonna
        drape your arm around the Mayor of
        Shantytown?

                    BARTLET
        I didn't know you were superstitious.

                    CHARLIE
        I'm not. Plus there are the tribes in
        South America that don't think a
        photograph's a good idea to begin with.

                    BARTLET
        Yeah.

                    CHARLIE
        You ever see any pictures on my desk?

                    BARTLET
        No.

                    CHARLIE
        You ever wonder why?

                    BARTLET
            (pause)
        Charlie, just out of curiosity, in your
        mind, how much time do I spend thinking
        about your desk?

                    CHARLIE
        Fair point, sir.

                                            (CONTINUED)

40   CONTINUED: (3)   40

                              BARTLET
                    How long have we been talking about this
                    now?

                              CHARLIE
                    A couple of minutes.

                              BARTLET
                    Okay, let's not tell anybody that.

                              CHARLIE
                    Yeah. Mr. Keith, I'm sorry, we're gonna
                    have to re-schedule this for tomorrow.

                              KEITH
                    Oh why?

              BARTLET   CHARLIE
        Just scheduling.   You're spookin' the hell out
                                      of the President.

                              KEITH
                    I'm--

                              CHARLIE
                    I'll explain it.

                              BARTLET
                         (exiting)
                    Thank you.

        And we

                                                              CUT TO:

41   **INT. SAM'S OFFICE - DAY**   41

        SAM's sitting on the floor near the bookshelf with a couple of
        briefing manuals. C.J. comes in.

                              C.J.
                    Sam?

                              SAM
                    Yeah.

                              C.J.
                         (beat)
                    Whatchya doin' on the floor?

                              SAM
                    I don't know, I think it was just the
                    closest thing.

                                                          (CONTINUED)

> C.J.
> Come on, you're gonna get your pants
> shmutsy.

SAM pulls himself up on C.J.'s arm.

> SAM
> Hey, the First Lady isn't a lesbian, is
> she?

> C.J.
> I don't know, I can ask her.

> SAM
> Why were there rolling pins?

> C.J.
> Brenda Swetland: "At this moment you're
> not licensed to practice medicine,
> correct?" A. Bartlet: "At this moment I'm
> just a wife and mother."

> SAM
>   (beat)
> I don't see it.

> C.J.
> Well you gotta want it.

> SAM
> Oh I see it.

> C.J.
> Yeah.

> SAM
> What are we doing?

> C.J.
> Well I wanted my office to issue a
> statement saying you're annoying, shut
> up, but Bruno said to wave at it and he's
> right.

> SAM
> Yeah.

(CONTINUED)

                       C.J.
Listen, I know this is the last thing you
want to hear right now but I want to get
Anthony a Big Brother and Charlie said no
and I thought if it was anything you
might be interested in I could talk to
you about it.
    (beat)
It's an hour a week. He doesn't have
anybody. And you know he hasn't gotten
over Simon.

                SAM
    (pause)
You asked Charlie first?

C.J. laughs...

                     C.J.
There's no way you have time for this.

                SAM
I might.

                     C.J.
You don't.

                SAM
    (calling)
Ginger.

                     C.J.
You just worked 48 hours straight.

                SAM
Yeah.

                     C.J.
And that was the *weekend*.

                SAM
    (pause)
Maybe he'd enjoy sitting and watching me
work. I could narrate what I was doing
for him. "Right now I'm reading
background intelligence on Central
America as it relates, believe it or not,
to textile imports. Oooh, intelligence,
007." See, and now I've got him going
with 007.

(CONTINUED)

41   CONTINUED: (3)   41

                         C.J.
              I'm sitting here listening, already I've
              turned to a life of crime.

                         SAM
              You know I'd do it if I could.

                         C.J.
              I do know that, shmutsy pants.

                         SAM
              That's gonna be around for a few days,
              right?

                         C.J.
              How's it goin' in there?

                         SAM
              Fine, it hasn't really started yet.
              Bryce, you know, is pushing him away from
              the unilateral standards and the rest of
              the meetings start in about 20 minutes.

GINGER comes in--

                         GINGER
              Josh is on the phone.

                         C.J.
              Thanks.

C.J. exits. SAM picks up the phone--

                         SAM
                    (into phone)
              Hey.

                                        INTERCUT WITH:

42   **EXT. COUNTRY ROAD - SAME TIME**   42

                         JOSH
              How's it going?

                         SAM
              Fine so far.

                         JOSH
              Just Bryce, right?

                                        (CONTINUED)

42   CONTINUED:

>   SAM
>   Yeah. Lemme ask you something. He was
>   saying that Commerce hasn't had enough
>   input on the stump speech and I started
>   to say that was my fault and the
>   President kinda ran me over.
>
>   JOSH
>   Yeah, he doesn't like the appearance that
>   his staff's covering for him.
>
>   SAM
>   It genuinely wasn't his fault.
>
>   JOSH
>   Nothing's not his fault in the Oval
>   Office.
>
>   SAM
>   Got it.
>
>   JOSH
>   Anything else before we get on the train?
>
>   SAM
>   Could you put Toby on?

JOSH hands the phone to TOBY--

>   TOBY
>   Was Bryce pissed?
>
>   SAM
>   Yeah. Listen, with his secretarial
>   candidates the last few weeks, Charlie
>   says he's been asking questions about
>   remembering names and numbers. He's
>   worrying about short term memory loss,
>   right, it's one of the effects of--
>
>   TOBY
>   Yeah.
>
>   SAM
>   Okay.
>
>   TOBY
>   Anything else?
>
>   SAM
>   Come home.

(CONTINUED)

42   CONTINUED: (2)   42

                              TOBY
                    We're on our way.

TOBY closes the phone and hands it to DONNA as the jeep pulls
into--

43   **INT. TRAIN STATION - CONTINUOUS**   43

--where the train is already sitting at the platform.

                              JOSH
                    Don't worry, I'll have Jews for the money
                    stuff?

TOBY looks at JOSH...

                              JOSH
                    You have an inadvertent habit of putting
                    down my Judaism by implying that you have
                    a sharper anti-Semitism meter than I do.

                              TOBY
                    You know the ancient Hebrews had a word
                    for Jews from Westport. They pronounced
                    it Presbyterian.

                              JOSH
                    And by saying things like that.

                              TOBY
                    I'm just sayin' I'm from Brighton Beach.

                              JOSH
                    Well Mohammed al Mohammed el Mohammed bin
                    Bizir doesn't make the distinction when
                    he suits up in the morning.

                              TOBY
                    As long as you have a good grasp of the
                    complexity of that situation.

                              DONNA
                    What the hell are the two of you talking
                    about?

                              TOBY
                    I assure you neither one of us knows.

                              CONDUCTOR
                         (shouting)
                    All aboard!

                                                          (CONTINUED)

                        JOSH
            Tyler, assure me there's gonna be no
            trouble.

                        TYLER
            There's gonna be no trouble.

                        JOSH
            The train runs on regular train fuel?

                        TYLER
            I'm pretty sure.

                        JOSH
            You guys don't have your very own
            international dateline in Bloomington or
            something?

                        TYLER
            No.

    The three of them have stepped up onto the train--

                        JOSH
            In that case, on behalf of Bartlet for
            America and the Democratic Party I want
            to thank you for your help and tell you
            you're a good guy and good luck to you.

                        TYLER
            Thank you.

                        DONNA
            I'm gonna find seats.

    DONNA goes into the train car.

                        JOSH
            Take it easy.

                        TYLER
            Mr. Lyman, Mr. Ziegler.

                        JOSH
            Call me Josh.

                        TOBY
            Toby. I work at the White House.

                                        (CONTINUED)

43   CONTINUED: (2)   43

                          TYLER
            Yeah, can I tell you something? People
            are gonna think you're a lot cooler if
            you don't say that yourself, but rather
            let them find out on their own.

                          TOBY
            Okay.

                          JOSH
            The engineer knows the route?

                          TYLER
            Josh, Toby, on my girlfriend's life, your
            troubles end 98 miles right down that
            track.

And at the very moment TYLER points, the train pulls out of
the station in the opposite direction.

TOBY and JOSH have nothing to say.

                                                        CUT TO:

44   **OMITTED (INCORPORATED INTO SCENE 47)**   44

45   **OMITTED**   45

46   **INT. SITUATION ROOM - DAY**   46

LEO and FITZWALLACE are alone. FITZWALLACE has a cup of
coffee. NANCY comes in.

                          LEO
            Nancy.

                          NANCY
            Leo. Yeoman Fitzwallace.

                          FITZWALLACE
            Dr. McNally.

                          NANCY
            Let's attack.

                          LEO
            Who?

                          NANCY
            Qumar, let's recommend to the President
            that we attack.

                                                    (CONTINUED)

46   CONTINUED: 46

                              LEO
          Why?

                              NANCY
          'Cause I've had it.

                              FITZWALLACE
          I don't think the U.N.'s gonna let us do
          it for that reason.

                              NANCY
          That's 'cause you're a sissy. You want
          peace in the Middle East, gimme a pair of
          third generation ICBMs and a compass.
          You've got B-2 Spirit stealth bombers
          over Qumar right now, as if the Qumari
          Air Defense System requires stealth
          capability. *Just fly in at night!* And
          while you're at it, could you order the
          USS Louisiana to fire off a D-5 Trident,
          just to see if it works, what's the worst
          that could happen.

                              FITZWALLACE
                    (pause)
          Is she talking to me?

                              NANCY
          Yes!!

                              FITZWALLACE
          Well 98% of all living organisms within a
          7 mile radius would die instantly in a
          torment of fire.

                              NANCY
          Admiral Sissymary...we're running out of
          options on the menu.

                              LEO
          What's happened?

                              NANCY
          There's intel that says that Qumar has a
          tape.

                              LEO
          Of what?

                              NANCY
          A cell phone call that Shareef made from
          the plane.

                                                          (CONTINUED)

> FITZWALLACE
> There isn't. We disabled the phones, we
> monitored communication from the plane,
> we bugged Shareef and we replaced his
> cell phone battery with a dummy. There's
> no tape, there was no phone call.

> LEO
> Why are they saying there is, it's to
> provoke a response, right?

> NANCY
> Yeah.

> LEO
> (pause)
> And they're using the Act V scene from
> *Hamlet*? Are these Batman villains?

> NANCY
> They're building a case for sure, but I
> think we have to start talking about
> there's something worse than Qumar saying
> it was us.

> FITZWALLACE
> She's right.

> LEO
> What.

> FITZWALLACE
> Qumar saying it was someone else.

> FADE TO BLACK:

END OF ACT FIVE

ACT SIX

From the BLACK we HEAR--

>   BARTLET (VO)
>   You can't say faith based initiatives to
>   me, you have to be more specific than
>   that. You can't offer a guy a hot meal
>   but first you have to accept God into
>   your heart, it's against the law. It's
>   also a little obnoxious.

TITLE:

>   P4:45 - **President met with Sen. Shuler,
>   Sen Choate.**
>
>   P4:50 - **President met with Ch. Lacey.**
>
>   P5:20 - **President met with Deborah
>   Fiderer.**

FADE IN:

47   **INT. THE OVAL OFFICE - DAY**   47

>   SENATOR #1
>   If a church runs a soup kitchen are they
>   serving Christian soup?
>
>   BARTLET
>   No, the soup is non-demoninational, Fred,
>   but I'm not talking about the soup, I'm
>   talking about the programs and another
>   problem is the Government can't subsidize
>   organizations that discriminate in hiring
>   practices as religious organizations are
>   allowed to do.
>
>   SENATOR #2
>   Mr. President, in my district the only
>   ones making inroads into keeping kids in
>   school and off drugs are the churches and
>   the synagogues and the mosques. They have
>   terrific programs and until we find a
>   better one, let me fund those.
>
>   BARTLET
>   We're gonna talk about it around here,
>   but I wouldn't--
>
>   SENATOR #2
>   Yes sir.

                                        (CONTINUED)

47   CONTINUED: 47

                         BARTLET
          Okay.

                         SENATORS
          Thank you, sir/Thank you

The Senators exit and BARTLET goes behind his desk.

                         SAM
          How are the interviews going?

                         BARTLET
          I met with two women this morning on the
          plane, I'm meeting another in a little
          bit.

                         SAM
          Are either of this morning's women
          possibilities?

                         BARTLET
          No.

                         SAM
          Why?

                         BARTLET
          Well the first one isn't easily
          impressed.

                         SAM
          What makes you say that?

                         BARTLET
          She told me. The second one wasn't funny.

                         SAM
          She wasn't funny.

                         BARTLET
          Or rather didn't think I was.

                         SAM
          You told a joke?

                         BARTLET
          She was the secretary to an Ambassador to
          France.
                         (MORE)

                                                    (CONTINUED)

47   CONTINUED: (2)

> BARTLET (cont'd)
> I told her that I'd had dinner with
> D'Astier at the Élysée Palace--she gently
> corrected me at that point, calling it
> the Palais de l'Élysée--for that alone I
> wanted to send for a parachute--and I
> made a joke to D'Astier having to do with
> cheese and I said that D'Astier was
> visibly insulted and that he was
> reconsidering my diplomatic status. And
> she said 'well did he.'

> SAM
> She didn't get that you were joking.

> BARTLET
> It didn't bode well for me.

> SAM
> Who's this afternoon.

> BARTLET
> A crazy woman that Charlie knows. Hey, do
> we have a GPS read-out on Josh and Toby,
> have they been sighted?

> SAM
> I talked to them a little while ago,
> they're on their way.

> BARTLET
> 300 IQ points between 'em they can't find
> their way home. I swear to God, if Donna
> wasn't there, they'd have to buy a house.

BARTLET's been shuffling through some papers on his desk
during this and a moment ago he came across the newspaper he
was carrying earlier.

> BARTLET
> "You've gotta be able to keep a lot of
> names and numbers in your head, can you
> do that?" "Oh I should think so." Oh
> should you. Okay, well I'm gonna
> interview a few more people and in the
> meantime you can get your ass back on the
> cover of the *The New Yorker* where it
> belongs.

> SAM
> Was that unimpressed one or humorless.

> BARTLET
> A third one. Charlie says I don't want
> anyone to replace her.

(CONTINUED)

47   CONTINUED: (3)

                    SAM
          You think that's true?

                    BARTLET
          I don't know, Sam, I'm a puzzle.

                    SAM
          Yes sir.

                    BARTLET
               (re: the newspaper)
          This Seth Weinberger thing makes me
          crazy.

                                                              CUT TO:

48   **INT. TRAIN - DAY**   48

JOSH, TOBY and DONNA are sitting across from each other, a
fold down card table between them. TOBY and JOSH each have
cups and a couple of little empty liquor bottles in front of
them. DONNA's got a map and a few schedules laid out in front
of her.

After a moment...

                    DONNA
          All right, I've got a plan.
               (pause)
          We're gonna switch trains in Bedford and
          we will then be going in the right
          direction. Now we're not gonna make the
          6:15, that was a pipe dream, that was
          folly. Now. There's a 9:30 leaving
          Indianapolis International with a 45
          minute layover in Chicago, though the
          ticket agent warned that the flight could
          be delayed due to bad weather.

                    JOSH
          What are the chances of *that*?

                    DONNA
          Well for what it's worth, the guy in the
          diner said the reason the picture on the
          TV was fuzzy--

                    JOSH
          No. No. Quaint is quaint, but we're not
          Navajo Indian Guides and when we want
          weather information we call the White
          House Operations Center.

                                                              (CONTINUED)

48   CONTINUED:

> DONNA
> We can do that when we get to a pay phone
> but we can't do that right now.

> JOSH
> Why not?

> DONNA
> Because my cell phone
> battery's out.

> JOSH
> Your cell phone battery's out.

> DONNA
> Yes.

> JOSH
> I need information. I need to know what's
> happening. I have no idea what's
> happening in the world.

> DONNA
> I bought you the paper.

> JOSH
> I read it. Preparations are under way for
> the fair. I'm briefed. Organizers say
> it's gonna be the best one yet. What else
> you got?

> TOBY
> Frivolous law firms.

TOBY's been examining the contents of his pockets during the
above, and now he's looking at a note he scribbled.

> JOSH
> What?

> TOBY
> He meant to say frivolous law suits and
> he said frivolous law firms.

> JOSH
> Who?

> TOBY
> Benjamin Disraeli.

> JOSH
> He misspeaks.

(CONTINUED)

48   CONTINUED: (2)

>   TOBY
> Yes he does. He also thinks that Sarajevo
> and Bosnia are two different countries,
> so that's a bit of a setback for the
> region.

>   JOSH
> Yes.

>   TOBY
> Chamberlain led England in World War II.
> I don't mind that he doesn't know
> history, I mind that he hasn't seen a
> movie. Mexico is part of NATO.

>   JOSH
> He meant they were an ally.

>   TOBY
> What'd they lob a chalupa at the Warsaw
> Pact?

>   JOSH
> I agree it's not impressive, but as you
> pointed out, he's gonna be surrounded by--

>   TOBY
> Do you think he's ever disagreed with one
> of his advisors?
>   (beat)
> Honestly?
>   (pause)
> Do you think he's ever said to one of his
> advisors, "I've got a different idea"?
>   (pause)
> But I don't care if he thinks Luxembourg
> is an uptown stop on the IRT, and I don't
> care about the Greco-Roman wrestling
> matches with the language--not that
> polished communication skills are an
> important part of this job--what I care
> about is when he was asked if he'd
> continue the current U.S. policy in China
> and he said, "First off, I'm gonna send
> 'em a message: Meet an American leader."
> I don't know what that means, but
> everybody cheered.

>   JOSH
> Which is one of the reasons I work full
> time for his opponent, I don't know what
> gave you the impression I had to be
> convinced. But I want to win.
>   (MORE)

                                                              (CONTINUED)

48 CONTINUED: (3)   48

> JOSH (cont'd)
> You want to beat him. And that's a
> problem for me 'cause I want to win.

> DONNA
> Can I get approval of my travel plan?

> JOSH
> Yeah.

They ride in silence a moment...

> TOBY
> (reading from another scrap)
> "A rising tide sinks all boats."

TOBY shows JOSH the piece of paper to demonstrate he's not
making it up as we

                                                        CUT TO:

49 **INT. MRS. LANDINGHAM'S OFFICE - EARLY EVENING**   49

FIDERER is sitting and waiting in a dark blue suit. CHARLIE's
sitting at his desk.

> FIDERER
> Is it all right to ask what he did for a
> year?

> CHARLIE
> What do you mean?

> FIDERER
> He's been without a secretary for a year.

> CHARLIE
> The President has five secretaries. Four
> of them funnel their work through the
> Executive Secretary.

> FIDERER
> He has five secretaries?

> CHARLIE
> He has two research secretaries, a social
> secretary and a scheduler. The scheduler
> has an assistant whose job it is to keep
> the book.

> FIDERER
> What's the book.

                                                    (CONTINUED)

49   CONTINUED:

                    CHARLIE
          It's the daily diary, it's a minute by
          minute accounting of what the President
          did that day. 10:25, placed a phone call
          to the Fed Chair.

                    FIDERER
          What about private stuff?

                    CHARLIE
          We've got euphemisms. Every once in a
          while they'll be a fluke cancellation,
          some kind of gap in the schedule and the
          President and First Lady might slip over
          to the residence, you know--

                    FIDERER
          --for a matinee?

                    CHARLIE
          Yeah.

                    FIDERER
          What do you call it?

                    CHARLIE
          Barbecuing.

                    FIDERER
          Okay.

                                        CUT TO:

50   **INT. THE OVAL OFFICE - EARLY EVENING**   50

      We're at the end of a meeting.

                    LACEY
          The payment and settlement systems worked
          fine. The Dow's price/earnings is around
          35, the historical average is 18. This
          isn't a crisis, it's investors getting
          back to common sense.

                    BARTLET
          Well it's an election year, Bill, and
          we'd rather people didn't exercise common
          sense but I agree with what you're
          saying.

                    LACEY
          Thank you, Mr. President.

                                        (CONTINUED)

50   CONTINUED: 50

          LACEY exits as do all STAFFERS who are there. CHARLIE's
          stepped in--

                              CHARLIE
                    Sir?

                              BARTLET
                    Yes.

                              CHARLIE
                    Deborah Fiderer.

                              BARTLET
                         (not wild about it)
                    Really?

                              CHARLIE
                    Yes sir.

                              BARTLET
                    All right.

          CHARLIE steps out and FIDERER comes in.

                              FIDERER
                    Mr. President.

                              BARTLET
                    Hi.

                              SAM
                    Debbie.

                              FIDERER
                    Hello.

                              BARTLET
                    You two know each other?

                              SAM
                    Debbie used to work for Donald
                    McKittridge. She's very interesting, her
                    resume's impressive. I remember thinking
                    she was efficient and creative, she's the
                    one who found Charlie. I remember people
                    talked about her a lot, they found her
                    pretty strange. But I remember thinking I
                    didn't find her that strange.

                              FIDERER
                    You know I can hear you, right?

                                                        (CONTINUED)

                    SAM
I'm in your corner.

SAM steps out...There's a long silence...

                    BARTLET
You're the alpaca farmer.

                    FIDERER
It was something I tried for a while.

                    BARTLET
You hired Charlie, huh.

                    FIDERER
Well I worked in the Office of
Presidential Personnel and he'd come into
the wrong office, he'd been called in
about a job as a messenger.

                    BARTLET
I didn't know that.

                    FIDERER
Yeah we started talking and it doesn't
take long to see he's a special kid so I
sent him to Josh Lyman.

                    BARTLET
Well...thanks for that.

                    FIDERER
Yes sir.

                    BARTLET
Who was in second place, who did I almost
get?

                    FIDERER
Sir?

                    BARTLET
I like to think about the road not taken.

                    FIDERER
You're testing my memory.

                    BARTLET
Yeah.

                    FIDERER
A young man named David Dweck.

                            (CONTINUED)

                        BARTLET
            David Dweck?

                        FIDERER
            Yes I called him David Dweck want a dwink
            of wa wa until I realized that wasn't
            really funny.

BARTLET smiles...

LARRY steps in--

                        LARRY
            Excuse me, Mr. President, you said you
            wanted--

                        BARTLET
            Yeah.

                        LARRY
            Hong Kong's down 4% but it's still over
            10,000 and it's too early to tell
            anything. The Nikkei's down 2%, the
            dollar's down point-3% against the yen,
            point-4% against the Euro. Frankfurt
            opens in eight hours.

                        BARTLET
            Thanks.

                        LARRY
            Thank you.

LARRY steps out.

                        BARTLET
            Sorry. Why were you fired?

                        FIDERER
            I'm sorry?

                        BARTLET
            Why were you fired?

                        FIDERER
            No particular reason.

                        BARTLET
            That doesn't sound quite right.

                        FIDERER
            No?

                                            (CONTINUED)

50   CONTINUED: (4)

                    BARTLET
         Why were you fired.

                    FIDERER
         Is it relevant?

                    BARTLET
         Only because you're asking for a job.

                    FIDERER
         Chronic lateness.

                    BARTLET
         I don't believe you.

                    FIDERER
         It's true.

                    BARTLET
         No it's not.

                    FIDERER
         You call me a liar to my face?

                    BARTLET
         Yes.

                    FIDERER
         Okay.

                    BARTLET
         Charlie said it was because of him.

                    FIDERER
         He did?

                    BARTLET
         He said you hired him and that's why you
         got fired.

                    FIDERER
         Charlie makes things up.

                    BARTLET
         No he doesn't.

                    FIDERER
         He's a bad seed and I knew it the moment
         I saw him.

                    BARTLET
         I'm now ordering you to tell me why you
         were fired.

                                        (CONTINUED)

50   CONTINUED: (5)   50

                              FIDERER
          Well I'm afraid we're at a classic
          impasse, Mr. President.

                              BARTLET
          You were strange the first time I met you
          and you're strange now.

                              FIDERER
          Hey, the first time you met me there was
          a good reason.

                              BARTLET
          What?

                              FIDERER
          I was high.

                              BARTLET
          Okay--

                              FIDERER
          This time it's just me.

                              BARTLET
          Tell me why you were fired.

                              FIDERER
          No sir.

                              BARTLET
          I'm gonna figure it out anyway. What I
          lack in memory I more than make up for
          with exceptional powers of deductive
          reasoning.

                              FIDERER
          That come with tights and a cape?

                              BARTLET
          All right, I think the interview's over.

                              FIDERER
          Yeah, but let's do this every once in a
          while.

                              BARTLET
          Thank you very much.

          CHARLIE's opened the door to let FIDERER out into--

51   **INT. LANDINGHAM'S OFFICE - CONTINUOUS**   51

--where MCKITTRIDGE is waiting with a WOMAN.

                    MCKITTRIDGE
          Debbie.

                    FIDERER
          Mr. McKittridge.

                    MCKITTRIDGE
          What are you doing here?

                    FIDERER
          I was--

                    CHARLIE
          I brought her in.

                    FIDERER
          I was interviewing for--

                    MCKITTRIDGE
          Charlie--

                    FIDERER
          Hang on.

                    MCKITTRIDGE
          How many times do we have to--

                    CHARLIE
          I know, but I brought her in.

                    FIDERER
          It doesn't matter, I'm not getting the--

                    MCKITTRIDGE
              (still to CHARLIE)
          It does matter, there's a way it works.

And BARTLET comes out of the Oval Office--

                    BARTLET
          BRIAN Dweck!!

Everyone turns and looks at him. Silence.

                                        (CONTINUED)

51   CONTINUED: 51

>   BARTLET
>   CFO of Colfax, and contributor to
>   Representative Mark McKittridge, whose
>   brother is the Director of the White
>   House Office of Presidential Personnel,
>   wants a job for his son, David...wants a
>   dwink of wa wa. My powers of deduction
>   are not to be mocked.
>
>   MCKITTRIDGE
>   Mr. President, I assure you, whatever she
>   told you--
>
>   BARTLET
>   She didn't tell me anything. I ordered
>   her to and she--
>   (to CHARLIE)
>   --by the way, my powers of ordering are a
>   joke. I can create an agency but I can't
>   get her to--
>   (to MCKITTRIDGE)
>   She didn't give you up. She, uh...

And then it sinks in a little, but he wants to cover.

>   BARTLET
>   (pause)
>   She didn't give you up.

BARTLET goes back inside. SAM follows him into--

52   **INT. THE OVAL OFFICE - CONTINUOUS**   52

BARTLET's standing there, troubled by the act of betrayal he's
about to commit. SAM only needs to push him the last inch...

>   SAM
>   (pause)
>   Was she funny?
>
>   BARTLET
>   (pause--then calling)
>   Charlie, have the agents stop her at the
>   door for a second.

BARTLET runs out into--

53   **INT. LANDINGHAM'S OFFICE/CORRIDORS - CONTINUOUS**   53

BARTLET hustles past people who wonder what the hell is going
on. He pushes open the doors into--

54   **INT. WEST WING LOBBY - CONTINUOUS**   54

                         BARTLET
                    (calling)
               Debbie.

FIDERER stops. As does anyone who's standing in the lobby.

                         FIDERER
                    (pause)
               Yes sir?

                         BARTLET
                    (pause)
               Where's the dollar?

                         FIDERER
               I'm sorry, sir?

                         BARTLET
               What's the dollar doing right now?

                         FIDERER
                    (pause)
               It's down point-3% against the yen, point-
               4% against the Euro.

BARTLET looks at her a moment longer, then points to CHARLIE,
and then FIDERER...a manager telling a pitching coach to bring
the lefty into the game.

BARTLET turns and exits. The silence in the room continues a
moment longer before a round of welcome to the job applause
starts to surround FIDERER and we

                                               CUT TO:

55   **INT. CORRIDOR - EARLY EVENING**   55

As BARTLET's making his way back to the Oval Office.

                         AIDE (NANCY)
               Mr. President, the First Lady's back.

                         BARTLET
               Heh heh. Bring her on.

And BARTLET disappears into the Oval Office as we

                                               FADE TO BLACK:

                         END OF ACT SIX

ACT SEVEN

TITLE:
          P8:25 - President attended DNC
                   fundraiser at Capital Hilton.

FADE IN:

56   **INT. RESIDENCE VESTIBULE - EVENING**   56

A BUTLER is taking a coffee tray out of the bedroom as BARTLET
comes around the corner.

                    BUTLER
          Good evening, Mr. President.

                    BARTLET
          Is the First Lady inside?

                    BUTLER
          Yes sir.

                    BARTLET
          Suppertime.

BARTLET goes into--

57   **INT. BARTLET'S BEDROOM - CONTINUOUS**   57

                    BARTLET
               (calling)
          Medea?! You home?!

ABBEY steps out of the bedroom--

                    ABBEY
          Jed--

                    BARTLET
          "Political experts seemed surprised by
          the Bartlet campaign's decision to
          position their candidate against
          motherhood. Said one spokesperson--"

                    ABBEY
          I'm so sorry. I'm sorry.

                    BARTLET
               (pause)
          What?

                    ABBEY
          I feel terrible, can I talk to the staff?

                                        (CONTINUED)

> BARTLET
> (pause)
> No, don't do this.

> ABBEY
> I'm not kidding, I'm sorry.

> BARTLET
> About what?

> ABBEY
> I screwed up.

> BARTLET
> How?

> ABBEY
> You know how.

> BARTLET
> What the hell are you--it was *benign*, it
> was totally benign what you said, these
> women are out of their minds, we're
> laughing about it here.

> ABBEY
> Nobody's laughing.

> BARTLET
> I'm telling you, watch--turn on C.J.'s
> press briefing, she's been doing 20
> minutes up there, they're booking her
> into Caesars.

> ABBEY
> You don't think it's gonna be a problem?

> BARTLET
> No.

> ABBEY
> *THEN GET OFF MY BACK, JACKASS!*

> BARTLET
> (frustrated and disgusted)
> Ahhh, you pulled the switcheroo.

> ABBEY
> You are so heartbreakingly easy at the
> end of the day.

> BARTLET
> You deceived me.

(CONTINUED)

                            ABBEY
            You called me Medea.

                            BARTLET
            You played upon my love for you.

                            ABBEY
            Ah, who gives a damn.

                            BARTLET
            Yeah. I hired someone today.

                            ABBEY
            Seriously?

                            BARTLET
            Yeah.

                            ABBEY
            Who?

                            BARTLET
            Her name is Debbie Fiderer and she used
            to work here.

                            ABBEY
            I don't remember her.

                            BARTLET
            It used to be DiLaGuardia.

                            ABBEY
            Debbie DiLaGuardia?

                            BARTLET
            Yeah.

                            ABBEY
            She's great.

                            BARTLET
            She doesn't scare you a little?

                            ABBEY
            She scares you?

                            BARTLET
            No.
                (pause)
            Okay I'm getting dressed for the thing.

                                            (CONTINUED)

57   CONTINUED: (3)   57

                        ABBEY
          I'm gonna make fun of you a little bit
          more while you do, okay?

                        BARTLET
          Yeah.

BARTLET goes in the bathroom and ABBEY changes the channel on
the TV to closed circuit to watch the press briefing--

                        C.J. (ON TV)
          The First Lady loves two out of the three
          of her children but she doesn't like to
          tell them which two.

                                                          CUT TO:

58   **INT. PRESS BRIEFING ROOM - SAME TIME**   58

                        C.J.
          Arthur.

                        ARTHUR
          The President's on the podium at 8:15?

                        C.J.
          That's when it's scheduled, probably more
          like 8:30 and he's gonna speak for 15
          minutes.

                        MARK
          Any comment on the CBO deficit numbers?

                        C.J.
          Last OMB was $11 billion off, CBO missed
          by 25 billion, there's gonna be a deficit
          but the CBO's numbers are off. Katie?

                        KATIE
          Legislative Appropriations?

                        C.J.
          He can't say until he sees the bill. All
          right, that's a full lid, I'll see you
          all over there.

CAROL's walked in with a note for C.J.

                        C.J.
          Hang on a second.

                                                     (CONTINUED)

58   CONTINUED: 58

C.J. looks it over. It takes a long moment. Then C.J. and
CAROL confer for an uncomfortably long moment as CAROL hands
her a cell phone with a small wire and earpiece connected.
Everyone in the press room knows they're about to hear news.

                    C.J.
                (from notes)
        Okay, today at 5:32 pm Central Savings
        Time, two pipe bombs were set off inside
        the Geiger Indoor Arena, which is the
        swimming team's facility at Kennison
        State University, the Kennison Hawkeyes.
        The women's team was hosting a match...a
        meet...with Illinois, Michigan and
        Minnesota, they're all Big Ten schools.
        44 people are dead, it looks like about a
        hundred injured...about 20 critically.

                    PRESS
        C.J.!

C.J. puts the wire in her ear now as she says--

                    C.J.
        I'm gonna have to listen in while I talk
        to you. Barry then Sydney then Fran.

                                                        CUT TO:

59   **INT. CORRIDOR - EVENING**   59

LEO and MARGARET are walking--

                    LEO
        I didn't say I wasn't going, I said I
        could live without it.

                    MARGARET
        It sounded like you weren't going.

                    LEO
        I forgot about it is all.

They walk into--

60   **INT. MARGARET'S OFFICE/LEO'S OFFICE - CONTINUOUS**   60

                    MARGARET
        Did you have other plans?

                    LEO
        As a matter of fact I did, I was planning
        a quiet night.

                                                        (CONTINUED)

60   CONTINUED: 60

                              MARGARET
                    Watching your cooking show.

                              LEO
                    It's not just a cooking show, all right,
                    it's very relaxing, the woman is sublime.

                              MARGARET
                    If you ask me it's soft porn. No one
                    needs to massage garlic oil into a leg of
                    lamb that much. On top of which--

                              LEO
                    Hang on.
                         (pause)
                    Why's she still on?

LEO's pointing to the TV which is showing C.J.'s briefing with
the sound off. He pops it on--

                              C.J. (ON TV)
                    Well the information that they were pipe
                    bombs is coming from--we're getting both
                    campus information and Cedar Rapids
                    Police and Fire...

...and as C.J. continues we HEAR the beginning of *I Don't Like
Mondays*, the song Donna was talking about at the diner.

                              VOCAL
                    *"The silicon chip inside her head has
                    switched to overload..."*

                              LEO
                    Find out what happened.

MARGARET exits and LEO stands helpless in front of the TV. The
song continues as we

                                                            CUT TO:

61   **EXT./EST. AIRPORT MARRIOTT - DUSK**   61

It's pouring rain.

62   **INT. MARRIOTT - SAME TIME**   62

TOBY, JOSH and DONNA, drenched, come in the front door.
DONNA's covered herself in JOSH's jacket. JOSH and TOBY are
oblivious to their condition because they've got soaking
evening newspapers in their hands.

                                                        (CONTINUED)

> DONNA
> I don't under*stand* the two of you.

> JOSH
> We had to get out, he can't read in a
> moving car.

> DONNA
> You can't read in a moving car, he can.
> He was reading to us.

> JOSH
> I need it to enter through my eyes.

> DONNA
> You couldn't wait three blocks.

> JOSH
> 685 points.

> TOBY
> Did it say how big a percentage drop it
> was?

> JOSH
> It did, but by the time I got there my
> newspaper had stopped having the
> molecular structure of a newspaper.

They've made it to the front desk.

> DESKMAN
> Yes, can I help you?

> DONNA
> Yes please, we need a room.

> DESKMAN
> Is that two rooms?

> DONNA
> No just the one for--
>   (to JOSH and TOBY)
> --what did we decide, a half hour?

> JOSH
>   (to the DESKMAN)
> Our flight's--
>   (pushes DONNA out of the way)
> Our flight's been delayed and we're just
> looking for someplace to dry off and
> watch the news.

(CONTINUED)

62   CONTINUED: (2)   62

                          DESKMAN
               Lemme see what I've got.

The DESKMAN starts tapping on his computer--

                          JOSH
               If the Nikkei doesn't react by--

But TOBY's not there. He's wandered over to be closer to the
TV in the lobby that's showing CNN's report of a pipe bombing
in Cedar Rapids.

JOSH and DONNA go over as the song continues...

                          VOCAL
               "Tell me why. I don't like Mondays..."

...and the three of them stand helpless in front of the TV as
we

                                                    CUT TO:

63   **OMITTED**   63

64   **INT. BALLROOM - NIGHT**   64

1000 tuxedoed Democrats who've paid plenty to be there.
BARTLET in a spotlight at the podium behind a big backdrop.

                          BARTLET
               Restoring abundance amid an economic
               shortfall, securing peace in a time of
               global conflict, sustaining hope in this
               winter of anxiety and fear. More than
               anytime in recent history, America's
               destiny is not of our own choosing. We
               did not seek, nor did we provoke, an
               assault on our freedoms and our way of
               life. We did not expect, nor did we
               invite, a confrontation with evil. Yet
               the true measure of a people's strength
               is how they rise to master that moment
               when it does arrive. 44 people were
               killed a couple hours ago at Kennison
               State University. Three swimmers from the
               men's team were killed and two others are
               in critical condition when, after having
               heard the explosion from their practice
               facility, they ran into the fire to help
               get people out.
                    (beat)
               Ran into the fire. The streets of heaven
               are too crowded with angels tonight.
                    (MORE)

                                            (CONTINUED)

64   CONTINUED: 64

> BARTLET (cont'd)
> They're our students and our teachers and
> our parents and our friends. The streets
> of heaven are too crowded with angels,
> but every time we think we've measured
> our capacity to meet a challenge, we look
> up and we're reminded that that capacity
> may well be limitless. We will do what is
> hard, we will achieve what is great. This
> is a time for American heroes and we
> reach for the stars. God bless their
> memory, God bless you and God bless the
> United States of America.

The place goes bananas. BRUNO's standing next to SAM.

> BRUNO
> When did you write that last part?

> SAM
> In the car.

> BRUNO
> (pause--to himself)
> Freak.

                                                            CUT TO:

65   **INT. JOSH'S BULLPEN - NIGHT**   65

ANTHONY's sitting outside C.J.'s office. He's looking older
than the last time we saw him. He's got a bruise over one eye.

After a moment the back doors open and we see the flashing
lights of the motorcade as C.J. and other STAFFERS start to
trickle in in evening dress.

> C.J.
> Anthony. I'm so sorry, thank you for
> waiting. This thing came up at the last
> minute, a bomb at a swimming meet, you
> probably...I can take you home now...you
> probably saw it here on the television
> sets.
> (pause)
> You know I really miss Simon, too. That's
> probably something we can talk about.
> (pause)
> I asked around today, I wasn't able to
> find anyone, but I'm not done, there are
> more people I'm asking tomorrow.
> (beat)
> I'll take you home now.

ANTHONY gets up and mumbles something we don't hear--

                                                       (CONTINUED)

65   CONTINUED: 65

                    C.J.
I'm sorry?

                    ANTHONY
I said I don't need a babysitter, bitch,
are you deaf?

                    C.J.
         (beat)
Well I don't think you do need a
babysitter but the ADA says--

BLAM!!

Here's what's happened. CHARLIE came in from the motorcade and
walked past C.J. and ANTHONY. When he got about five feet past
them he heard him call her a bitch, did an immediate and
casual 180 degree turn, walked back, grabbed ANTHONY by the
shirt and shoved him against the filing cabinet.

                    ANTHONY
What the hell's the matter with you,
dog?!

                    CHARLIE
This is Ms. Cregg, she's the White House
Press Secretary and Senior Counselor to
the President and if she wasn't she'd
still be Ms. Cregg. I don't mind your not
respecting people, I mind your doing it
out loud, I mind your doing it in this
building. You wanna be a punk, fine, but
I don't think you've got the size for it.
You wanna go to juvey, get out deal and
kill cops, okay, but every time you do a
crime you get caught so I think you're
gonna have to do something else. Nine
o'clock Saturday mornings I eat breakfast
at Cosmos on Delaware, I come here for an
hour and do office work and then I go to
St. Judes for an hour and play
basketball. You can go to juvey or you
can be at Cosmos nine o'clock on
Saturday, it's entirely up to you.

And CHARLIE walks away as we

                                    FADE TO BLACK:

                   <u>END OF ACT SEVEN</u>

ACT EIGHT

FADE IN:

66   **INT. CORRIDORS/COMMUNICATIONS BULLPEN - NIGHT**   66

It's started to rain outside. SAM's coming out of Landingham's office and is heading to his own. He's done for the day. He undoes his bow tie as he heads into--

67   **INT. SAM'S OFFICE - CONTINUOUS**   67

There's a single lamp on in the room, and as he goes to his desk, he hears someone behind him say--

                WOMAN (OS)
      Shmutsy pants.

SAM stops...

                SAM
      I know that voice.

He turns around. It's MALLORY. She was just at the fundraiser. Need we say she looks fine.

                MALLORY
      I was at the dinner.

                SAM
      I didn't see you.

                MALLORY
      Nice job on the speech.

                SAM
      What makes you think I wrote it?

                MALLORY
      "We did not seek, nor did we provoke, we
      did not expect, nor did we invite..."

                SAM
      A little thing called cadence.

                MALLORY
      It works for you.

                SAM
      How's New York.

                MALLORY
      Richard got traded to the Blackhawks.

                      (CONTINUED)

                      SAM
For a Zamboni battery?

                    MALLORY
And Garniér and a first round draft pick.

                      SAM
So you're moving to Chicago.

                    MALLORY
Richard and I split.

                      SAM
That is terrible. That is the worst--I am
so sorry. I liked him too, his brooding
stare in the penalty box, is there
anything I can--

                    MALLORY
Shut up!

                      SAM
Okay.

                    MALLORY
I came by to say hi, I came by to tell
you I liked the speech.

                      SAM
Well thank you very much.

                    MALLORY
My dad said you staffed the President
today.

                      SAM
Yes.

                    MALLORY
How was it?

                      SAM
        (pause)
You know anything about chaos theory?

                    MALLORY
        (pause)
I know it has to do with fractal
geometry.

                                      (CONTINUED)

67   CONTINUED: (2)   67

                    SAM
          That's about all I know too. But it has
          to do with there being order, even great
          beauty, in what looks like total chaos.
          And if we look closely enough at the
          randomness around us, patterns will start
          to emerge.
                    (pause)
          I love Josh like a brother and he's a
          world class political mind but until
          today I didn't know he was smarter than I
          was. I've worked here three years and
          eight months, and until you sit in the
          room all day you can't comprehend the
          chaos of the Oval Office. I had one good
          moment, talking about the global ripple
          of a budget deficit, but that was it, the
          rest of the day was just keeping up. And
          this was a pretty light day.

                    MALLORY
          One good moment is good.

                    SAM
          I'm not complaining, I'm saying one good
          moment is great, it was a golf shot. I've
          gotta get back in there. That's where
          it's happening.
                    (pause)
          You came by just to say you liked the
          speech?

                    MALLORY
          This is a time for American heroes and we
          reach for the stars? I'm weak.

                    SAM
          Yeah I think I stole that from Camelot.

                    MALLORY
          Lemme get you home, I don't think you're
          gonna make it.

                    SAM
          Yeah, I don't think I'm gonna make it
          either.

     They head out into--

68   **OMITTED**   68

69   **INT. CORRIDOR - CONTINUOUS**   69

>   MALLORY
>   Camelot?

>   SAM
>   Good writers borrow from other good
>   writers. Great writers steal from them
>   outright.

>   MALLORY
>   G'night, Charlie.

>   SAM
>   G'night, Charlie.

>   CHARLIE
>   Take it easy.

CHARLIE was coming along and now he heads into--

70   **INT. MRS. LANDINGHAM'S OFFICE - CONTINUOUS**   70

There's a wrapped gift on the desk. CHARLIE goes behind the
desk and opens it. It's a framed picture but we don't see of
what. CHARLIE looks at it...he's never seen this one before...

C.J. appears in the doorway...

>   C.J.
>   The picture's from Deanna, I just put it
>   in a frame. I've had it in my office for
>   a week I just keep forgetting to give it
>   to you.

>   CHARLIE
>   Thanks, it's nice.

>   C.J.
>   Have a good night.

>   CHARLIE
>   G'night.

C.J. exits. CHARLIE stands the picture up on his desk. He
touches it to make sure it's in just the right place. Then
grabs some paperwork he's gonna take home and we see the
picture: A uniformed policewoman and a five year old boy named
Charlie.

>   CUT TO:

71   **INT. MARRIOTT BAR - NIGHT**   71

The place is half empty as the thunderstorm continues outside.
DONNA's bought herself a dry Indiana sweatshirt at the gift
shop which she's wearing right now.

JOSH and TOBY are still slogging through it.

                         JOSH
              Campaigns aren't about the candidates.

                         TOBY
              No?

                         JOSH
              They're about the voters. How are we
              gonna create jobs, how are we gonna fix
              health care, how are we gonna make the
              lights go on, how are we gonna protect
              ourselves.

                         TOBY
              Don't we want to ask if the plumber knows
              which direction the pipes run? Don't we
              want to--forget the plumber--don't we
              want leadership to sound and to *feel*
              like--instead of appealing to our least
              expensive, however legitimate, desire to
              feel good about ourselves, don't we want--

                         DONNA
              All right, that's it, I can't take it.

                         TOBY
              He started it.

                         DONNA
              I'm not kidding. I have such an impulse
              to knock your heads together. I can't
              remember the last time I heard you two
              talk about anything other than how a
              campaign was playing in Washington. Cathy
              needed to take a second job so her dad
              could be covered by her insurance. She
              tried to tell you how bad things were for
              family farmers and you told her we
              already lost Indiana. You made fun of the
              fair but you didn't see they have
              livestock exhibitions where they give
              prizes for the biggest tomato and the
              best heirloom apple. They're proud of
              what they grow.
                         (MORE)

                                                          (CONTINUED)

71   CONTINUED:

> DONNA (cont'd)
> Eight modes of transportation, the
> kindness of six strangers, random
> conversations with twelve more and nobody
> brought up Bartlet versus Ritchie but
> you. I'm writing letters on your behalf
> to the parents of the kids who were
> killed today, can I have the table
> please?

And TOBY and JOSH silently agree she's got 'em and they get up
and walk over to the bar where they sit a few stools apart.
There's a man sitting close to TOBY.

After moment...

> MAN
> Flight's delayed?

> TOBY
> Yeah.

> MAN
> Me too. I'm going to St. Louis.

> TOBY
> Washington.

> MAN
> I'm with my daughter. She's upstairs in
> the room but we were out here looking at
> Notre Dame.

> TOBY
> Yeah?

> MAN
> You got kids?

> TOBY
> No.

> MAN
> Wait'll you take your oldest to look at
> colleges. It's an incredible feeling. You
> wish they'd go to college across the
> street from your house, but you know...

> TOBY
> Yeah.
>   (to the BARTENDER)
> Jack Daniels rocks.

> BARTENDER
> Yeah.

                                                          (CONTINUED)

> TOBY
> My boss went to Notre Dame.

> MAN
> Beautiful campus, I've never seen
> anything like it. She's not gonna be able
> to get to sleep tonight.

TOBY smiles...

> MAN
> You see what happened in the market
> today?

> TOBY
> Yeah I saw. You invested.

> MAN
> A mutual fund that's supposed to send her
> to college. I never imagined $55,000 a
> year I'd have trouble making ends meet.
> And my wife brings in another 25. My
> son's in public school it's no good.
> They've got 37 kids in a class, no art
> and music, no advanced placement courses.
> Other kids, their mother has to make 'em
> practice the piano, you can't pull my son
> *away* from a piano, he needs teachers. And
> I spend half the day thinking about what
> happens if I slip and fall down on my own
> front porch.
> (pause)
> It should be hard. I like that it's hard.
> Putting your daughter through college,
> that's a man's job, that's a man's
> accomplishment. But it should be a little
> easier. Just a little easier. 'Cause in
> that difference is everything.
> (pause)
> I'm sorry, I'm Matt Kelley.

TOBY's just looking at this man...then looks over at JOSH
who's been just as focused on it.

JOSH nods his "No, forget the bet"...

Then for a totally different reason, TOBY says...

> TOBY
> (pause)
> I'm Toby Ziegler.
> (MORE)

(CONTINUED)

71   CONTINUED: (3)   71

                              TOBY (cont'd)
          I work at the White House. Do you have a
          minute to talk, we'd like to buy you a
          beer.

                                                    FADE TO BLACK:

        TITLE:
                        A5:05 - The President met with Mr.
                        McGarry, Ch. Fitzwallace and
                        Dr. McNally.

        FADE IN:

72   **EXT. PORTICO - EARLY MORNING**   72

        It's still dark outside as BARTLET makes his way to the Oval
        Office in jeans and a sweatshirt. He walks into--

73   **INT. THE OVAL OFFICE - CONTINUOUS**   73

        --where LEO, FITZWALLACE and NANCY are waiting.

                              ALL THREE
          Good morning, sir/Good morning/Good
          morning, Mr. President.

                              BARTLET
          It's the happy fun group.

                              LEO
          We have reason to believe that in the
          next 48 hours, the Qumari rescue team
          will announce that they've recovered a
          military-issue, Israeli-made parachute.

                              BARTLET
                (pause)
          They're just allowed to make things up
          now?

                              NANCY
          As long as we won't step up and say it
          was us they do.

                              BARTLET
                (to LEO)
          They know it was us, right?

                              LEO
          Yeah.

                              BARTLET
                (to NANCY)
          Is that what you think we should do?

                                                    (CONTINUED)

73   CONTINUED:

                    NANCY
Me?

                    BARTLET
Yeah.

                    NANCY
No I don't. I am however beginning to
lean toward reducing our nuclear arsenal
one at a time if you know what I mean,
sir.

                    BARTLET
          (to FITZWALLACE)
What about you?

                    FITZWALLACE
Well I'm with Dr. Strangelove on keeping
our military secrets secret but Nancy and
Leo and I think there's a third option
which is to say it was us but insulate
you.

                    BARTLET
          (smiling)
I signed a piece of paper, Fitz.

                    FITZWALLACE
We can get around that.

                    BARTLET
          (pause)
You just hated my living guts when I got
this job, didn't you.

                    FITZWALLACE
No sir.

                    BARTLET
Yeah you did. I didn't know anything and
I didn't have any respect for the Chiefs.
You became my counselor and you wrangled
the Chiefs and you brought 'em to me.

                    FITZWALLACE
You got the Chiefs, sir, they respect
you.

                    BARTLET
You brought 'em. And you talked Leo into
Shareef and he talked me into it.
          (MORE)

                                              (CONTINUED)

73   CONTINUED: (2)   73

                          BARTLET (cont'd)
          It was my order and you executed it
          flawlessly and I stand by it, I stand by
          you, I stand by you all, I stand by it
          till I die.
                    (pause)
          Plus I'm gonna need some cell mates in
          Holland.
                    (pause)
          So what do we do now?

                          LEO
          We're in the situation room.

                          BARTLET
          Let's go.

And the four of them exit as we

                                                          CUT TO:

74   **EXT. PARKWAY - EARLY MORNING**   74

And it's still dark as an airport van makes its way.

75   **INT. THE VAN - EARLY MORNING**   75

JOSH, TOBY and DONNA are sitting with two other passengers and
a driver.

                          JOSH
          You're telling me we couldn't have just
          gone to the nearest Chinese restaurant,
          picked up some Kikkoman and poured it in
          that soy diesel thing.

                          DONNA
          I don't think it works like that. Plus
          how close do you think the nearest
          Chinese restaurant was.

                          JOSH
          Well we should start making cars that run
          on ketchup.

                          DONNA
          When I get home I'm taking the longest
          hot bath of my life.

                          TOBY
                    (calling up to the DRIVER)
          Excuse me, would you mind letting me off
          up there at the bridge?

                                                     (CONTINUED)

75   CONTINUED: 75

                          DRIVER
              You sure?

                          TOBY
              Yeah, I can walk to work from
              there.

JOSH looks out the window and sees what TOBY's talking about.

                          JOSH
              Yeah, I can hop out there too.

                          DONNA
              Please not this again.

                          JOSH
              Hey, you're the one who did the number
              back at the bar.

                          DONNA
              It didn't have anything to do with
              eliminating modern conveniences.

                          JOSH
              He can drop you off at home.

                          DONNA
                  (pause)
              I'll get out with them up here.

The van pulls over and the three of them get out onto--

76   **EXT. ROADSIDE - CONTINUOUS**   76

                          TOBY
              If our jobs teach us anything it's that
              we don't know what the next President's
              gonna face. If we choose someone with
              vision, someone with guts, someone with
              gravitas who's connected to other
              people's lives and cares about making
              them better, if we choose someone to
              inspire us, then we'll be able to face
              what comes our way and achieve things
              we can't imagine yet. Instead of
              telling people who's most qualified,
              instead of telling people who's got the
              better ideas, let's make it obvious.
              It's gonna be hard.

                                                              (CONTINUED)

76   CONTINUED:

                         JOSH
              Then we'll do what's hard.

We pull back and the three of them have just begun crossing
the Memorial Bridge on foot. The Washington skyline is in
front of them. The sun's just starting to come up.

                                        FADE TO BLACK:

                         <u>END OF SHOW</u>

HOLY NIGHT

I grew up with the Malina kids, Rachel, Stuart and Joel, and met their cousin Josh in 1989 at a poker game at my apartment in New York. Josh was an actor who'd just graduated from Yale and I was casting understudies for the Broadway production of *A Few Good Men*, which would be going into rehearsals in August.

Josh competed against a few hundred other actors and got the job. After six months, he moved into a principal role and then a bigger principal role and then a bigger principal role in the National Tour.

He did the film version, as well as *Malice* and *The American President*, playing several other roles in several other pieces not written by me in between.

When Tommy and I began casting *Sports Night*, we both liked Josh for the part of Dan Rydell, one of the two anchors, but the network (ABC) was insisting on a more conventional leading man and the role went to Josh Charles.

At the same time, though, we were having a lot of difficulty casting the role of Jeremy, an intern at the fictional sports channel with half a dozen lines.

I turned to Tommy and said, "What if I re-write Jeremy as one of the leads and we go back to Josh Malina?"

I went home that afternoon and wrote Jeremy's second act interview scene that appears in the pilot. I faxed the pages to Josh, who came in the next morning and read with Sabrina Lloyd for ABC production head Jamie Tarses and he had the job.

Four years later I was sitting in the conference room in the bank of offices John Wells keeps on the Warner Bros. lot. It had come time to get serious about replacing Rob, who'd been given permission to vacate his contract with a year and a half remaining so that he'd be available for the pilot season to get his own show.

Rob and I had hit it off from the first day of work. He loved the show and I loved him in the show. What little off-the-set socializing time there was we often spent together. Our wives had become friends. I didn't want him to leave and I told him that, creatively, I was leaving the door open for the character to come back anytime he chose. But for now, at least, he was leaving and he had to be replaced.

In addition to John and Tommy, we were joined by our casting director, Tony Sepulveda, who had a list of actors.

Dermot Mulroney...C. Thomas Howell...Stephen Eckholdt...Judd Nelson...Macaulay Culkin...Jon Cryer...Names were being read off as suggestions for a role I'd yet to invent. Tommy looked over at me and mouthed, "What about Josh?"

It's a 40-second golf cart ride from John's office to my office and that's how long it took for Josh to get the part (though I still hadn't written it yet). He would fit in beautifully with the ensemble both on and off the screen and the casting had integrity.

He was offered a contract for four "trial" episodes, after which we had to make a decision on whether he'd be a series regular. After looking at dailies from Josh's first episode, *Game On*, specifically the last scene where Josh's character, Will Bailey, stands up to Sam Seaborn for the third and final time, the try-out was over. John Wells ordered the company that produces our main title sequence to put together a mini-montage for Josh. I sealed the casting by having Will Bailey take over Sam's office in the Christmas episode.

Here's *Holy Night*.

The West Wing

Holy Night

CHERRY REVISIONS:	12/04/02
SALMON REVISIONS:	12/04/02
BUFF REVISIONS:	12/03/02
GREEN REVISIONS:	12/03/02
YELLOW REVISIONS:	12/01/02
PINK REVISIONS:	11/26/02
BLUE REVISIONS:	11/26/02

<u>THE WEST WING</u>

"Holy Night"

(formerly "Ursa Major in the Northern Sky")

Written by
Aaron Sorkin

Directed by
Thomas Schlamme

PRODUCTION #175-311
Episode Ten

JOHN WELLS PRODUCTIONS
in association with
WARNER BROS. TELEVISION
4000 Warner Blvd.
Burbank, CA 91522

<u>Final Shooting Script</u>
November 25, 2002
Copyright © 2002
Warner Bros. Television
All Rights Reserved

THE WEST WING
"Holy Night"
Script Revision History

DATE	COLOR	PAGES
11/26/02	BLUE PAGES	CAST,33,34,35-36
11/26/02	PINK PAGES	CAST,SETS,56,56A,61, 62-63,64,64A,65,66-67, 68-69
12/01/02	YELLOW PAGES	1,9,10,38,38A,39,40,45, 48,53,56,57,58,59,60, 61-64,64A,65,66-67,68-69
12/03/02	GREEN PAGES	28,58
12/03/02	BUFF PAGES	61-64,64A
12/04/02	SALMON PAGES	61-64,64A
12/04/02	CHERRY PAGES	61-64,64A

SET LIST

INTERIORS
CAR
WHITE HOUSE
    Mural Room
    Corridors
    Leo's Office
    Conference Room
    Press Briefing Room
    Lobby
    Communications Bullpen
    Toby's Office
    Bartlet's Private Study
    Fiderer's Office
    Oval Office
    C.J.'s Office
    Sam's Office
    Roosevelt Room
    Josh's Office
    Josh's Bullpen
    Residence Foyer

EXTERIORS
BROOKLYN BRIDGE - NIGHT
PORTICO – LATE AFTERNOON
PORTICO – NIGHT

THE WEST WING

"Holy Night"

CAST LIST

PRESIDENT JOSIAH BARTLET
LEO McGARRY
JOSH LYMAN
SAM SEABORN
TOBY ZIEGLER
C.J. CREGG
CHARLIE YOUNG
DONNA MOSS

CAROL
MARK
KATIE
DANNY CONCANON
WILL BAILEY
GINGER
DR. STANLEY KEYWORTH
ZOEY
BONNIE

ZEV
JULES
JACOB
LARRY CLAYPOOL
RON
JULIE ZIEGLER
JEAN PAUL
WHIFFENPOOF #1

"Holy Night"

<u>TEASER</u>

FADE IN:

1   **EXT. BROOKLYN BRIDGE - NIGHT**   1

It's a drizzly, misty night by the East River as the camera
cranes down to a small, not very populated street.

TITLE:

New York City
Christmas Eve

Where we see an old Packard Yellow Cab pick up two sailors and
their dates coming out of a bar.

Across the street from the bar a car is parked and three men
in their early 20's sit inside.

2   **INT. CAR - SAME TIME**   2

English subtitles go up on the screen as we join the three
young men who are speaking only in Yiddish. JULES sits in
back. Despite the dark and professional circumstances, JULES
has an almost sunny spirit about him. His friend in the front
passenger seat is ZEV. JACOB's at the wheel, and is less
interested in the conversation between JULES and ZEV.

>   ZEV
>   Vos far a mentch hut a numen Cole un vos
>   far a mentch hut a numen Sandy. Dos is
>   mein frageh tzu dir.
>   (English translation)
>   *[What kind of person is named Cole and*
>   *what kind of person is named Sandy? This*
>   *is my question to you.]*
>
>   JULES
>   Du kenst unshtellen die radio-- yeh?
>   *[Why don't you turn on a radio?]*
>
>   ZEV
>   Ich vell es unshtellen ven gelt vet
>   unheiben tzu fallen arois fun es.
>   *[When money starts coming out of it,*
>   *that's when I'll turn one on.]*
>   (laughing - to JACOB)
>   Du hust gehert vos ich hub gezugt?
>   *[You hear what I said?]*

(CONTINUED)

>   JACOB
>   Yeh.
>   *[Yeah.]*

>   JULES
>   Cole Porter is a barimter Americaner. Er
>   shreibter leeder vos meh speilt oif der
>   radio, un in ois-shtelung vos shpilen oif
>   Broadway.
>   *[Cole Porter is a great American song
>   writer on the radio. And for the Broadway
>   shows.]*

>   JACOB
>   Er is nisht dorten.
>   *[He's not in there.]*

>   ZEV
>   Der leidig geyer?
>   *[The bum?]*

>   JACOB
>   Der leidig geyer is nisht dorten.
>   *[The bum's not in there.]*

>   ZEV
>   Yoh-- er is.
>   *[Yeah he is.]*

>   JACOB
>   Far vos kumt er nisht arois?
>   *[Then why isn't he coming out?]*

>   ZEV
>   Far vos?
>   *[Why?]*

>   JACOB
>   Yoh.
>   *[Yes.]*

>   ZEV
>   Vile er is dorten.
>   *['Cause he's in there.]*

And JULES couldn't muzzle a short laugh. JACOB turns his head
and gives him half a look but it was enough.

>   JULES
>   Un Cole Porter hut gezungen in a grupeh
>   in zein universitet ubber es hut a nomen
>   vos ich ken nit zugen.
>   (MORE)

                                                    (CONTINUED)

2   CONTINUED: (2)   2

> JULES (cont'd)
> *[And Cole Porter was in a singing group at his university but it's got a name I can't pronounce well yet.]*

> ZEV
> Zug es in Yiddish.
> *[Say it in Yiddish.]*

> JULES
> Yiddish hut nit dos vort.
> *[Yiddish doesn't have the word.]*

> JACOB
> Vos meinst du Yiddish hut nit dos vort, es hut alleh verter.
> *[What do you mean Yiddish doesn't have the word, it has all the words.]*

> JULES
> Whiffenpoof.

JACOB doesn't know what to make of that, doesn't care and goes back to watching the bar.

> ZEV
> (to JULES)
> Du host gegangen tzu an ois-shtelung?
> *[You been to a show?]*

> JULES
> Ich hub gekoift an album fun leider.
> *[I got a record album.]*
> (singing a little in English)
> "In olden days a glimpse of stocking was looked on as something shocking though heaven knows--"

> ZEV
> Ich hub leib dos leid.
> *[I like that song.]*

> JULES
> Dos is Cole Porter.
> *[That's Cole Porter.]*

> JACOB
> Ir baydeh-- zei shtill.
> *[Would the two of you shut up.]*

> ZEV
> Nu-- far vos bistu azoi? Zein veib hut geboiren a yingele, es is im gut, far vos ken es im nit zein gut?
> *[Hey, why do you have to be like that?*
> (MORE)

(CONTINUED)

2   CONTINUED: (3)   2

                          ZEV (cont'd)
              His wife just had a boy, he's feeling
              good, why can't he feel good?]

                          JACOB
              Er is nit duh.
              [He's not in there.]

                          ZEV
              Der leidig geyer is dorten, Jacob, ich
              hub arumkekukt far im un er is dorten.
              [The bum is in there, Jacob, I scouted
              the bum and he's in there.]
                    (long pause)
              Ver is Sandy?
              [Who's Sandy?]

                          JULES
              Er is a pitcher vos die Dodgers huben
              angeshtelt-- zei giben im fertzin toizent
              dollar un er is ninetzen yor alt, er is
              tzvei yor yunger far unz.
              [He's a pitcher the Dodgers just signed.
              14,000 dollars he got he's 19 years old,
              he's two years younger than me and you.]

                          JACOB
              Genug, dos is alles, ich gei ruffen
              Anastasia.
              [All right, that's it, I'm calling
              Anastasia.]

                          ZEV
              Meh darf nit rufen Anastasia.
              [You don't gotta call Anastasia.]

                          JACOB
              Er is nit dorten.
              [The guy isn't in there.]

                          ZEV
              Du vaist dos nit.
              [You don't know that.]

                          JACOB
              Du zogst az meineh eigen arbeten nit gut?
              Es is dorten duh a telephone, gerecht?
              [You're saying my eyes don't work the
              regular way? There's a phone in back of
              the thing, right?]

                          ZEV
              Yeh.
              [Yeah.]

                                                    (CONTINUED)

> JACOB
> Du hust a kopikeh?
> *[You got a nickel?]*

> ZEV
> Du darfst nit ruffen--
> *[You don't have to call--]*

> JACOB
> Du hust a kopikeh?
> *[You got a nickel?]*

> ZEV
> (pause)
> Yeh ich hub a kopikeh.
> *[Yeah, I got a nickel.]*

> JACOB
> Far vos kumst du nit mit mir.
> *[Then why don't you come with me.]*

Takes a long time...there's no way to avoid it...he's done.

> ZEV
> Yeh.
> *[Yeah.]*

All three start to get out of the car.

> JACOB
> Du bleib duh.
> *[You stay here.]*

> JULES
> Ich kum as du vilsst.
> *[I can come if you want.]*

> ZEV
> Nein Julie, do bleib duh, un zeh vos es
> tut zich beim tir, mir vellen gliech
> tzurik cummen.
> *[No Julie, you stay here, keep an eye on
> the door, we'll just be a minute.]*

JACOB and ZEV get out of the car and disappear behind a chain
link fence, some rusted stuff and mist.

JULES is alone. He pops an unfiltered camel into his mouth and
lights it. He looks over at the door to the bar. Nothing going
on. Then he says something just to try it on for size.

                                                        (CONTINUED)

2   CONTINUED: (5)   2

                        JULES
               Tuvia.
               [Tobias.]

POP! POP!--

We hear the muffled sound of two small caliber bullets being fired. JULES turns quickly then jumps out of the car.

He looks around, and starts to step very tentatively toward where the two disappeared--

And suddenly JACOB comes walking up.

                        JACOB
               Gei tzurik in aftomobile.
               [Get back in the car.]

                        JULES
               Vu is Zev?
               [Where's Zev?]

                        JACOB
               Gei tzurik in aftomobile.
               [Get back in the car.]

They get in the car.

                        JULES
               Vu is Zev?
               [Where's Zev?]

                        JACOB
               Vos kentst du tohn?
               [What can you do?]

                        JULES
               Vos?
               [What?]

                        JACOB
               Ich hub gezugt-- vos kentst du tohn.
               [I said what can you do.]

He starts the car.

                        JACOB
               Nu-- vos far a nomen hust do gegeben dein
               zun?
               [So what did you name your son?]

JULES doesn't answer...

                                                (CONTINUED)

2   CONTINUED: (6)   2

                        JACOB
                   (pause--English)
           Jules. What did you name your son?

                        JULES
                    (English)
             Tobias. Little Toby.

The car pulls away and we

                                       SMASH CUT TO:

MAIN TITLES

<u>END OF TEASER</u>

<u>ACT ONE</u>

FADE IN:

3   **INT. MURAL ROOM - DAY**   3

The room is packed with people who right now are listening to
12 YOUNG MEN in white tie and tails sing *Bye Bye Blackbird* a
capella. It's snowing outside.

C.J. comes in the doorway and stands there and smiles as she
listens. Then she makes eye contact with CAROL and they step
outside.

4   **INT. CORRIDOR - CONTINUOUS**   4

                    C.J.
          It's really starting to get socked in out
          there and I'm worried about the airports.

                    CAROL
          You think they should wrap it up?

C.J. listens to the music she loves...

                    C.J.
          Well one more after this.

                    CAROL
          I know, aren't they great?

                    C.J.
          You just want 'em to take you to their
          place and--

                    CAROL
          They're 20 years old, ma'am.

                    C.J.
              (gimme some of that)
          Yes.
              (pause)
          Sing...is what I was gonna say. Take you
          to their place and sing.

JOSH is walking by--

                    C.J.
          Josh, you should come in and hear them
          sing.

                    JOSH
          In a minute, Leo's got me.

                                        (CONTINUED)

4   CONTINUED: 4

We hear the WHIFFENPOOFS sing a little longer before we

                                                    CUT TO:

5   **INT. LEO'S OFFICE - DAY**   5

--as JOSH taps on the door.

                         LEO
               Come on in.

                         JOSH
               What do you need?

                         LEO
               Hey, are you staying in town?

                         JOSH
               No, she's meeting Jack Reese at the
               Washington Inn. How does he get a room at
               the Wash--*I* can't get a room at the
               Washington Inn.
                    (pause)
               Me? I don't know yet, what do you need?

                         LEO
               Israel's closed the Church of the
               Nativity, you wanna believe that at
               Christmas?

                         JOSH
               It's ironic.

                         LEO
               Why?

                         JOSH
               'Cause Mary and Joseph couldn't get a
               room at the inn and they went to this
               place which is now on Christmas--the
               irony isn't self-explanatory?

                         LEO
               This isn't funny.

                         JOSH
               I know.

                         LEO
               It's not funny.

                         JOSH
               Why did they close it?

                                            (CONTINUED)

5   CONTINUED: 5

                    LEO
          I don't know, can you find out?

                    JOSH
          Yeah.

                    LEO
          Thank you.

                                        CUT TO:

6   INT. CONFERENCE ROOM - DAY   6

    The snow continues as TOBY and his lawyer, RON, sit across
    from LARRY CLAYPOOL. A COURT REPORTER takes it down.

                    CLAYPOOL
          Good morning, this is a deposition in the
          matter of Laurie Milton and Citizens for
          Full Disclosure v. Congresswoman Andrea
          Wyatt in U.S. District Court for the
          District of Columbia and taken at the
          offices of Freedom Watch. The Court
          Reporter today is Patricia Goldstein from
          the firm of Alpha Reporting. Your name
          is?

                    TOBY
          Toby Ziegler.

                    CLAYPOOL
          Is that your full name?

                    TOBY
          Tobias Zachary Ziegler.

                    CLAYPOOL
          Date of birth?

                    TOBY
          December 23rd, 1954.

                    CLAYPOOL
          Today's your birthday?

                    TOBY
          Yes.

                    CLAYPOOL
          What is your relationship to
          Congresswoman Wyatt?

                                        (CONTINUED)

6   CONTINUED:

                         TOBY
          She's my ex-wife.

                         CLAYPOOL
          And is she pregnant right now?

                         TOBY
          You would have to ask her.

                         CLAYPOOL
          Why's that?

                         RON
          He's not answering the question.

                         CLAYPOOL
          It's been widely reported.

                         TOBY
          Yes.

                         CLAYPOOL
          You won't confirm it?

                         TOBY
          No.

                         CLAYPOOL
          Why's that?

                         TOBY
          It's private.

                         CLAYPOOL
          There's no right to privacy in a
          deposition.

                         TOBY
          But you have to demonstrate relevancy.

                         CLAYPOOL
          Miss Wyatt is being sued by her
          constituents for failing to disclose a
          medical disability while asking for their
          votes and we're trying to discover the
          extent of the conspiracy.

                         TOBY
          The conspiracy was massive.

                         CLAYPOOL
          How pregnant is your ex-wife?

                                                              (CONTINUED)

6   CONTINUED: (2)   6

                         TOBY
               As I understand pregnancy, it's a binary
               state, you either are or you aren't.

                         CLAYPOOL
               You are the father, are you not?

                         TOBY
               Once again, there are medical records.

                         CLAYPOOL
               You and Miss Wyatt conceived this baby
               out of wedlock.

                         TOBY
                    (pause)
               There are two babies.

An assistant has come in and handed RON a slip of paper.

                         RON
               They're closing Dulles. I'd like to
               suggest that we pick this up again after
               the holiday.

                         CLAYPOOL
               That's fine.

They gather up their things...

                         TOBY
                    (to CLAYPOOL)
               I'm told that on my sunniest of days I'm
               not that fun to be around. I wonder
               what's gonna happen when you make my
               children a part of your life.

They walk out and we

                                                         CUT TO:

7   **INT. PRESS BRIEFING ROOM - DAY**   7

C.J. at the podium.

                         C.J.
               The President and First Lady will board
               Air Force One this evening at 7:30 for
               their flight to Manchester and attend
               midnight mass tomorrow at the Church of
               the Sacred Heart. Mark, what are you
               doing?

                                                      (CONTINUED)

7   CONTINUED: 7

                              MARK
                    What do you mean?

                              C.J.
                    You're supposed to come in here as Santa
                    Claus right now.

                              MARK
                    We did it already.

                              C.J.
                    Where was I?

                              KATIE
                    You were with the President and we
                    started worrying about the weather.

                              C.J.
                    You exchanged gifts?

                              MARK
                    Sorry.

                              C.J.
                    Well this is exactly what happened to
                    Ebenezer Scrooge who was a perfectly nice
                    little guy until something happened with
                    Mr. Fezziwig that I can't remember. All
                    right, back to business.

And from the back of the room--

                              SANTA
                    Ho ho ho.

And everyone applauds...

                              C.J.
                    Aww, you see...

                              SANTA
                    Ho ho ho.

And SANTA goes up on stage...

                              C.J.
                    Santa, you'll be mindful of security,
                    right?

                              MARK
                    He's cleared.

                                                            (CONTINUED)

7   CONTINUED: (2)   7

                          SANTA
             Have you been a good girl?

                          C.J.
             I've been bad, I've been very bad.

                          SANTA
             Even better.

SANTA takes a small box from his bag and hands it to C.J. She
opens it--

                          C.J.
             It's a goldfish pin. Thank you everyone,
             it's beautiful. Merry Christmas, this was
             so sweet, thank you. That's a full lid.

                          PRESS
             Merry Christmas/Merry Christmas, C.J.

The PRESS get up and exit.

                          C.J.
                    (to SANTA)
             They gave me a goldfish pin 'cause I like
             goldfish. Actually what I like are the
             crackers, but there was a guy--

And SANTA kisses C.J. on the lips...

                          C.J.
                    (pause)
             Danny?

DANNY takes the wig and beard off...

                          DANNY
             What's goin' on?

C.J. smiles a big smile and we

                                                    CUT TO:

8   **INT. WEST WING LOBBY - DAY**   8

WILL's sitting in the lobby making some last minute notes to
himself as TOBY comes in from outside.

                          WILL
             How'd it go?

                                              (CONTINUED)

> TOBY
> Why do you sit in the lobby instead of my
> office?

> WILL
> The Holy Line of Demarcation.
>   (showing him on the floor)
> Right there. It's where the West Wing
> starts and I won't go past it.

> TOBY
> I wasn't listening to anything you just
> said.

> WILL
> I said the Holy Line of Demarcation--

> TOBY
> It's 'cause I didn't care.

> WILL
> You got notes back on the Congressional
> section.

> TOBY
> This has become inconvenient for me.

> WILL
> What has.

> TOBY
> Your being at OEOB and me having meetings
> in the lobby, I'm moving you closer.

TOBY heads, and WILL follows, into--

9   **INT. CORRIDOR - CONTINUOUS**   9

> WILL
> To where?

> TOBY
> The empty office next to me.

> WILL
> I'm not moving into the Deputy's office.

> TOBY
> Why?

(CONTINUED)

9   CONTINUED: 9

                         WILL
           A) I'm not the Deputy, B) It's Sam's
           office and finally it's way, way over the
           Holy Line of Demarcation.

                         TOBY
           You'll move your stuff in today.

                         WILL
           That's the Oval Office over there, right?

                         TOBY
           Yeah.

                         WILL
           I'm averting my eyes.

                         TOBY
           Okay.

                         WILL
           Seriously, Toby, you put me in that
           office and everyone who works on the
           speech writing staff is gonna resent me.

                         TOBY
           Don't be ridiculous, it's a West Wing
           office, everyone who works in the White
           House is gonna resent you.

                         WILL
           That's right.

                         TOBY
           Yet curiously I don't care.

                         WILL
           All right, the notes on the Congressional
           section--

                         TOBY
           Get your stuff and we'll talk about the
           notes.

                         WILL
           Thank you.

     TOBY continues into--

10   **INT. COMMUNICATIONS BULLPEN - CONTINUOUS**   10

     --where he opens his office door and walks into--

11   **INT. TOBY'S OFFICE - CONTINUOUS**   11

--where he's surprised, to say the least, to see a 79 year-old
man named JULIE standing there.

                    JULIE
          Toby.

They look at each other for a long, silent moment before TOBY
calls out--

                    TOBY
              (calling)
          Ginger.

                    JULIE
          I'm not here through any funny business,
          I have an appointment tag that was gotten
          for me by Mr. Joshua Lyman.

                    TOBY
          Josh got you in, you talked to Josh?

                    JULIE
          Yes sir.

GINGER steps in--

                    GINGER
          Yeah.

There's a long silence...

                    JULIE
          I'm Toby's father, I'm Julie Ziegler.

                    GINGER
          It's great to meet you, Mr. Ziegler, I'm
          Ginger, I'm a staff assistant.

                    TOBY
          Ginger, tell security to stand by at
          Station 6.

                    GINGER
          Yes sir.

GINGER exits--

                    JULIE
          I've got an appointment tag, Toby, don't
          do this.
                  (MORE)

                                              (CONTINUED)

11   CONTINUED: 11

                         JULIE (cont'd)
            Your brother, your sisters, they let me
            in their lives and I play with the
            grandchildren.
                    (beat)
            And now you're gonna have...*twins*...I
            read it in the newspapers. I'm so happy
            for you son, you should hear how I talk
            about you.

                                          FADE TO BLACK:

                        END OF ACT ONE

ACT TWO

FADE IN:

12   **INT. BARTLET'S PRIVATE STUDY - DAY**   12

BARTLET's in a session with STANLEY as the snow continues
outside.

> BARTLET
> There's a new International Math and
> Science study. We ranked 19th out of 21
> countries.

> STANLEY
> That's not very good.

> BARTLET
> This is what I'm talking about.

> STANLEY
> Who did worse?

> BARTLET
> South Africa and Cyprus.

> STANLEY
> See that's questionable company 'cause
> you don't really think of Cyprus as a
> leader in the field.

> BARTLET
> No you don't. Nor us anymore for that
> matter. A third of all math teachers and
> half of all science teachers didn't major
> or minor in that subject.

> STANLEY
> I did very well in math and science. I
> don't know why.

> BARTLET
> And we'll want to get to the bottom of
> that but we've increased education
> spending to 100 billion dollars a year
> and as a result we're now using 7th grade
> textbooks in 9th grade and the same
> answers get a higher score on the SATs.

> STANLEY
> *That* pissed me off.

(CONTINUED)

12   CONTINUED:

                    BARTLET
         Right, but I'm talking about children
         now.

                    STANLEY
         What'd you get?

                    BARTLET
         On the SATs?

                    STANLEY
         Yeah.

                    BARTLET
         You don't want to know.

                    STANLEY
         You got a double 800 didn't you.

                    BARTLET
         I got 800-790. For the life of me I can't
         imagine what I got wrong. Then I took 'em
         again and I got 800-790. I mean is it
         possible there was some sort of number-2
         pencil...*anomaly* that could have--

                    STANLEY
         Excuse me, I'm sorry to interrupt. You
         got an 800-790 and took the test again?

                    BARTLET
         Yeah, I know, it's a little...something.

                    STANLEY
         It's a little something, yeah.

                    BARTLET
         So the schools have reached a crisis
         state and our infant mortality rate is
         two and a half times what it is in
         Singapore. So what I think we should do
         for starters is, we should keep more
         people alive. Then send them to school.
         Get a little peace and prosperity going.

                    STANLEY
         You feeling like you haven't been doing
         enough about it yet?

                    BARTLET
         Stanley, the width...and depth of what I
         haven't done about it yet...You know you
         can't do anything about hurricanes.
                    (MORE)

                                   (CONTINUED)

12   CONTINUED: (2)

                          BARTLET (cont'd)
          The President can't do anything about
          nature or bad luck. I oughta be able to
          do something about the airplane.

STANLEY lets the non-sequitor hang there for a while before he
says...

                          STANLEY
               (quietly)
          Uh-oh.

                          BARTLET
          Wait, what did I just say?

                          STANLEY
          Hard to figure, sir, but you've
          introduced a new word into the
          conversation.

                          BARTLET
          What do airplanes signify?

                          STANLEY
          Death.

                          BARTLET
          Really.

                          STANLEY
          Well that's in dreams I think. I don't
          know.

                          BARTLET
          Stanley, I never thought to ask, but
          you're a doctor, right?

                          STANLEY
          Me?

                          BARTLET
          Yeah.

                          STANLEY
          How do you mean?

BARTLET leans back in his chair. He's gotta confess something
to STANLEY and for him it's like confiding a sexual problem.
He lowers his voice...

                          BARTLET
          I've been spacing out for a minute at
          meetings. Three times this week. I'll
          hear someone talking and realize I wasn't
          listening to part of it.

                                              (CONTINUED)

12   CONTINUED: (3)   12

                           STANLEY
                  That's unusual?

                           BARTLET
                  Very.

         BARTLET's intercom beeps. He picks up the phone.

                           BARTLET
                      (into phone)
                  Hi.
                      (beat)
                  Yeah.
                      (hangs up--to STANLEY)
                  Leo.

         And the door opens and LEO steps in--

                           LEO
                  Mr. President.

                           BARTLET
                  What's goin' on?

                           LEO
                  The Church of the Nativity is closed, you
                  wanna believe that?

                           BARTLET
                  Why?

                           LEO
                  I'm finding out. Dr. Keyworth, Dulles and
                  National are both closed.

                           STANLEY
                  Ahhhh.

                           LEO
                  You mind being our guest for a little
                  while.

                           STANLEY
                  Thank you.

                           BARTLET
                  And now we're a third of the way through
                  an Agatha Christie story.
                      (as Igor)
                  "Wernt noobody be goin' nowhere, the
                  bridge is warshed out."
                      (long pause)
                           (MORE)

(CONTINUED)

12   CONTINUED: (4)   12

> BARTLET (cont'd)
> Well I'm finished now but I was doing the
> guy who says that in Agatha Christie
> stories. Stanley, as always. Leo, I'll be
> in the office.

> LEO
> Thank you, sir. Stanley, do me a favor
> would you. As you wander about the
> building, why are you here. You're from
> the American Psychiatric Association
> Medicare Task Force. You're lobbying me
> on behalf of the APA for a prescription
> drug benefit. Where do you stand?
> Copayments should apply to mental
> treatment, right now it's just at a rate
> of 50%.

> STANLEY
> That's just plain wrong.

> LEO
> Well stay here and fight the good fight.
> We have sandwiches.

LEO exits and we

                                                              CUT TO:

13   **INT. CORRIDOR - DAY**   13

CHARLIE's walking down the hall with some files. He's in a
perfectly pleasant mood. He walks into--

14   **INT. FIDERER'S OFFICE - CONTINUOUS**   14

--where ZOEY's sitting with her boyfriend JEAN PAUL, straight
off a page of *GQ* with a thick French accent.

> ZOEY
> Hey Charlie.

> CHARLIE
> Hey Zoey.

CHARLIE continues into--

15   **INT. THE OVAL OFFICE - CONTINUOUS**   15

--where he gets as far as the desk and is about to put the
file down when he realizes that was just ZOEY. He walks back
out into--

16   **INT. FIDERER'S OFFICE - CONTINUOUS**   16

>   CHARLIE
> Hello.
>
>   ZOEY
> Hi. This is Jean Paul. Jean Paul, this is
> Charlie Young.
>
>   CHARLIE
> How do you do.
>
>   JEAN PAUL
> Zoey talks about you all the time. She
> talks about you so much I think sometimes
> I want to kill you.
>
>   CHARLIE
> Hey, that's nice of you, thanks.
>
>   ZOEY
> It's a common emotion.
>
>   CHARLIE
> Is there a particular way I'm supposed to
> address you.
>
>   JEAN PAUL
> Oh don't be silly.
>
>   ZOEY
> He's very casual about it. The average
> passerby would never know he was French
> royalty. Unless, you know, they looked at
> him.
>
>   JEAN PAUL
> Yes.
>
>   CHARLIE
> Well Jean Paul, I read 150 words about
> you in *US Weekly* and I feel like I know
> you already.
>
>   JEAN PAUL
> Thank you.
>
>   CHARLIE
> Excuse me.

CHARLIE goes back into--

17   **INT. THE OVAL OFFICE - CONTINUOUS**   17

--where he now puts the file on the desk. ZOEY comes in.

> ZOEY
> So I need you to give me the coverage on
> my father's mood.

> CHARLIE
> Why?

> ZOEY
> 'Cause I want to ask him something.

> CHARLIE
> What?

> ZOEY
> Do you need to know?

> CHARLIE
> No, I just want to.

> ZOEY
> If I tell you why will you tell me his
> mood?

> CHARLIE
> Yes.

> ZOEY
> I want to ask my dad if Jean Paul can
> come to New Hampshire with us.

> CHARLIE
> He hasn't met him yet.

> ZOEY
> He's gonna meet him today.

> CHARLIE
> *Now* we got ourselves a show.

> ZOEY
> My dad's gonna love him.

> CHARLIE
> Oh yeah.

> ZOEY
> I love him. And so my father will love
> him.

(CONTINUED)

17   CONTINUED: 17

                        CHARLIE
          That's absolutely the way it works.

                        ZOEY
          Will you just tell me his mood.

                        CHARLIE
          No, I'm afraid you fell for the oldest
          trick in the book. I *work* for the
          President, I don't discuss his mood, but
          I wish you all the luck in the world. I
          like Jean Paul, we've got a lot in
          common.

                        ZOEY
          You're the worst kind of snob.

                        CHARLIE
          Well I think there are snobs who are way
          worse, but thank you.

     CHARLIE exits and we

                                              CUT TO:

18   **INT. C.J.'S OFFICE - DAY**   18

     DANNY's wearing his Santa pants and a red thermal undershirt.

                        DANNY
          When I left they had 97 runs.

                        C.J.
          The score gets that high?

                        DANNY
          A high score is 400.

                        C.J.
          When did you start liking cricket?

                        DANNY
          I haven't yet, but last week I took four
          days in Bermuda.

                        C.J.
          I love Bermuda, I like the scooters.

                                              (CONTINUED)

> DANNY
> Me too and I got one and was riding into
> Hamilton when I saw a bunch of people
> playing cricket and I like sports though
> it turns out not as much as I thought,
> but that's not the point.

> C.J.
> What was the point?

> DANNY
> I met a guy there. A Bermudian whose name
> I'm not gonna tell you right now. He was
> explaining the game to me, he's a cricket
> nut, he plays in a league. And he's a
> ramp signal agent at a small airstrip, he
> marshalls the planes as they're coming
> in. He was telling me a story to
> illustrate how much he loves cricket.
> There was a day his supervisor told his
> four-person crew they had tomorrow off
> 'cause a training crew was coming in to
> work their shift. The next day the guy
> realized he'd left his cricket bat in his
> locker at work and his wife had the car
> so he walked six miles to the airstrip to
> get it. Except when he got there, he
> wasn't allowed in. Three men in coveralls
> who identified themselves as being with
> the training crew were standing out
> front. All three were white, two of them
> had Southern accents. On May 21st he was
> told to take tomorrow off. On the 22nd
> Abdul Shareef's plane went off radar 85
> miles from Bermuda.

> C.J.
>   (pause)
> This is like something you'd get on the
> Internet.

> DANNY
> I'm back and I'm happy about it and I
> think you know how I feel about you but
> don't mess me around on this story, okay.
> The three guys out front were U.S. Army
> Rangers. I gotta go change my clothes.

C.J. watches DANNY as he heads out, passing by CAROL--

> CAROL
> He's back!

(CONTINUED)

18   CONTINUED: (2)   18

                          DANNY
              I go where you are, Carol, you're where
              the story is.

                          CAROL
              I'm blushing.

                          DANNY
                   (calling back without turning
                    around)
              Well that's a job well done.

     C.J. watches DANNY disappear as we

                                                            CUT TO:

19   **INT. LEO'S OFFICE - DAY**   19

                          JOSH
              The Israelis say it's unsafe.

                          LEO
              They're worried about an attack?

                          JOSH
              They're worried about the roof caving in,
              part of it collapsed this morning.

                          LEO
              Why can't they fix it?

                          JOSH
              'Cause they'd have to bring in hammers
              and nails.

                          LEO
              They're worried someone's gonna use the
              stuff for bombs?

                          JOSH
              Of course that's what they're worried
              about. Leo, there are about 93,000 other
              churches within rock throwing distance of
              this place and I'm not sure if--

                          LEO
              I don't think that's the point. I'm not
              trying to create a plan for a lasting
              cease-fire, right now I'm just trying to
              fix a roof. Is that really not possible
              down there? See if you can find a U.N.
                   (MORE)

                                                            (CONTINUED)

19 CONTINUED: 19

                          LEO (cont'd)
            Relief and Recovery Unit anywhere around
            there...or an NGO that could serve as
            neutral-*God*-as a neutral party to oversee
            transportation, storage and repair. Thank
            you.

                          JOSH
            Thank you.

JOSH exits into--

20 **INT. CORRIDOR - CONTINUOUS**   20

--and is almost immediately guided/pushed by TOBY into the
wall--

                          TOBY
            What the hell are you doing, what were
            you doing?

                          JOSH
            Yes, I'm sorry, yes. I did.

                          TOBY
            I wish you hadn't and you knew that.

                          JOSH
            I did.

                          TOBY
            Yeah.

And TOBY continues into--

21 **INT. COMMUNICATIONS BULLPEN - CONTINUOUS**   21

--and GINGER hands him a slip of paper as he continues into--

22 **INT. TOBY'S OFFICE - CONTINUOUS**   22

                          TOBY
            Your flight's canceled, all the shuttles
            are canceled for a while.

                          JULIE
            I can take the train.

                          TOBY
            No you can't, the tracks are frozen in
            Trenton. What hotel are you staying at,
            we'll see if we can get you the room for
            a few hours more.

                                                          (CONTINUED)

22   CONTINUED: 22

                         JULIE
               I didn't take a room.

                         TOBY
                    (calling)
               Ginger.

                         JULIE
               I could be quiet while you worked.

GINGER appears in the doorway.

                         TOBY
               Would you call around to the hotels we
               know, see if anybody's got a room for me.

                         GINGER
               Yeah.

GINGER pops back out.

                         JULIE
               You got some pull in this town, huh?

                         TOBY
               Excuse me.

TOBY heads out and into--

23   **INT. SAM'S OFFICE - CONTINUOUS**   23

--or at least as far into it as he can get, because a couple
of dozen people have moved their bicycles in there. WILL's
behind the desk.

                         TOBY
               Hey.

                         WILL
               Good.

                         TOBY
               It looks like some of the junior staffers
               may have moved their bicycles in here in
               protest.

                         WILL
               Yeah, it looks like that may have
               happened.

                         TOBY
               You know--

                                                    (CONTINUED)

23   CONTINUED: 23

                        WILL
I don't care, I want to talk about the
notes.

                        TOBY
I agree with all three of them.

                        WILL
I agree with two of the three. He says
"No leading with reform. Fix the pipes,
don't buy a new toolbox." You have to
talk about the toolbox now, at the
beginning of an administration is the
only time you can.

                        TOBY
Except if you say at the beginning of the
administration that you want campaign
reform and nothing happens then you just
spent four years doing nothing about
campaign reform.

                        WILL
Yeah, you gotta get on the field and then
you gotta win.

                        TOBY
I still think he's right but it gets a
conversation. Someone'll tell you what
time the meeting is.

                        WILL
With who?

                        TOBY
The President.

                        WILL
And who?

                        TOBY
Us.

                        WILL
No, I shouldn't be there for that.

                        TOBY
You can tell 'em I said move the bicycles
you know.

                                (CONTINUED)

23   CONTINUED: (2)   23

                         WILL
            Can we forget about that. I'm not
            prepared, nor I must say do I feel
            comfortable at this point--

                         TOBY
            Yeah.

TOBY goes back into the bullpen and is handed another note as
he walks into--

24   **INT. TOBY'S OFFICE - CONTINUOUS**   24

                         TOBY
                    (off the note)
            We're striking out on hotels.

                         JULIE
            If you like, I can wait someplace else
            around here.

                         TOBY
            Okay, that's a good idea. You've been
            convicted of multiple felonies, you think
            the U.S. Secret Service lets you walk
            around this building unescorted? You
            can't.
                    (beat)
            You're a threat to the President.

There's a long, long silence before JULIE maybe even smiles a
little and says...

                         JULIE
            I'm really not.

                         TOBY
            I'm gonna work for a while now.

                                        FADE TO BLACK:

                         END OF ACT TWO

33.

ACT THREE

FADE IN:

25   **EXT. PORTICO - LATE AFTERNOON**   25

BARTLET's standing outside in his shirtsleeves and watching
the snow. It's an odd sight.

CHARLIE steps out from the office--

                    CHARLIE
          Sir?

                    BARTLET
          Yeah.

                    CHARLIE
          Would you like a coat?

                    BARTLET
          It's not that cold.

CHARLIE steps inside and we

                                                        CUT TO:

26   **INT. ROOSEVELT ROOM - LATE AFTERNOON**   26

The WHIFFENPOOFS haven't gained access to their street clothes
yet and are sitting around in various stages of white tie,
some of them at the table, some of them on the floor, with
books in front of them. They're singing *Girl From Ipanema* for
DONNA, who's dressed as if she's about to head out the door
for a winter weekend getaway, which she is.

                    DONNA
          No, no, nope, I'm sorry, it's not doing
          it for me. This is a Ralé Chalet in the
          mountains with four-poster beds and dust
          ruffles. There's a 14,000 bottle wine
          cellar, you got anything like that?

                    WHIFFENPOOF #1
          We can work something up from *The Mikado*.

                    DONNA
          No. What about a naval officer. You must
          have songs about handsome young naval
          officers?

                    WHIFFENPOOF #1
          We'll put our heads together ma'am.

                                                    (CONTINUED)

26   CONTINUED:

                         DONNA
            I appreciate that.

CAROL comes in with a box of sandwiches and begins passing
them out--

                         CAROL
            Sandwiches, here we go.
                 (to DONNA)
            You should leave right now.

                         DONNA
            I'm leaving right now.

                         CAROL
            Your roads are all right?

                         DONNA
            I-66, which they've been salting since
            this morning.

CHARLIE comes in--

                         CHARLIE
            Carol?

                         CAROL
            Yeah.

                         CHARLIE
            He'd like to do the *Times* closer to six,
            can C.J. or a deputy sit in?

                         CAROL
            Yeah.
                 (to the WHIFFENPOOFS)
            You guys are all set?

                         WHIFFENPOOFS
            Thank you/Yes ma'am/etc.

                         DONNA
            I can stay here till you get back.

                         CAROL
            I'll just be a second.

CAROL exits.

                         DONNA
            Can you think of an appropriate song they
            can do for me before I go?

                                              (CONTINUED)

26   CONTINUED: (2)   26

> CHARLIE
> You guys know *Girl From Ipanema?*

> WHIFFENPOOFS
> (singing)
> *"Tall and tan and young and lovely--"*

BARTLET sticks his head in--

> BARTLET
> Charlie.

And the WHIFFENPOOFS shut up...

> CHARLIE
> Yes sir.

> BARTLET
> I'm going to see Josh in his office, tell
> him I'm on my way.

> CHARLIE
> Yes sir.

BARTLET's gone. DONNA doesn't have a good feeling about this.
CHARLIE knows what DONNA's thinking...

> CHARLIE
> (quietly)
> Go ahead, go now.

> DONNA
> (pause)
> I'll wait.

CUT TO:

27   **INT. JOSH'S OFFICE - LATE AFTERNOON**   27

JOSH is on the phone.

> JOSH
> No. No actually, three units are in the
> Sudan and a fourth is in Turkey which--
> (off an index card)
> --has just had a 6-2 Seismic Experience,
> that's an earthquake, right?
> (beat)
> Okay, and make sure they know it's just
> transportation and oversight, we don't
> need materials.

There's a KNOCK on the door.

(CONTINUED)

> JOSH
> Come in.
> (into phone)
> Becky, also--excuse me, I'll call you
> back. Good afternoon, Mr. President.

> BARTLET
> Listen, this is gonna sound crazy, but
> Olympia Buckland had an infant mortality
> bill that we asked her not to take out of
> Committee 'cause it was too expensive.

> JOSH
> Yeah.

> BARTLET
> I'd like her initiative, or something
> similar, to be folded into the HHS
> budget.

> JOSH
> Yes sir, we can make it a priority with
> the next Congress.

> BARTLET
> No I mean...I want it...*for* the next
> Congress. You understand what I'm saying?

> JOSH
> (beat)
> I--Yes, I think you're saying that before
> it goes to the printer on January 1st,
> you want to re-write the Federal Budget.

> BARTLET
> A little bit, yeah. If we nip and tuck in
> different departments we can do it. It'll
> take a 'round-the-clock kind of effort.
> Yes it's a holiday, but OMB works for us,
> right?

> JOSH
> (beat)
> For the moment, yes.

> BARTLET
> You think this is crazy?

> JOSH
> No, certainly not crazier than Leo going
> for peace in the Middle East by close of
> business.

(CONTINUED)

27   CONTINUED: (2)   27

                         BARTLET
              You can get it started?

                         JOSH
              Yes sir, I can.

                         BARTLET
              Thank you.

                         JOSH
              Thank you, Mr. President.

BARTLET exits. JOSH takes a moment and rubs his eyes 'cause
the worst part is what he has to do right now.

He steps out into--

28   **INT. BULLPEN - CONTINUOUS**   28

And DONNA's already there. JOSH looks at her. This isn't one
of the funny ones.

After a long moment...

                         JOSH
              I'm sorry, it's not what it looks like.

                         DONNA
              It's okay.

                         JOSH
              It's the--

                         DONNA
              What?

                         JOSH
              --HHS budget, it seems very important to
              him and there's a hard deadline.

                         DONNA
              It's really okay.

                         JOSH
              I'll have you on the road as soon as I
              possibly can.

                         DONNA
              Where do we start?

                                                        (CONTINUED)

28   CONTINUED: 28

                        JOSH
           (pause)
        Call all the policy councils, tell 'em we
        need to package an initiative on infant
        mortality. I'll walk 'em through it.

                      DONNA
        Yeah.

                                            CUT TO:

29   **INT. LEO'S OFFICE - LATE AFTERNOON**   29

STANLEY sits at the round table with a mug of coffee and a *New York Times*. The winter storm hitting the northeast has become 24 hour news coverage which is playing silently on the monitor.

LEO comes in--

                      LEO
        Stanley, everything all right?

                      STANLEY
        Everything's fine.

                      LEO
        Come to my office. Three sophomores at
        the University of Michigan hacked into
        something called the Navstar Global
        Positioning System at the Colorado
        Springs Monitor Station.

                      STANLEY
        Did they get anything?

                      LEO
        Yeah, yeah they got something called the
        OS/comet program.

                      STANLEY
        Is it important?

                      LEO
        Yeah, you know, you'd have to say it is.
        It has the source codes to missile
        navigation systems.

                      STANLEY
            (pause)
        You know, if on these extended visits I
        could not see quite so much of the
        sausages being made--

                                       (CONTINUED)

> LEO
> I understand.

> STANLEY
> It's just that when I leave here I live
> out there.

> LEO
> Hey they're in FBI custody, the system
> worked.

> STANLEY
> So if our missile defense fails at least
> we'll know the guys who did it are in
> custody.

> LEO
> Oh you can run, but you can't hide.

> STANLEY
> Well I may want to be doing a little bit
> of both.

> LEO
> Plus when something like this happens we
> have to spend hundreds of millions of new
> dollars on security. You know what that
> means?

> STANLEY
> Higher taxes for me?

> LEO
> I was gonna say committee meetings, but
> yeah. And I still can not, I can never
> work up any real anger against these
> guys. In their minds it was just a
> formidable challenge.

> STANLEY
> So's robbing a bank.

> LEO
> I'm telling you these guys are sitting in
> custody still not thinking they did
> anything wrong.

> STANLEY
> Criminals don't experience a lot of guilt
> over the crimes they've committed and
> it's not because they don't experience
> guilt.

(CONTINUED)

29   CONTINUED: (2)   29

                         LEO
              How do you know what goes on in their
              heads?

                         STANLEY
              By being a psychiatrist.

                         LEO
              You know what's terrible? I just this
              week was sitting in on a meeting where
              they were talking about security with
              these systems and I lost the train in the
              middle. I've done that a couple of times
              this week, I'll be in a meeting and--

There's a KNOCK on the door--

                         LEO
              Yeah.

C.J. steps in--

                         C.J.
              I'm sorry, can I have a minute?

                         STANLEY
              Take the office.

                         LEO
              No we'll step outside.

LEO gets up and we

                                                    CUT TO:

30   **INT. FIDERER'S OFFICE - LATE AFTERNOON**   30

CHARLIE's working at his desk when WILL comes in.

                         CHARLIE
              Hello.

                         WILL
              Good afternoon, I'm Will Bailey.

                         CHARLIE
              Oh it's good to meet you. Charlie Young.

                         WILL
              Hi.

                                                    (CONTINUED)

30   CONTINUED: 30

                         CHARLIE
          The President's gonna see you in just a
          minute.

                         WILL
          Oh no. No. I'm meeting Toby Ziegler here.

                         CHARLIE
          Yeah, Toby's not coming, he called, Leo
          needs him on the Hill.

                         WILL
          Really.

                         CHARLIE
          Yeah.

                         WILL
          Really.

                         CHARLIE
          Yeah.

                         WILL
          Well this should be rescheduled for a
          time when that's not happening.

The Oval Office door opens and a meeting spills out--

                         WILL
          So I'll go back to my office and--

BARTLET pops his head out--

                         BARTLET
          Toby here yet?

                         CHARLIE
          No sir, but this is Will Bailey.

                         BARTLET
          So finally we meet.

                         WILL
          Hello.

                         BARTLET
          You wanna come in?

                         WILL
          Oh no. No. No no no.

                                              (CONTINUED)

30   CONTINUED: (2)   30

                         BARTLET
            Okay, well I sent some notes on the
            Congressional section.

                         WILL
            Did you?

                         BARTLET
            Isn't that why you're here?

                         WILL
            Actually I was just meeting Toby Ziegler.

                         BARTLET
            To see me.

                         WILL
            Yes.

                         BARTLET
            I thought it was about the notes on the
            Congressional section.

                         WILL
            I'm pretty sure it is.

                         BARTLET
            Okay, would you like to come back with
            Toby?

                         WILL
            I think so, sir, yes.

                         BARTLET
            Well thanks for stopping by.

                         WILL
            Thank you, Mr. Justice. Mr. Bartlet. Mr.
            President, actually.

BARTLET nods that yes, that's the one, and goes back into the
Oval Office.

WILL stands there a moment...

                         WILL
            Oh my God...

                         CHARLIE
            You know what, I've seen worse.

                         WILL
            Really?

                                                    (CONTINUED)

30 CONTINUED: (3)   30

                              CHARLIE
                    Well--
                         (thinking)
                    --no.

                              WILL
                    Yeah.

WILL goes out into--

31 **INT. CORRIDOR - CONTINUOUS**   31

--and immediately sees TOBY coming along.

                              WILL
                    Hey! I thought you were up at the Hill.

                              TOBY
                    On the Hill, you're not at the Hill. I'm
                    back, how did it go?

                              WILL
                    It didn't go very well.

                              TOBY
                    A presidential flame-out?

                              WILL
                    It doesn't matter, look--

                              TOBY
                    Makes you feel like you'll never know the
                    love of a real woman.

They go into--

32 **INT. COMMUNICATIONS BULLPEN - CONTINUOUS**   32

--where all of the glass facing the bullpen from Will's office
has been covered in "Seaborn for U.S. Congress" posters.

                              WILL
                    Can we not talk about it.

                              TOBY
                    Sure. What did he say about the
                    Congressional section?
                         (beat)
                    Never quite got there?

                              WILL
                    No.

                                                        (CONTINUED)

>   TOBY
>   Yeah, that's a harsh look in the mirror,
>   that'll be with you the next time you try
>   to make love to a real woman.

>   WILL
>   Look, it doesn't matter about me, I think
>   this thing is important.

>   TOBY
>   Bonnie, would you get Mr. Bailey and
>   myself a few minutes with the President
>   this evening.

>   BONNIE
>   Yeah.

>   TOBY
>   (to everyone)
>   And people, there are laws against
>   campaigning in Federal buildings. If
>   you're gonna cover Will's office, please
>   use plain oak tag or shaving cream if you
>   need to.
>   (to WILL)
>   Okay?

>   WILL
>   Yeah.

WILL goes into his office--

>   GINGER
>   Hey Toby, Lisa Lilly's on the phone. The
>   Justice Department's having some kind of
>   thing tonight with skits and she wants to
>   know when Albert Anastasia was killed. I
>   can't find it, do you know?

>   TOBY
>   No, but hang on a second.

TOBY opens the door to his office--

>   TOBY
>   When was Albert Anastasia killed?

>   JULIE
>   I'm sorry?

>   TOBY
>   When was Anastasia killed?

>   (CONTINUED)

32   CONTINUED: (2)   32

                         JULIE
              October of 1957.

TOBY closes the door.

                         TOBY
              October '57.

                         GINGER
              Thanks.

                         BONNIE
                 (handing TOBY a slip of paper)
              Here you go.

                         TOBY
              Thank you.

TOBY steps into--

33   **INT. SAM'S OFFICE - CONTINUOUS**   33

                         TOBY
              Seven-thirty.

                         WILL
              You'll be there?

                         TOBY
              Yes.

                         WILL
              You promise?

                         TOBY
              Yes.

                         WILL
                 (pause)
              I really thought I was gonna do a lot
              better than that.

                         TOBY
              Listen, when you get home tonight you're
              gonna be confronted by the instinct to
              drink alone. Trust that instinct, manage
              the pain, don't try to be a hero.

                         WILL
              Who rides a bicycle to work when there's
              gonna be a foot and a half of snow?

(CONTINUED)

33   CONTINUED: 33

> TOBY
> These are all good questions.

> WILL
> Okay.

TOBY starts to leave--

> WILL
> Hey, your dad seems like such a nice guy.
> I was talking to him before.

> TOBY
> Yeah.

> WILL
> Is he retired?

> TOBY
> Yeah.

> WILL
> What did he do?

> TOBY
> He made ladies' raincoats and before that
> he worked for Murder Incorporated.
>   (pause)
> Boy it really is snowing.

FADE TO BLACK:

<u>END OF ACT THREE</u>

ACT FOUR

FADE IN:

34   **INT. JOSH'S OFFICE - NIGHT**   34

JOSH is on the phone.

> JOSH
> (into phone)
> The problem is there's been an earthquake
> in Turkey and those units are occupied.
> (a little louder)
> I say there's been an earthquake, a 6-2
> seismic experience.
> (beat)
> Thank you, I realize the hour and it's a
> holiday but if you can get back to me.
> Thank you.

DONNA's come in at the end of this.

> DONNA
> Well they've got three PADs working on it
> and both deputies at DPC. So far the
> policy councils are having a hard time
> taking action without identifying
> offsets.

> JOSH
> What are they talking about?

> DONNA
> Early childhood nutrition.

> JOSH
> They want to cut early childhood
> nutrition? The kids'll just die later.

> DONNA
> They don't want to cut anything.

> JOSH
> What does OMB have?

> DONNA
> They want to explore a dedicated tax.

> JOSH
> A tax on poor people 'cause they can't
> afford medical care?

(CONTINUED)

> DONNA
> I wouldn't try to sell it that way.

> JOSH
> (pause)
> I'll get you there first thing in the
> morning.

> DONNA
> What did you mean when you said it's not
> what it looks like?

> JOSH
> Jack's already down there?

> DONNA
> Yeah.

> JOSH
> I'll call him and apologize.

> DONNA
> What did you mean?

> JOSH
> I meant that I wasn't keeping you here on
> purpose.

> DONNA
> Why would I think you were doing that?

> JOSH
> I wasn't.

> DONNA
> Why would I think you were?

> JOSH
> I don't know, it was just something I
> said. Listen, this doesn't have to be a
> disaster, you know. C.J.'s staff is gonna
> make little snowmen and stick them on the
> seats in the Press Briefing Room and take
> a picture.

DONNA laughs...

> JOSH
> We can do that and then I'll get you
> drunk at the Hawk and Dove.

> DONNA
> That sounds nice.

(CONTINUED)

34   CONTINUED: (2)   34

                         JOSH
          I have to go see the President.

                         DONNA
          Okay.

JOSH walks out into--

35   **INT. CORRIDOR - CONTINUOUS**   35

--where C.J.'s coming along.

                         C.J.
          How's it going?

                         JOSH
          Leo and the President have gone Christmas
          Crazier than usual.

                         C.J.
          You know Danny's back.

                         JOSH
          I got an e-mail from him. Any sparks?

                         C.J.
          C'mere for a second.

They step to a quiet place.

                         C.J.
          He's chasing a story that says the day
          Shareef's plane went down there was an
          airstrip in Bermuda that was secured by
          Rangers.

                         JOSH
          You told Leo?

                         C.J.
          I told him and I didn't ask him any
          questions.

                         JOSH
          Danny thinks that we somehow got a
          Gulfstream to land in Bermuda,
          assassinated Shareef, then disassembled
          the plane and distributed the pieces
          throughout the Bermuda triangle?

                         C.J.
          Yeah.

                                        (CONTINUED)

35   CONTINUED: 35

                              JOSH
          I think he spent too much time in the
          Africa hot.

                              C.J.
          The thing is?

                              JOSH
          Yeah?

                              C.J.
          I'm absolutely certain that's what
          happened.

                              JOSH
              (pause)
          We're not supposed to be talking about
          this.

                              C.J.
          If it's true we need to say so before
          Danny does. We've been here before.

                              JOSH
          Not here, but I get your point.

                              C.J.
          Okay.

     JOSH moves on and we

                                                                 CUT TO:

36   **INT. RESIDENCE FOYER - NIGHT**   36

     BARTLET is hosting ZOEY and JEAN PAUL.

                              JEAN PAUL
          It is better to work to live, I think,
          than to live to work. In France we have a
          35 hour work week.

                              BARTLET
          Right, on the other hand 20% of your
          youth is unemployed. They're just *living*
          to live.

                              JEAN PAUL
          Yes, that is right, but sir we have the
          best public health care and pension in
          the world. State financed pensions, they
          are equal almost to income levels.

                                                            (CONTINUED)

36   CONTINUED: 36

                        BARTLET
          Yeah, it helps when someone else is
          picking up those bigger ticket items like
          a national defense.

                        ZOEY
          I love seeing my two men sparring.

                        BARTLET
          I'm sorry?

                        JEAN PAUL
          She's very fond of you.

                        BARTLET
          Excellent. Listen, Zoey's mom badly wants
          to meet you and I badly wanted to be here
          when that happened, but I'm still on the
          clock so Jean Paul, I'm gonna ask you to
          make yourself comfortable here in the
          family quarters till my wife shows up,
          Zoey why don't you walk your old man back
          to the office.

                        ZOEY
                (to JEAN PAUL)
          You'll be all right here?

                        JEAN PAUL
          Of course.

                        ZOEY
          I'll be right back.

     BARTLET and ZOEY head off into--

37   **INT. CORRIDOR - CONTINUOUS**   37

                        ZOEY
          What do you think so far?

                        BARTLET
          He's the best looking person I've ever
          seen in real life.

                        ZOEY
          You want me to tell you about his
          lineage?

                        BARTLET
          Oh would you?

                                            CUT TO:

38   **EXT. PORTICO - CONTINUOUS**   38

--as ZOEY and BARTLET head down the path. The snow is still
coming down, but gently.

                    ZOEY
          Jean-Paul-Pierre-Claude Charpentier
          Vicomte de Conde de Bourbon. He is the
          22nd Vicomte de Bourbon. Though obviously
          that got interrupted by the French
          Revolution.

                    BARTLET
          Yeah, that was a setback for the
          Bourbons. Listen--

                    ZOEY
          So I have to ask you and I'm nervous but
          I'd like Jean Paul to come stay with us
          in Manchester this Christmas.

                    BARTLET
              (beat--sweetly)
          Zoey...I think it's really sweet that you
          still come to me for permission. You're
          classy and you're old fashioned.

                    ZOEY
          So it's okay?!

                    BARTLET
          Not in a million years.

                    ZOEY
          Dad--

                    BARTLET
          Listen.

BARTLET wants to say something. He takes his suit jacket off
and puts it over her.

                    BARTLET
          Siddown for a second. When you were
          little, like two, I really wanted you to
          like me and I wasn't sure you did. With
          Liz and Ellie my act just worked and with
          you I had to try harder.

                    ZOEY
              (pause)
          Dad, what's wrong?

                                              (CONTINUED)

38 CONTINUED: 38

                         BARTLET
                    (almost a whisper)
               I did something a few months ago, and I'm
               sure I was right and I'd do it again but
               it's hard to live with.

There's a long silence...

                         BARTLET
               This is ridiculous, you're freezing, come
               inside.

                         ZOEY
               No, Dad--

                         BARTLET
               Come inside.

They walk into--

39 **INT. THE OVAL OFFICE - CONTINUOUS**   39

--where LEO's waiting.

                         LEO
               Good evening, Mr. President. Zoey.

                         ZOEY
               Hi Mr. McGarry, Dad--

                         BARTLET
               You know why don't you go back to the
               Residence and make sure your mom hasn't
               killed your boyfriend. Yeah, he can come
               to Manchester, he's gonna have more
               Secret Service stuff to do and he sleeps
               in the root cellar which, like your
               bedroom door, will be guarded 'round the
               clock by two U.S. Marshals.

                         ZOEY
                    (pause)
               Okay.

ZOEY exits...

                         LEO
               She looks great.

                         BARTLET
               I almost told her.
                    (beat)
               I've been feeling it a little lately.
                    (MORE)

                                                              (CONTINUED)

39   CONTINUED:

                    BARTLET (cont'd)
          I've been exorcising my guilt by having
          Josh crowbar infant mortality money into
          the HHS budget on Dec. 23rd at eight
          o'clock.

                    LEO
          For me he's trying to get Arabs and
          Israelis to like each other.

                    BARTLET
          How's it going?

                    LEO
          It's a challenge.

                    BARTLET
          Yeah.

                    LEO
          Danny Concanon knows a guy who couldn't
          get to his locker.

                    BARTLET
          Yeah. We'll figure it out.

                    LEO
          Yeah.

                    BARTLET
          Stanley thought it was weird that I took
          the SATs again too.

                    LEO
          It is.

                    BARTLET
          You don't think it's possible that the
          answer to the remaining question was
          important?

                    LEO
          No.

                    BARTLET
          Really?

                    LEO
          Yeah.

                    BARTLET
             (pause)
          How the hell would *you* know, you got
          1400.

                                              (CONTINUED)

39   CONTINUED: (2)   39

               LEO
         True.

CHARLIE steps in--

               CHARLIE
         Sir?

               BARTLET
         Yeah, send 'em in.

TOBY comes in with WILL. BARTLET will be involved with this
verbally, but he's doing other stuff at his desk and most of
his head is otherwise engaged.

               TOBY
         Good evening, Mr. President.

               BARTLET
         Listen, my reasons for not wanting to
         talk about campaign reform at the
         Inauguration is simple. It's not a
         legislative speech and when we cite
         issues it should be the ones that affect
         people's lives. You agree?

               TOBY
         Yes.

               BARTLET
         Anything else?

               TOBY
         No sir.

Everyone stands still for a moment, then WILL turns to leave,
even takes a few steps, but no one else does.

               TOBY
         In his defense he caught the bad note, he
         came to me, he made it important.

               LEO
         Yeah.

WILL creeps back in...

               TOBY
         He wasn't distracted by the fact that his
         office was filled with bicycles.

                                              (CONTINUED)

39   CONTINUED: (3)

> WILL
> (to TOBY)
> Excuse me.

> TOBY
> (to WILL)
> Yeah.

> WILL
> You said I caught the bad note.

> TOBY
> Yeah, that was planted there to see how
> you'd do telling truth to power.

> BARTLET
> Not very well so far.

> WILL
> The junior staff, they're faking it too?

> TOBY
> No, they legitimately hate you.

> WILL
> I have no difficulty, sir, telling truth
> to power.

> BARTLET
> Okay, except when I asked you to come in
> the Oval Office you said "No. No no. No,
> no, no. No."

> WILL
> And I was firm in my convictions.

> BARTLET
> And you called me Mr. Justice.

> TOBY
> Frankly, sir, I think that problem's
> easily solved with a post-it on the
> bathroom mirror every morning. "Remember,
> he's a President. Remember, he's a
> President."

> LEO
> Can we get back to why you think--

(CONTINUED)

39   CONTINUED: (4)   39

                          WILL
           Because yes, you do want to talk about
           issues that affect people and this is the
           issue that affects everyone and you can't
           raise the subject halfway through a term.

                          LEO
           Maybe, but I'm not convinced and that's
           'cause you haven't convinced me. This
           isn't Tillman at the Stanford Club or the
           California 47th, this is big-boy school,
           Mr. Bailey, you understand?

                          WILL
           Yes sir I do.

                          LEO
           All right, it's Christmas, you've
           probably got someplace to go.

                          BARTLET
           Thank you.

                          TOBY/LEO
           Thank you, Mr. President.

They all exit and TOBY goes out into--

40   **INT. CORRIDOR - CONTINUOUS**   40

--where he's immediately guided/shoved into the wall by JOSH's
arm.

                          JOSH
           I just need to tell you this.

JOSH takes a moment but decides this isn't the right spot.

                          JOSH
           C'mere.

They arrive at another spot. Settle in. And JOSH doesn't like
it.

                          JOSH
           Sorry, c'mere.

                          TOBY
           Josh--

                          JOSH
           All right. It was desperation, it wasn't
           out of a desire to do evil.
                            (MORE)

                                              (CONTINUED)

40   CONTINUED: 40

                         JOSH (cont'd)
          He had a young family and he barely spoke
          the language. He went to jail. He went to
          jail and you went to school and it was
          all a half a century ago. Look what he
          did in two generations. What room did you
          just walk out of?

                         TOBY
          I appreciate that that's what you think.
          Do I get to think what I think?

                         JOSH
          No you don't, because you don't know what
          I know.

                         TOBY
          What?

                         JOSH
          That I'd give anything to have a living
          father who was a felon. Or a sister with
          a past.
                    (beat)
          That's it.

TOBY walks away. JOSH heads back into--

41   **INT. FIDERER'S OFFICE - CONTINUOUS**   41

--as LEO's coming out.

                         LEO
          I'm just coming to see you, you're off
          the hook with both of us, we'll go for
          infant mortality after the 1st.

                         JOSH
          I don't mind. People are working on it
          and Donna's here with me. We've got a
          whole night planned around it.

                         LEO
          Yeah I'm callin' it off. And I hooked
          Donna up with a news helicopter that's
          landing about two miles from the inn
          she's going to.

                         JOSH
          Donna left?

                         LEO
          Yeah. Anyway, forget the Nativity, we'll
          get 'em next time.

                                                    (CONTINUED)

41   CONTINUED: 41

                         JOSH
              Yes sir.

                                                          CUT TO:

42   42
and   **OMITTED**   and
43   43

44   **INT. TOBY'S OFFICE - NIGHT**   44

Where JULIE can hear the singing too. TOBY comes in.

                         TOBY
              It's getting too late to do anything. Why
              don't you sleep on my couch and we'll get
              you out in the morning.

                         JULIE
              You know I think it might make it easier
              if you *knew* some of the history. You
              shouldn't have to ask when Anastasia was--

                         TOBY
              Oh God Dad, I know when Anastasia was
              killed. I know about the candy store in
              Brownsville. I know about Louie Amberg. I
              know the Half Moon Hotel, sixth story
              window, Coney Island.

And from the lobby we HEAR the WHIFFENPOOFS singing *Oh Holy
Night*.

                         JULIE
              Can I tell you, you're romanticizing my--
              Dutch Schultz ain't never heard a me,
              Toby.
                   (hardly a whisper)
              My crew...it only happened to terrible
              people. Terrible people. Murderers
              themselves.

                         TOBY
              Dad, please--

                         JULIE
              Loan sharkers, heroin, these were our
              neighborhoods--

                         TOBY
              We don't have to do this all in one
              night?

                                                     (CONTINUED)

                         JULIE
                    (pause)
          What?

                         TOBY
          Come on.

                         JULIE
                    (pause)
          I should stay tonight with you?

                         TOBY
          You should stay with me.

                         JULIE
          Andrea's healthy?

                         TOBY
          Very healthy.

     They walk out into--

45   **INT. CORRIDOR - CONTINUOUS**   **(FORMERLY BULLPEN/CORRIDORS)**   45

                         JULIE
          You got names picked out?

                         TOBY
          No, not yet.

                         JULIE
          Toby, who is that that's been singing all
          day?

                         TOBY
          It's a group called the Whiffenpoofs.
          They're from Yale. They came to do a
          series of concerts and the snow--

                         JULIE
          Did you say the Whiffenpoofs?

                         TOBY
          The Whiffenpoofs. I'm surprised you
          haven't heard of them, you used to like
          Cole Porter a lot.

                         JULIE
          They're singing right now in this
          building?

                         TOBY
          Right in here.

                                                      (CONTINUED)

45   CONTINUED: 45

And they walk into--

46   **INT. LOBBY - CONTINUOUS**   46

--where STAFFERS are gathered casually around listening to *Oh Holy Night.*

                    JULIE
               (to himself)
          Ich hub uuz duh gebracht.
               (English translation)
          [I got us here.]

                    TOBY
          What does that mean?

                    JULIE
          I'm having the strongest memory.

                    TOBY
          Let's go.

TOBY catches JOSH's eye across the room and makes a subtle "what do you want me to say" gesture. JOSH smiles.

LEO comes along and taps him on the shoulder--

                    LEO
          C'mere for a second.

JOSH follows LEO into--

47   **INT. BULLPEN - CONTINUOUS**   47

--where the singing continues.

                    LEO
          Was I insensitive before about telling
          you Donna was gone?

                    JOSH
          No, what do you mean?

                    LEO
          I don't know, I thought--

                    JOSH
          It's fine, of course it's fine. It's
          great, I was feeling guilty and now this
          is good. It's better than good, it's the
          way it should--

                                              (CONTINUED)

47   CONTINUED: 47

                        LEO
          Oh get it together, would you please?

                             JOSH
          I'm trying.

                             LEO
          Okay.
               (pause)
          There's something we have to talk about.

LEO stares at him silently for a long moment...

                             JOSH
               (long pause)
          You'll tell me when you need to.

                             LEO
               (pause)
          It's four years later and there are
          things that are worse and things that are
          exactly the same. Where do you start?

                             JOSH
          By fixing a roof.
               (beat)
          I'm staying on the phones, you wanna stay
          with me?

                             LEO
          Yeah.

LEO grabs a phone and punches a button as JOSH similarly gets
to work and the singing continues as we

                                                        CUT TO:

48   **OMITTED (INCORPORATED INTO SCENE 47)**   48

49   **INT. FIDERER'S OFFICE - NIGHT**   49

As CHARLIE hesitates a moment, then shuts off the lights on
his desk and walks out into--

50   **INT. CORRIDOR - CONTINUOUS**   50

As CHARLIE makes his way past the communications bullpen, now
dark except for the light coming from WILL's office and
CHARLIE takes brief note of WILL still being there, pacing and
working on the speech and the song continues as CHARLIE walks
into--

51   **INT. WEST WING LOBBY - CONTINUOUS**   51

--and through the open doors to JOSH's bullpen we can see JOSH being handed a mug of coffee as he hands off his cell phone to LEO who just passed through the frame and we

                                                        CUT TO:

52   **EXT. PORTICO - NIGHT**   52

And BARTLET stares out at the snow and the singing continues and we

                                                        CUT TO:

53   **INT. LOBBY - NIGHT**   53

As JULIE stands in the same room as his son and the WHIFFENPOOFS and we pull back and

                                                        FADE TO BLACK:

                          <u>END OF SHOW</u>

COMMENCEMENT

In the fourth act of a first season episode called *Mr. Willis of Ohio*, Bartlet tells his youngest daughter, Zoey, that he's increasing her Secret Service protection after an incident in a Georgetown bar where a couple of frat boys who are drunk and stoned (and who don't recognize her) start to pose a physical threat.

Zoey objects to the increased protection, wanting the freedom of her youth, and her father scares her into agreeing by telling her about the Treasury Department's "nightmare scenario," which isn't that the President gets killed, but rather that the child of a President gets kidnapped and the country's held hostage with an emotionally unstable Commander in Chief directing the action.

I'd always wanted to dramatize that hypothetical, and around March I told Tommy and the staff that, along with the birth of Toby's two children, that's how we were going to end the season.

The pieces had to be put in place. In Episode 19 (*Evidence of Things Not Seen*), Zoey announced that she was going to spend the summer in France with a boyfriend of questionable repute. In 20 (*Life on Mars*), I had the Vice President (John Hoynes) resign, paving the way for a large Constitutional obstacle in the final two episodes.

Alex Graves turned in an episode as good as anything he'd ever done, and the last act of this episode was, for my money, his best work to date.

Here's *Commencement*.

The West Wing

Commencement

BUFF REVISIONS:	05/05/03
GREEN REVISIONS:	04/25/03
YELLOW REVISIONS:	04/08/03
PINK REVISIONS:	04/07/03

THE WEST WING

"Commencement"

Written by
Aaron Sorkin

Directed by
Alex Graves

PRODUCTION #175-322
Episode Twenty-One

JOHN WELLS PRODUCTIONS
in association with
WARNER BROS. TELEVISION
4000 Warner Blvd.
Burbank, CA 91522

Final Shooting Script (BLUE)
April 6, 2003
Copyright © 2003
Warner Bros. Television
All Rights Reserved

THE WEST WING

"Commencement"

Script Revision History

DATE	COLOR	PAGES
04/06/03	FULL BLUE	1-64
04/07/03	PINK PAGES	6,7,9,10,10A,12,13,14-15, 16,20,23,24,26,27,38,39, 40,41,50,51,60,61
04/08/03	YELLOW PAGES	CAST,SETS,45,46,49,52,53, 54,55,56,56A,57,58,59, 59A,59B,60,62,63,64
04/25/03	GREEN PAGES	SETS,26,45,54,54A,55,55A, 56,56A
05/05/03	BUFF PAGES	TITLE PAGE

SET LIST

INTERIORS
WHITE HOUSE
 Situation Room
 Fiderer's Office
 Oval Office
 Back Lobby
 Lobby
 Residence Foyer
 Bartlet's Private Study
 Josh's Office
 Corridors
 C.J.'s Office
 Leo's Office
 Great Hall
 Upper Press Room
 Press Briefing
 Josh's Bullpen
 Stairway

TOBY'S HOUSE

BARTLET'S LIMO

HOSPITAL ROOM

TECHNO CLUB
 Main Area
 Corridor/Restroom Area

EXTERIORS
THE POTOMAC - DAY

PENNSYLVANIA AVENUE - DAY

STREET/TOBY'S HOUSE - DAY

TOBY'S HOUSE - DAY

WHITE HOUSE/BACK DRIVEWAY - DAY

GEORGETOWN UNIVERISTY - DAY

NATIONAL ARBORETUM - NIGHT

NATIONAL ARBORETUM/ASIAN GARDEN - NIGHT

TECHNO CLUB/FRONT - NIGHT *

STREET (WESLEY'S CAR) - NIGHT

PORTICO - NIGHT

TECHNO CLUB/ALLEY - NIGHT

TECHNO CLUB/BACK - NIGHT *

THE WEST WING
"Commencement"
CAST LIST

PRESIDENT JOSIAH BARTLET
LEO McGARRY
JOSH LYMAN
SAM SEABORN
TOBY ZIEGLER
C.J. CREGG
CHARLIE YOUNG
DONNA MOSS
ABIGAIL BARTLET
AMY GARDNER

NANCY MCNALLY
FITWALLACE
WILL BAILEY
BUTTERFIELD
ZOEY
CAROL
DANNY CONCANON
ANDREA WYATT
MARGARET
JEAN PAUL

AVERY
WESLEY DAVIS
JAMIE REED
MOLLY O'CONNOR
RANDY WEATHERS
DR. GLAZER
COOPER
AIDE
CHANCELLOR
WAITRESS
CIVILIAN

"Commencement"

<u>TEASER</u>

FADE IN:

1   **EXT. THE POTOMAC - DAY**   1

We see a couple of skulls race by before we see JOSH and
AVERY, a young Senator, who are sharing a jog.

> JOSH
> I haven't spoken to the President about
> this. Or Leo McGarry. I haven't spoken to
> Toby or Leadership. The only person I've
> talked to about this is C.J. Cregg. She
> got excited about it and sent me to you
> to take your temperature.

> AVERY
> Well I'd love to be the President's Vice
> President, Josh, most people would, but
> I'm unconfirmable.

> JOSH
> Why?

> AVERY
> 'Cause someone's gonna ask me if I'm
> homosexual and I'm gonna say yes.

> JOSH
> Why would you say yes?

> AVERY
> Josh?

> JOSH
> You're gay?

> AVERY
> Yeah.

> JOSH
> I didn't know that.

> AVERY
> That would make you about the only one
> left in the Federal government who
> didn't.

> JOSH
> Gee.

(CONTINUED)

1   CONTINUED: 1

                         AVERY
               Yeah.

                         JOSH
               Well I don't know why that should make a
               difference, after all--

                         AVERY
               Are you out of your mind?

                         JOSH
               Yeah, it's an obstacle to confirmation,
               it's an impediment.

                         AVERY
               Yeah.

                         JOSH
               What do you know, well good for you, good
               luck with that.

                         AVERY
               Thanks.

                         JOSH
                'Scuse me.

JOSH pulls up and takes his cell phone out of his pocket. He
sits at the side of the river as he dials and we

                                              INTERCUT WITH:

2   **EXT. PENNSYLVANIA AVENUE - SAME TIME**   2

C.J.'s walking toward the White House as her cell phone rings.
She's wearing Saturday clothes.

                         C.J.
                    (into phone)
               WCJC, the number one station with the
               number one sound in progressive rock.

                         JOSH
               You <u>think</u> you're funny.

                         C.J.
               Oh I know I'm funny.

                         JOSH
               Where are you?

                         C.J.
               I'm going in, did you get paged?

                                              (CONTINUED)

2   CONTINUED: 2

                         JOSH
             No.

JOSH's pager goes off--

                         JOSH
             Yes.
                 (beat)
             Hang on.

JOSH clicks the phone--

                         JOSH
                 (into phone)
             Hello?

                                        INTERCUT WITH:

3   **INT. SITUATION ROOM - SAME TIME**   3

A briefing is underway for several people including BARTLET.
LEO's on a phone at the side.

                         LEO
             Yeah, come in, would you.

                         JOSH
             What's goin' on?

                         LEO
             The commencement speech.

                         JOSH
             You're calling everyone in on a
             commencement speech?

                         LEO
             Just come on in.

JOSH clicks back to C.J.--

                         JOSH
             That was Leo.

                         C.J.
             About the Georgetown speech?

                         JOSH
             Yeah, I don't think it's about the
             speech. I'm getting in a cab, I'll see
             you in a minute.

                                        (CONTINUED)

3   CONTINUED: 3

And we

                                                          CUT TO:

4   **INT. SITUATION ROOM - DAY**   4

The briefing continues. We see now that FITZWALLACE and NANCY
are there.

                    NANCY
          ·No, the FBI found the van abandoned in
          Sacramento.

                    BARTLET
               (frustrated)
          How were they able to rent a van?

                    NANCY
          Sir, I'm joining those who are
          recommending Threat Condition Bravo. I
          think at the very least we have to
          increase security at the sea ports and
          the airports.

                    BARTLET
               (pause--reading off a cable)
          "A torrential downpour in the Pacific
          Northwest."

                    NANCY
          Yes sir.

                    BARTLET
               (pause)
          A torrential downpour.

                    NANCY
          Yes.

                    BARTLET
               (pause)
          And they're just missing.

                    FITZWALLACE
          Yes sir.

                    BARTLET
          The five of them. They're just missing.

                    FITZWALLACE
          Yes sir.

                                              (CONTINUED)

4   CONTINUED: 4

                         BARTLET
          We're gonna work on that?

                         CIVILIAN
          Yes sir.

                         BARTLET
          ThreatCon Bravo. Find them. ThreatCon
          Bravo. Leo and I'll be back. We have to
          tell the Senior Staff that we killed
          Abdul Shareef now.

And as BARTLET and LEO start out, we

                                                  SMASH CUT TO:

MAIN TITLES

                         <u>END OF TEASER</u>

ACT ONE

FADE IN:

5   **INT. FIDERER'S OFFICE - DAY**   5

TOBY's standing and waiting. C.J. comes in.

>   C.J.
> Good morning.

>   TOBY
> Good morning.

>   C.J.
> Big day.

>   TOBY
> Yes.

>   C.J.
> Are you nervous?

>   TOBY
> How do you know about this?

>   C.J.
> The house?

>   TOBY
> Yeah.

>   C.J.
> Not because *you* told me.

>   TOBY
> That's right.

WILL comes in.

>   WILL
> Hey.

>   TOBY/C.J.
> Hey.

>   WILL
> I'm glad he's finally asking for help
> with this speech.

>   TOBY
> It's not gonna be about commencement.

(CONTINUED)

                         WILL
            Why not?

                         TOBY
            'Cause he doesn't call the four of us in
            Saturday morning at eight to work on a
            commencement speech.

                         WILL
            Aren't you nervous you haven't seen it?

                         TOBY
            I'm choosing to be nervous about other
            things today.

                         WILL
            Oh hey, that's right, big day.

                         TOBY
                 (to C.J.)
            Is he talking about the house?

                         WILL
            It's romantic romantic.

JOSH has come in, showered and changed.

                         TOBY
                 (to JOSH)
            They know about the house.

                         JOSH
                 (beat)
            Did you tell them?

                         TOBY
            No. Did you?

                         JOSH
            It's a bold, romantic gesture, I spread
            it around, got you some good will. I
            think I softened some people up on you.

                         TOBY
            How'd your morning jog go with Vice
            President Avery?

                         JOSH
            That was you too?

                         TOBY
            Mostly her.

                                              (CONTINUED)

5   CONTINUED: (2)   5

CHARLIE steps out of the Oval Office--

                         CHARLIE
               You can go in.

The four of them head into--

6   **INT. OVAL OFFICE - CONTINUOUS**   6

--where BARTLET and LEO are waiting. BARTLET's on the phone.

                         LEO
               Go ahead and siddown, he's gonna be a
               second.
                    (to TOBY)
               How you doin'.

                         TOBY
               Good.

                         LEO
               What is it, two weeks?

                         TOBY
               In ten days, we can pick a day on the
               calendar and they'll induce.

                         LEO
               You can pick a day?

                         TOBY
               Yeah.

                         LEO
               That's great, so you can do it on a
               Friday, let the kids get their feet wet
               over the weekend.

                         TOBY
               Yeah.

                         LEO
               Ten days.

                         TOBY
               Yeah.

                         LEO
               Lemme tell you somethin', you know what
               I'd do, I'd check into the hospital
               today. You can't do it too soon. Mallory
               was very nearly born at Exit 32 on the
               Long Island Expressway.

                                                      (CONTINUED)

6   CONTINUED: 6

                              BARTLET
                         (hanging up)
                    Thanks.

Everyone stands--

                              BARTLET
                    Yeah, listen, I don't think this is gonna
                    come as a galloping shock to anyone here,
                    but last May I ordered a Special Ops unit
                    to kill Abdul Shareef and that's what
                    they did and we made it look like what
                    got reported.

                              LEO
                    Anybody need him to stop?

                              JOSH
                    No sir.

                              LEO
                    Anybody need a minute?

                              TOBY
                    No sir.

                              C.J.
                    No sir.

                              LEO
                    There was considerable evidence presented
                    to a group that included Fitzwallace,
                    Nancy, Berryhill, Babish, the Attorney
                    General and a few others, we gave it to
                    the gang of eight. The man had committed
                    crimes and remained a threat, for
                    instance we stopped him from blowing up
                    the Golden Gate Bridge. Were U.S. laws
                    broken, no. International law, possibly.

                              BARTLET
                         (pause)
                    See, I said we took Shareef and they said
                    fine, and then you went on talking for
                    another five, ten minutes.

                              C.J.
                    Mr. President.

                              BARTLET
                    Yeah.

                                                      (CONTINUED)

6   CONTINUED: (2)   6

                                  C.J.
                 Why the decision to tell us this morning?

                                  BARTLET
                 Well I just ordered ThreatCon Bravo so
                 people are gonna be seeing some
                 heightened security this weekend.

                                  C.J.
                 What's the threat?

                                  LEO
                 Increased chatter about torrential rain
                 in the Pacific Northwest. It's pouring
                 rain in the Pacific Northwest.

                                  WILL
                 I'm sure the analysts have already
                 thought of this but, you know, it *is*
                 raining in the Pacific Northwest.

                                  LEO
                 For a couple of years we've been keeping
                 an eye on five possible Bahji sleepers in
                 Central New York. And last night they
                 disappeared, we lost 'em.

                                  JOSH
                 We lost 'em.

                                  BARTLET
                 We did.

                                  JOSH
                 And we're worried about retribution for
                 Shareef.

                                  LEO
                 Yes.

                                  JOSH
                 Can I ask, how hard can it be to keep an
                 eye on five Qumari religious fanatics in
                 Schenectady?

                                  BARTLET
                 Tell him sister.

                                  LEO
                 I think you'd both be surprised. Anything
                 else?

                                                         (CONTINUED)

6   CONTINUED: (3)   6

> WILL
> How'd you get Shareef's plane to land?

> LEO
> Thank you.

> ALL
> Thank you, Mr. President/Thank you,
> sir/etc.

> BARTLET
> Oh, hey, Toby, big day.

> EVERYBODY
> Big day/Big, big day.

> BARTLET
> The house. A masterstroke. Come on, give
> us a kiss.

> TOBY
> Thank you, sir, no.

> BARTLET
> Okay.

Everyone exits but WILL...

> BARTLET
> Yes?

> WILL
> Well, sir, I have time today. Right now.
> And I was wondering if you'd like me to
> look over the Georgetown speech.

> BARTLET
> No, I don't need help.

> WILL
> Yes sir.

> BARTLET
> Yeah, I need help.

> WILL
> Yes sir, I'd be happy to. Why don't you
> let me read what you have.

> BARTLET
> What I have?

(CONTINUED)

6   CONTINUED: (4)   6

                        WILL
          Yes.

                        BARTLET
               (pause)
          Well it's been said I have a pleasant
          speaking voice and oratorical style.

                        WILL
               (beat)
          You don't have anything?

                        BARTLET
          On paper?

                        WILL
          Yeah.

                        BARTLET
          No.

                        WILL
          It's at four o'clock.

                        BARTLET
          Yeah.

                        WILL
          We should probably get started.

                        BARTLET
          Yeah, right away I would think.

                        WILL
          Yeah.

                        BARTLET
          Except this minute I have to go over and
          meet the agents who are being detailed to
          Zoey for France. They speak French.
               (beat)
          As *well* as being Secret Service agents, I
          didn't mean that they speak French and so
          therefore are guarding Zoey in France.

                        WILL
          Yeah, I got it, sir.

                                              (CONTINUED)

6   CONTINUED: (5)   6

> BARTLET
> I've been thinking I'd like to talk about creativity. Why don't you get started on some thoughts and I'll join you.

> WILL
> Yes sir.

BARTLET exits and we

                                                CUT TO:

7   **OMITTED**   7

8   **INT. BACK LOBBY - DAY**   8

Special Agent WESLEY DAVIS, a handsome 39 year old black man wearing the dark-suited uniform of a Secret Service agent is walking in. He gets all the way in before JOSH comes around the corner and sees him from behind.

> JOSH
> Wes. Wesley.

> WESLEY
> Hey, Josh, what's goin' on?

> JOSH
> You back?

> WESLEY
> No, I go to France tomorrow morning. I'm leading Bookbag's paparazzi patrol for three months.

> JOSH
> Really.

> WESLEY
> Yeah.

> JOSH
> That's a bit of a powder puff detail there, isn't it, fella?

> WESLEY
> I go where I'm told.

9   **INT. LOBBY - CONTINUOUS**   9

                      JOSH
        So, in your training, what are you taught
        to do, say, if a stringer for *Town &*
        Country were to get in her face?

                      WESLEY
        You know I can kill you and just make *up*
        the reason why I did, right?

                      JOSH
        Oh yeah.

WESLEY keeps going and we

                                        CUT TO:

10   **INT. RESIDENCE FOYER - DAY**   10

Two WOMEN and a MAN, all in their late 20s but who look
younger and are dressed like college students, are standing at
the far end of the room and not talking.

BARTLET comes in and stops when he sees them. It's a slightly
confusing moment but he's gotten used to strangers walking
through his house.

                      BARTLET
          (beat)
        Hi.

                      JAMIE
        Good morning, Mr. President.

                      BARTLET
        Are you friends of Zoey's?

                      JAMIE
          (producing I.D.)
        No sir, Special Agent Jamie Reed, U.S.
        Secret Service.

                      MOLLY
        Molly O'Connor, sir.

                      RANDY
        Randy Weathers.

And as RANDY puts her ID back, BARTLET catches a glimpse of
the one accessory that separates them from the other college
graduates the town's filled with today--the shoulder holster
and the 9-millimeter.

                                (CONTINUED)

10   CONTINUED:

                        BARTLET
          Good.

WESLEY comes around the corner with BUTTERFIELD--

                        BUTTERFIELD
          Excuse me, Mr. President.

                        BARTLET
          Hey.

                        BUTTERFIELD
          You remember Wesley Davis.

                        BARTLET
          Wes, thanks so much for doing this, I
          know it's not what you like.

                        WESLEY
          No sir, I'm flattered you asked.

                        BARTLET
          So let's talk about how this is gonna
          work.

                        BUTTERFIELD
          These four agents will be assigned to the
          current team of 14 that gets supplemented
          by a rotating back-up group from the
          Paris office that's more familiar with
          the region. Wes is the Special Agent in
          Charge.

                        BARTLET
          Well, here's my question. These guys look
          pretty young to me and I'm looking for
          something very specific with this detail.
          This is a father/daughter situation so I
          think what I'm looking for in terms of
          protection would best be characterized as
          well...overwhelming force. Do they have
          that, do they have the ability to just
          overwhelm any...danger that might
          suddenly--do you have overwhelming--do
          they have overwhelming force?

                        BUTTERFIELD
             (to WESLEY)
          Attack Randy.

                                     (CONTINUED)

10   CONTINUED: (2)   10

And on that order WESLEY makes a sudden move toward RANDY, but
in a flash, MOLLY, the most diminutive and quietest seeming of
the three, has him flipped on his back, her knee in his chest
and her gun in his face.

                    BARTLET
              (a kid seeing fireworks)
          Wow!

                    ZOEY
          Oh God, Dad, what are you doing?

ZOEY's appeared from her bedroom down the hall. BARTLET
doesn't care, he's in heaven.

                    BARTLET
          This one here tossed Wesley like a bag of
          potato chips.

                    ZOEY
          Molly, get off of Wesley.

MOLLY gets off. BUTTERFIELD helps WESLEY up.

                    WESLEY
              (to BUTTERFIELD)
          You like calling on me for that one,
          don't you?

                    BARTLET
          You guys know each other?

                    ZOEY
          Molly was on Ellie's detail for a while.

                    BARTLET
          Oh good, okay, well Ellie's still up and
          running.

                    ZOEY
          Hi Wes, sorry about this.

                    WESLEY
              (to ZOEY)
          We're gonna be fine, it's wide perimeter
          protection, I just need you to show me
          your panic button everyday.

And ZOEY dangles her small panic button which she has on a key
chain.

                    BARTLET
          When do you start?

                                                        (CONTINUED)

10   CONTINUED: (3)

                    WESLEY
          1800, sir, 6PM tonight.

                    BARTLET
               (to ZOEY)
          Are you going back to the campus?

                    ZOEY
          Yeah.

                    BARTLET
          Okay, well lemme ask you this. Would you
          consider, instead of living in France
          with your boyfriend for three months,
          uhh...staying here. Living in your room
          and being a candy striper?
               (beat)
          Or surfing?

                    ZOEY
               (laughing)
          A candy striper?

                    BARTLET
          Or surfing. You could spend the summer
          working in a pet shop. We could play
          Yahtzee and watch movies at night.

                    ZOEY
               (sweetly amused)
          Dad, what fantasy is it that's going on
          in your head right now?

                    BARTLET
          What daughters would do their whole lives
          if I had my way.

                    ZOEY
          I'll see you later.

     ZOEY exits...

                    BARTLET
               (back to the AGENTS)
          Before I forget, if something comes up
          and you're faced with the choice of
          killing the boyfriend or not killing the
          boyfriend, kill the boyfriend. Nah, I'm
          just--no, no, kill the boyfriend.

                    LEO
          Excuse me, sir.

                                        (CONTINUED)

10   CONTINUED: (4)   10

LEO and FITZWALLACE have appeared.

                         BARTLET
              Excuse me.

                         BUTTERFIELD
              Thank you, Mr. President.

                         FITZWALLACE
              How you doin', Wes.

                         WESLEY
              Well, Mr. Chairman, thank you.

                         FITZWALLACE
              You take care on this new detail now,
              they've got some mimes over there that
              can be pretty nasty.

                         WESLEY
              Yes sir.

BARTLET, LEO and FITZWALLACE go into--

11   **INT. BARTLET'S PRIVATE STUDY - CONTINUOUS**   11

                         LEO
              Harbor patrol in Portland is reporting
              that the *Agile*, a cargo ship in port for
              fourteen hours now, has a container
              missing. They're supposed to have 46,
              they have 45.

                         BARTLET
              What's the registry?

                         FITZWALLACE
              They're flying a Nigerian flag but it's
              Syrian ownership.

                         BARTLET
              What are we doing on the ground?

                         FITZWALLACE
              The FBI's hunting down everyone who was
              on the ship.

                         BARTLET
              How long have they been at it?

                         FITZWALLACE
              An hour.

                                              (CONTINUED)

11   CONTINUED:

> BARTLET
> All right, let's give 'em another hour
> and then have the Coast Guard close the
> Port of--is it the Port of Portland, is
> it really the Port of Portland?

> LEO
> Yeah.

> BARTLET
> They're gonna lose 700 million dollars a
> day 'cause these five guys are missing.
> And I just now got why we're having this
> meeting.

> LEO
> What do you mean?

> BARTLET
> Portland. Torrential rain in the Pacific
> Northwest.

> LEO
> Yeah.

> BARTLET
> Screw the hour, let's close it down.

> FITZWALLACE
> Yes sir.

> BARTLET
> Thanks.

> FITZWALLACE
> Thank you, Mr. President.

FITZWALLACE exits...

> LEO
> Hey, did you know that ten days from now,
> Toby and Andy can pick a day and the
> doctor's gonna induce. They can decide
> what day the twins are gonna be born.

> BARTLET
> Well that's about the last thing they're
> gonna get to decide. So you choose
> Tuesday. Twenty years later look what
> happens.

(CONTINUED)

11   CONTINUED: (2)   11

They've exited and we

                                                                    FADE TO BLACK:

                                   <u>END OF ACT ONE</u>

<u>ACT TWO</u>

FADE IN:

12   **INT. JOSH'S OFFICE - DAY**   12

JOSH is sitting and staring at one of his walls, on which has
been tacked the names and photos of people in the VP derby.
Maybe a few words have been written next to one picture or
another, maybe a line's been drawn through AVERY. There's
probably a woman up there.

He surveys what he's got so far. Then unrolls what looks like
a blueprint on his desk which has been cleared for the day.
It's a seating chart of the U.S. Senate and he's been working
it for a few days 'cause there are already lines through a
number of the names that they've disqualified.

He starts again as CHARLIE steps in--

                    CHARLIE
          Josh?

                    JOSH
          Yeah.

                    CHARLIE
          The President wants to know if we still
          have the vetting files from five years
          ago.

                    JOSH
          For Vice President, you mean?

                    CHARLIE
          Yeah. You crossed off McKenna?

                    JOSH
          For health.

                    CHARLIE
          Ryan Lyndell?

                    JOSH
          I'm a fan of Lyndell's, so's the
          President, but the Speaker's not and this
          guy has to get confirmed.

                    CHARLIE
          Too much of a moonshot for the Speaker?

                                              (CONTINUED)

12   CONTINUED: 12

                         JOSH
          He's got an Asian garden in back of his
          house where he meditates.

                         CHARLIE
          Asian garden. Asian garden, I know what
          the--a note fell out of my wallet
          yesterday and I couldn't remember what
          it--
                  (he's gotten the note out)
          5-7. 10PM. Paeonia Japonica/Bamboo.

                         JOSH
          Both of which one would find in an Asian
          garden.

                         CHARLIE
          Next to each other at the Arboretum. I
          wrote this note three and a half years
          ago, right after Zoey started school. We
          buried, like, a 14 dollar bottle of
          champagne and decided we'd dig it up and
          drink it after she graduated.

                         JOSH
          You buried the champagne at the
          Arboretum.

                         CHARLIE
          Right between the Paeonia Japonica and
          the Bamboo.

                         JOSH
          How did you get away with digging up the
          National Arboretum?

                         CHARLIE
          Oh well you gotta do it at night.

                         JOSH
          Today's 5/7.

                         CHARLIE
          I know.

                         JOSH
          You gotta get the bottle back.

                         CHARLIE
          No.

                         JOSH
          You do.

                                              (CONTINUED)

                         CHARLIE
          No, I'm done. I gave it a shot. She's
          said no. She said it clearly.

                         JOSH
          You should dig it up, it's a good idea.

                         CHARLIE
          She's going to France tomorrow with
          Tartuffe, I'm gonna eat the fourteen
          bucks.

                         JOSH
          No, I mean as a friend and you give it to
          her as a graduation present. You give it
          to her at one of the parties tonight.
          That way she goes off without thinking
          you're mad at her.

                         CHARLIE
          I am mad at her.

                         JOSH
          Yeah, but that's not really her fault and
          she's goin' away for a while and anyway I
          don't know what I'm talkin' about, lemme
          ask you something. Between you and me,
          and I'm not looking for this particular
          promotion, but between you and me, what
          would you think about *this* choice.

While JOSH was talking, he's torn the lead photo in today's
paper out and tacked it up on the wall. It's a picture of LEO
standing next to BARTLET and looking very Vice Presidential.

CHARLIE smiles--

                         CHARLIE
          They'll confirm a gay Senator before an
          alcoholic addict.

                         JOSH
          Oh no they won't.

                         CHARLIE
          You got the vetting file?

                         JOSH
                  (handing it to him)
          I'll see you later.

CHARLIE exits into--

13   **INT. CORRIDOR - CONTINUOUS**   13

--where he passes AMY--

                    CHARLIE
        Hey.

                    AMY
        Hey, Charlie. Donna, the First Lady
        wanted you to know that Mary and Fred
        Wellington are back on the trip, so we
        need to deal with that.

                    DONNA
                (writing it down)
        All right.

                    AMY
        Yeah. You know Josh came by this morning
        to show me a list of six possible
        nominees. And I thought it was a very
        good list and I said, "Wow, well this is
        a windfall." And he got very quiet and it
        occurred to me after he left that he may
        have thought I meant, "It's great that
        the Vice President had to resign because
        now we get one of *these* guys". Did he
        happen to mention anything about that?

                    DONNA
        No.

                    AMY
        I didn't mean it was good the Vice
        President had to resign.

                    DONNA
        I'll tell Josh about the Wellingtons.

                    AMY
        Okay.

AMY heads off and we

                                                        CUT TO:

14   **INT. C.J.'S OFFICE - DAY**   14

DANNY is dead asleep on the couch and it appears that he's
been that way for a little while. He's got his coat over him
as a blanket and at the moment we can barely see his face,
which is buried in a pillow.

                                                    (CONTINUED)

14   CONTINUED: 14

C.J. walks in without noticing the body on the couch. She goes
behind her desk, picks up something to read, leans back in her
chair, kicks her shoes off and--

                          C.J.
              AAAAGGHH!

And DANNY wakes up terrified--

                          DANNY
              AAGHH!

                          C.J.
              You scared me!

                          DANNY
              I was sleeping!

                          C.J.
              What are you doing in here?

                          DANNY
              Hang on a second, I'm not sure.

                          C.J.
              CAROL!

CAROL runs in--

                          CAROL
              Sorry. Yes. Danny's here.
                   (beat)
              Sorry.

CAROL exits...

                          C.J.
              Can I help you?

                          DANNY
              I'm a little groggy. It's from when you
              wake up after you've *just* fallen--you know
              it's one of those where it really takes
              you a good long while to snap out of--

                          C.J.
                   (shouting)
              Can I help you?

                          DANNY
              All right. I just flew back from Boston.
                   (beat)
                        (MORE)

                                              (CONTINUED)

14   CONTINUED: (2)   14

>   DANNY (cont'd)
> No. Not Boston. Augsburg, Germany, I just
> flew back from Augsburg, Germany.

>   C.J.
> Danny, you wanna go home for a while and
> then talk to me.

>   DANNY
> No, this is important to you, I've been
> on trains and planes.

>   C.J.
> What?

>   DANNY
> I have a link between the U.S. Government
> and Abdul Shareef's plane and it's enough
> and we're gonna print it so I'm here to
> ask the White House if they'd like to
> comment.

>   C.J.
> We'll comment as soon as you show me the
> link.

>   DANNY
> I have a link, it's the pilot, it's Jamil
> Bari.

>   C.J.
> You've been saying that from the
> beginning.

>   DANNY
> I've got it now.

>   C.J.
> Well show it to me and I'll comment on
> it.

>   DANNY
> We don't need a White House comment to
> run it.

>   C.J.
> Well you're not gonna run it like this,
> there are National Security issues
> involved.

>   DANNY
> My paper isn't gonna hold off on it
> unless lives are in immediate danger.

>   (CONTINUED)

14   CONTINUED: (3)   14

                    C.J.
          They are.

                    DANNY
          Show me.

                    C.J.
          Classified security information? I don't
          think I'm allowed to do that.

                    DANNY
          Then what do we do?

                    C.J.
          Don't run it, not this weekend. I'm not
          lying to you about security concerns.

                    DANNY
          Except you've been faffing me around for
          months.

                    C.J.
          Of course I have.

                    DANNY
          I'm gonna give you a couple of hours to
          siddown with Leo and figure out what you
          can tell me that'll convince me I
          shouldn't print what I have. Otherwise
          comment on it or don't comment on it but
          it's the lead in tomorrow's paper. And by
          the way, that is the brand of courtesy
          you have never extended me.

                    C.J.
          I extend you courtesy all the time.

                    DANNY
          When?

                    C.J.
          You just slept on my couch.

                    DANNY
          Yeah all right.

                    C.J.
             (pause)
          All right, you'll gimme a couple of
          hours?

(CONTINUED)

14   CONTINUED: (4)   14

                         DANNY
                    You know I've got it, so off the record,
                    did we kill Shareef?

                              C.J.
                    Yeah.

And she exits as we

                                                              CUT TO:

15   **EXT. STREET - DAY**   15

TOBY and ANDY are getting out of TOBY's car. ANDY's
blindfolded. TOBY's helping her.

                         TOBY
                    All right, careful stepping out, there's
                    a street right there, there you go.

                         ANDY
                    You know if someone sees this they're
                    gonna call the police.

                         TOBY
                    I actually hadn't factored that into the
                    plan but that blindfold's about to come
                    off if you'll just come on over here and
                    go ahead...

ANDY takes the blindfold off and looks at what TOBY's brought
her there to see. A small but beautiful stone colonial at the
corner of a tree lined street.

                         ANDY
                       (pause)
                    You brought me to Jefferson Wyler's
                    house?

                         TOBY
                    Yeah.

                         ANDY
                    Why?

                         TOBY
                    Well every time we drive past you say
                    that it's your dream house.

                         ANDY
                    It is.

                                                              (CONTINUED)

15   CONTINUED: 15

                         TOBY
            And every time the Congressman's had us
            over you've said it was your dream house.

                         ANDY
            I wasn't lying.

                         TOBY
            You told Jeff Wyler that if he ever put
            it on the market you wanted to buy it.

                         ANDY
            I do.

                         TOBY
            Well it turns out he was gonna put it on
            the market but he's not anymore 'cause I
            bought it.

                         ANDY
            You bought this house?

                         TOBY
            Yeah.

                         ANDY
            You <u>bought</u> this house.

                         TOBY
            It's--yes, I did.

                         ANDY
            How did you afford it?

                         TOBY
            Well I put together some money for the
            down payment by selling my soul.

                         ANDY
            Can we go in?

                         TOBY
            Yeah.

      They walk into--

16   **INT. TOBY'S HOUSE - CONTINUOUS**   16

      The place is completely empty.

                         ANDY
            This is your house now.

                                                        (CONTINUED)

16   CONTINUED: 16

                          TOBY
             Well as a matter of fact it'll be your
             house if you say yes to this. Uh. Will
             you marry me?

                          ANDY
                    (pause)
             Oh. Toby. You gotta tell me that you
             didn't buy the house to...

                          TOBY
             No I mean--

                          ANDY
             I thought you were just moving out of the
             apartment and wanted to--

                          TOBY
             If we could get back to the original
             question.

                          ANDY
             Can you get the down payment back?

                          TOBY
             You're saying no.

                          ANDY
             Yeah, Toby, I've said no many times. I
             mean this is an incredible gesture, but--

                          TOBY
             I don't think you've noticed the things
             I've done to alter the behavior that's
             troubled you in the past. Giving up what
             you felt was a bachelor apartment is only
             the most recent of gestures, which
             include eating salads.

                          ANDY
             I have no problem with where we lived or
             what you ate. I do, but I don't care *that*
             much.

                          TOBY
             Then why aren't you remarrying me.

                          ANDY
             You don't really want to talk about this,
             do you?

                                              (CONTINUED)

                         TOBY
          Yeah, I do. Yeah. I thought you were just
          being cute. I just thought you were
          making me chase you as a punishment for
          the first marriage and that was okay with
          me, but--

                         ANDY
          I wasn't being cute, no.

                         TOBY
          Why?

                         ANDY
          You're just too sad for me, Toby.

                         TOBY
               (pause)
          What?

                         ANDY
          You're too sad for me. You're just sad,
          you bring the sadness home with you and
          you're sad.

                         TOBY
               (pause)
          I'm *not* sad.

                         ANDY
          You are. And I don't know if anything can
          change that but I can't.

                         TOBY
          I'm not sad, I take things seriously.

                         ANDY
          I take things seriously too.

                         TOBY
          I'm not comparing myself to anyone, I'm
          saying--

                         ANDY
          You're sad and you're angry and you're
          not warm. You take forever to trust
          someone.

                         TOBY
          Well my father used to kill people for a
          living so generationally the Zieglers are
          making lots of progress. I wouldn't worry
          about the kids.

                                          (CONTINUED)

                    ANDY
          I *do* worry about the kids.

                    TOBY
          Don't.

                    ANDY
          Because instead of showing them that the
          world is for *them*, you're gonna be
          telling them that they have to work hard
          in school so they can bone up for a life
          of hopelessness and despair.

                    TOBY
          Well wouldn't it be ironic if our kids
          were the only ones who were properly
          prepared.

                    ANDY
          Toby, I'm as serious a person as you are
          and I'm able to see the glass half full.

                    TOBY
          Great, half full, half empty, can we at
          least agree it's not full yet.

                    ANDY
          Well this is what I'm talking about.

                    TOBY
          That was a joke.

                    ANDY
          You indicated you wanted to talk about
          this seriously. I wish I hadn't said all
          that. That was a lot.

                    TOBY
              (pause)
          You--and you felt this way also when we
          were married, I mean it's not just now?

                    ANDY
          Come on. I'm sorry about that all. I'm
          really pregnant. Please. I take it all
          back.

                    TOBY
          Really. Come on. Did you feel that way
          when we were married? That I was sad?

                                        (CONTINUED)

16   CONTINUED: (4)   16

> ANDY
> No. I'm gonna go sit in the car. My
> ankles are starting you know--

> TOBY
> Do my friends feel like that?

> ANDY
> I'm so sorry I said that. Really. Come
> out to the car.

ANDY exits and TOBY stands alone in the house. He looks around
and thinks. And then--

> ANDY (OS)
> (yelling)
> *Toby!*

It takes TOBY a quick second to snap into it before he runs
outside to--

17   **EXT. HOUSE - CONTINUOUS**   17

--and ANDY's bracing herself against the car--

> ANDY
> My water broke.

FADE TO BLACK:

<u>END OF ACT TWO</u>

ACT THREE

FADE IN:

18   **INT. CORRIDOR - DAY** **(FORMERLY EXT. BACK DRIVEWAY)**   18

ABBEY, dressed for graduation, is heading to the motorcade and reading the speech with WILL next to her.

> WILL
> We just wrote 3900 words in five hours.

> ABBEY
> Well this is terrific so far.

> WILL
> Later, he quotes Cicero, Thomas Aquinas and Rudy Vallee in the space of two pages.

> ABBEY
> How does he connect them?

> WILL
> Three people you've never heard of.

> ABBEY
> It's about creativity.

> WILL
> Well he decided that's what he wanted to talk about, now the trick is he's gotta not change his mind.

And WILL says this as they walk into--

18A **INT. BACK FOYER - CONTINUOUS**   18A

--where BARTLET and his AGENTS are coming from the other corridor.

> BARTLET
> Good, you're here, I want to make some changes.

> ABBEY
> Jed--

> BARTLET
> Look at you, there is no way you have three adult children.

(CONTINUED)

18A CONTINUED: 18A

                          ABBEY
            You like the suit?

                          BARTLET
            I do, but the neck.

                          ABBEY
            What.

                          BARTLET
            It seems empty to me. Attention should be
            drawn to it.

And BARTLET takes a box out of his pocket...

                          BARTLET
            Nice job with the, you know, raising of
            the kid.

ABBEY takes a pearl necklace out of the box...

                          ABBEY
            They're beautiful.

                          BARTLET
            They're real, too, they can cut glass.

                          ABBEY
            That's diamonds that can cut glass.

                          BARTLET
            Well dammit what are these then?

                          WILL
            Excuse me, you said you wanted to make
            some changes, sir?

                          BARTLET
            Yeah, get in the car, we'll do it on the
            fly.

They walk out into--

18B **EXT. BACK DRIVEWAY - CONTINUOUS**   18B

--where the motorcade's waiting.

                          WILL
            Sir--

                          BARTLET
            Get in the car.

                                              (CONTINUED)

18B CONTINUED: 18B

They climb into--

19   **INT. BARTLET'S LIMO - CONTINUOUS**   19

                         WILL
              What kind of changes did you have in
              mind, sir.

                         BARTLET
              Small ones. Instead of talking about the
              internal muse I want to talk about the
              limits of reason and about passion and
              intuition in American life.

                         ABBEY
                    (looking in a mirror)
              These are just gorgeous.

                         BARTLET
              You can eat them, too, they're gumballs.

                         WILL
                    (into a phone)
              Ginger, tell site advance we're gonna
              need a really fast printer in the staff
              hold, there's no way this thing's gonna
              make it on the prompter, so let's get a
              nice leather folder with the Seal and, I
              don't know, a couple of cartons of
              cigarettes--

                         BARTLET
              I've got a folder. A Father's Day present
              from *another* one of my children who
              decided that living in their room for the
              rest of their life wasn't good enough.
                    (to the DRIVER)
              Coop?

                         COOPER
              Shoot 1, we're gonna go.

And the motorcycles roar past as the car pulls out--

                         WILL
              The limits of reason and passion and
              intuition in American life.

                         BARTLET
              Yes. Let's think.

                                                    CUT TO:

20   **INT. HOSPITAL ROOM - DAY**   20

ANDY's been hooked up to the things she needs to be hooked up
to and nurses are preparing the room for a delivery. TOBY's
there, obviously, but we get the sense that he's been benched
for this series of plays.

DR. GLAZER comes in. He's in his mid-30s and wears a baseball
cap.

                    GLAZER
          Andrea, what are you doing to me, we've
          got schedules, we've got bookkeepers.

                    ANDY
          What happened?

                    GLAZER
          Nothing happened, you're having a baby.
          Two of 'em as a matter of fact.

                    ANDY
          But it was supposed to be ten days?

                    GLAZER
          Yeah, well, what do you know.

                    ANDY
          Should I come back to the hospital?

                    GLAZER
          Come back to the--*Andy, your water broke.*
          You're having the baby now. This isn't
          gonna happen the way we talked about but
          it's gonna happen and it's gonna happen
          right now. You're at 10 centimeters,
          their heads are down there's no reason to
          do a C-section--Hey, Toby, I'm sorry, I
          didn't even see you there.

                    TOBY
          Is she gonna be able to get the epidural?

                    GLAZER
          Nah, we're gonna tough it out.

                    TOBY
          And when you say 'right now', what do you
          mean?

                    GLAZER
          Well you're gonna see at least one of
          your kids in about 15 minutes.

                                        (CONTINUED)

20   CONTINUED: 20

And TOBY may not know it yet, but the abstract nature of the
last nine months just got its first definable dimensions.

                    ANDY
          Toby.

TOBY comes over to the bed--

                    ANDY
          I can't believe--if I'd known this was
          gonna happen today I would never have--

                    TOBY
          No don't, what are you talkin' about,
          don't worry about it.

                    ANDY
          No, I know I hurt you back at the house.
          And I can't believe you bought the house.
          AAAGGHHH!
                    (to GLAZER)
          ALL RIGHT, YOUR HANDS ARE CLEAN ENOUGH,
          LET'S GO!!!

                    GLAZER
          Suction.

TOBY wraps a hand towel around his hand...

                    TOBY
          Bite my hand when it hurts.

                                                      CUT TO:

21   **INT. LEO'S OFFICE - DAY**   21

LEO's quickly signing some things and putting his jacket on so
that he can get to the graduation. MARGARET comes in with a
giftwrapped box.

                    MARGARET
          Here...is the pen.

                    LEO
          Look--

                    MARGARET
          I've giftwrapped the pen.

                    LEO
          It's a good pen.

                                                      (CONTINUED)

21 CONTINUED: 21

                         MARGARET
              You're giving Zoey a pen.

                         LEO
              It's not just a pen.

                         MARGARET
              Does it do other things?

                         LEO
              No, I meant it's a really good pen.

C.J. pops in the door--

                         C.J.
              He's meeting us in the Upper Press Room.

LEO walks out into--

22 **INT. CORRIDOR - CONTINUOUS**   22

                         LEO
              He said his link was the pilot?

                         C.J.
              Yeah, you know what he has?

                         LEO
              Well Shareef's pilot who died in the
              crash was Jamil Bari who had a Qumari
              passport and is alive, an American and
              not named Jamil Bari so he could have any
              number of things.

                         C.J.
                    (pause)
              Man...the things we can do.

                         LEO
              Yeah.

                         C.J.
              You're giving Zoey a pen?

                         LEO
              Yeah.

                         C.J.
              Does it do anything?

--and they turn a corner as we

                                                                       CUT TO:

22A **INT. PRESS BRIEFING ROOM/UPPER PRESS AREA - DAY**   22A

Monitors are showing a blue screen with the graphic:
PRESIDENT'S COMMENCEMENT ADDRESS AT GEORGETOWN UNIVERSITY. A
few REPORTERS are working in their seats.

DANNY's at a cubicle in front of his laptop. He's wearing
sunglasses and a baseball cap.

C.J. and LEO come in and LEO speaks quietly to DANNY--

> LEO
> Danny, C.J.'s gonna talk to you for a
> second and then you and I are gonna work
> together.
> (beat)
> Danny?

> C.J.
> He's asleep.

> LEO
> What are you talkin' about?

> C.J.
> He was in Augsburg, he hasn't slept yet.

> LEO
> So here's the national security threat?

> C.J.
> Well you gotta figure he's gonna wake up
> eventually.

> LEO
> When?

> C.J.
> (slapping the cubicle)
> *Wake up!*

> DANNY
> I heard every word you said, my covert
> skills are honed.

> LEO
> Good for you, follow me.

The three of them step outside into--

22B **INT. CORRIDOR - CONTINUOUS**   22B

They make sure it's private.

(CONTINUED)

                    C.J.
          We're at Threat Condition Bravo right
          now.

                    DANNY
          Why?

                    C.J.
               (making LEO say it)
          Why.

                    LEO
          'Cause five Bahji sleepers we were
          watching disappeared.

                    DANNY
          They disappeared?

                    LEO
          Yeah and it coincides with increased
          chatter we're hearing. You print we did
          this right now and I'm worried what the
          five guys are gonna do.

                    DANNY
          Three days, and I get an exclusive on the
          sleepers.

                    LEO
          Done.

                    C.J.
          Thank you.

                    LEO
          So you found the pilot?

                    DANNY
          Special Ops in Florida. He had an
          American passport when he went to flight
          school.

                    LEO
          In Augsburg.

                    DANNY
          Yeah.

                    LEO
               (smiling)
          The things we can do.

                                              (CONTINUED)

22B   CONTINUED: (2)   22B

They keep walking and we

                                                       CUT TO:

22C   **INT. LOBBY - CONTINUOUS**   22C

DONNA, dressed for graduation and heading for the door, is
intercepted by AMY, who's also dressed for the graduation.

                          AMY
                     (calling)
               Donna, I was just coming to see you. I
               love what you're wearing.

                          DONNA
               You too. I haven't been able to talk to
               Josh yet about the Wellingtons.

                          AMY
               Yeah, you don't need to, they're off the
               trip again, that's why I was coming.

                          DONNA
               Okay then, one less thing.

                          AMY
               Josh was offended 'cause I called the
               list a windfall, wasn't he.

They walk out onto--

22D   **EXT. BACK DRIVEWAY - CONTINUOUS**   22D

                          DONNA
               I'm sure he's not.

                          AMY
               I meant the list of candidates was good,
               I didn't mean--aye yi yi, why does he
               take these things this seriously?

                          DONNA
               If it bothered him he's forgotten about
               it by now. Like the car that was supposed
               to be here.

                          AMY
               Come in mine.

                                                       CUT TO:

23 **EXT. GEORGETOWN UNIVERSITY - DAY**   23

3000 seats have been set up for SPECTATORS and another 750 are
sitting empty, waiting for the GRADUATES of the College of
Arts and Sciences. The usual carnival atmosphere of graduation
day is increased by the presence of the national media and
threat level security. A double brass quintet is playing
Handel next to the stage that's been beautifully erected.

There's an area where the faculty, in their gowns, are waiting
for the processional. This is where we find BARTLET and WILL,
still working on the speech.

> BARTLET
> What do you think about using the Eudora
> Welty quote instead of the Gandhi.

> WILL
> Well I think they both work but since I
> wouldn't make any more changes, I'd stay
> with--

> BARTLET
> "You must be the change"--is that it--
> "You must be the change you wish to see
> in the world," it sounds too much like
> Eastern philosophy.

> WILL
> Well it was bound to, sir.

> BARTLET
> 'Cause Gandhi lived in India.

> WILL
> Yeah. Sir, this speech is about
> creativity and in my judgement it's a
> home run. Now what it *isn't* is a speech
> that will convince Zoey not to go to
> France tomorrow.

> BARTLET
> *Well let's write that one.*

And we HEAR the double quintet strike up *Pomp and
Circumstance.*

> AIDE
> Mr. President?

BARTLET understands it's time. He zips up his gown, which
includes the requisite chevrons for his degrees, honors and
disciplines and two cowls. The uniform of academic knighthood.

(CONTINUED)

23   CONTINUED: 23

                         CHANCELLOR
              Are you ready, Mr. President?

                         BARTLET
              Yeah. Thanks, Will, for the help.

                         WILL
                   (smiles)
              Use the Eudora Welty, it's better.

                         BARTLET
              Thank you.

And BARTLET and the CHANCELLOR, also impressively decked out
in academic badges, lead the procession of FACULTY in their
gowns and as they come out, the SPECTATORS all stand and
APPLAUD.

                         CHANCELLOR
              I understand you're not using the
              TelePrompter.

                         BARTLET
              Yeah, no, I've got it down here in this
              folder...and on some napkins in my
              pockets.

                         CHANCELLOR
              Are you gonna be all right with that?

                         BARTLET
              Oh yeah, I'll be fine, you know unless
              something comes up.

                         CHANCELLOR
              Like what?

                         BARTLET
              Well for instance I just realized I don't
              have access to my pockets anymore, but
              you know, what are you gonna do.

                                        FADE TO BLACK:

                       END OF ACT THREE

ACT FOUR

FADE IN:

24   **EXT. NATIONAL ARBORETUM - NIGHT**   24

The place is closed, deserted and dark, with all the nocturnal
sounds of nature. From the darkness we hear--

                    JOSH
          Charlie?

                    CHARLIE
          Yeah.

                    JOSH
          I need you to tell me now that you have
          some sense of where we're going and that
          we're not, you know, spending the night
          here, that we're not making *camp*.

JOSH and CHARLIE are walking fairly slowly, both because they
don't want to make any noise and because it's incredibly hard
to see.

                    CHARLIE
          You were the one who said dig up the
          champagne and give it to her tonight.

                    JOSH
          But didn't I almost immediately take it
          back?

                    CHARLIE
          No, I liked it, it was a good idea, send
          her off knowing we're cool.

                    JOSH
          Are you sure?

                    CHARLIE
          No.

                    JOSH
          It's pretty dark.

SPLASH splash SPLASH SPLASH--

                    JOSH
          Yeah, we're in a brook now.

                    CHARLIE
          Good, I think it was near a brook.

                                        (CONTINUED)

24   CONTINUED: 24

And CHARLIE and JOSH are indeed standing knee deep in a brook
about the size and danger of what you'd find on a public golf
course.

And we HEAR a call hoo-*HOO*.

                    JOSH
          It's like I'm in 'Nam basically, I'm in a
          rice paddy.

                    CHARLIE
          Yeah, you'd have done well there.

                    JOSH
          I didn't put on socks, I'm really happy
          with that decision.

                    CHARLIE
          Did you just hear something?

                    JOSH
          No, did you?

                    CHARLIE
          Like a radio crackle?

                    JOSH
          Or a buzzard?

                    CHARLIE
          Over there, there's a car.

                    JOSH
          We're busted. Thank God.

                    CHARLIE
          No that car isn't marked.

                    VOICE (JAMIE)
          Is someone there?

                    CHARLIE
               (pause)
          Hello?

                    VOICE (JAMIE)
          Yeah, I'm a Federal Officer, is someone
          there?

                    CHARLIE
          Jamie?

                                                      (CONTINUED)

24 CONTINUED: (2)   24

                        JAMIE
              Charlie?

                        CHARLIE
              What are you doing here?

                        JAMIE
                   (into sleeve)
              P3, Charlie Young's coming.

                        CHARLIE
              You're kidding me.

And CHARLIE takes off...

                        JOSH
              Josh Lyman. I'm with him. I'm gonna stay
              here, though, 'cause you know...

                                                        CUT TO:

25 **EXT. ASIAN GARDEN - NIGHT**   25

CHARLIE hustles in. He sees a sign that says *Paeonia Japonica*
and then hears--

                        ZOEY (OS)
              You're late.

CHARLIE turns to see ZOEY sitting on the ground against a rock
with a bottle of champagne.

                        CHARLIE
              You're here.

                        ZOEY
                   (pause)
              It's 10:07, I've been here for seven
              minutes.

                        CHARLIE
              Well you drove in in a sedan, I had to
              climb over the wall.

                        ZOEY
              Shouldn't you have allowed for that.

CHARLIE smiles...

                        CHARLIE
              I didn't think you were gonna be here.

                                                   (CONTINUED)

25   CONTINUED:

                              ZOEY
          Why'd you come?

                              CHARLIE
          I was gonna dig up the bottle and give it
          to you as a graduation present, why'd you
          come?

                              ZOEY
          Oh. To drink it.
               (beat)
          I'm kidding, I came 'cause I thought you
          might too.
               (beat)
          Though I have been drinking it.

                              CHARLIE
          You know there are people at a party that
          radio station's throwing. At that techno
          place that looks like the end of the
          world. I think they went 'cause you said
          you'd be winding up there.
               (beat)
          I didn't come 'cause I thought you'd be
          here, I wasn't trying to--

                              ZOEY
          You don't want to have the champagne with
          me?

                              CHARLIE
          No, no, I do.
               (beat)
          I do. I just thought if I should call
          people and tell 'em--

                              ZOEY
          You're such a good guy. You were raised
          in horror, what is it along the way that
          made you a good guy?

                              CHARLIE
               (pause--then offering some
                possibilities)
          I try to eat right.
               (pause)
          You know what's funny is, when I first
          saw the note--

     And ZOEY kisses CHARLIE for a long moment and then CHARLIE
     pulls away--

                                                        (CONTINUED)

                    CHARLIE
        We shouldn't do that.

                    ZOEY
        I know.

                    CHARLIE
        What's going on?

                    ZOEY
        Nothing.

                    CHARLIE
        Come on.

                    ZOEY
        Don't ask me that now.

                    CHARLIE
        I am asking you.

                    ZOEY
        Nothing, just you know, a lot of things.
        Dumb stuff. Jean Paul wants me to take a
        hit of ecstasy with him tonight.

                    CHARLIE
        Okay, but your kids are gonna have gills.

                    ZOEY
        I don't care about that, I'm honestly,
        I'm worried a little about my father.
        You've seen his hand shaking and his
        vision go. My leaving for three months
        isn't gonna do him any favors.
            (beat)
        And I'm confused about you.

                    CHARLIE
        Well, I can't advise you on that.

                    ZOEY
        Why not?

                    CHARLIE
        Because I think this is tonight and
        tomorrow you're on the Concorde.

                    ZOEY
        I deserved that.
            (pause)
        You think we could just sit here and
        enjoy the night for a while?

                                        (CONTINUED)

25   CONTINUED: (3)   25

                              CHARLIE
                    Actually, I think this is a bad time in a
                    person's life to stop showing up at
                    places they say they're gonna show up.

                              ZOEY
                    I should go to the party.

                              CHARLIE
                    Yeah.

ZOEY takes CHARLIE and kisses him again, then goes off
silently into the darkness. After a moment we hear a flash of
radio crackle.

CHARLIE leans back against the rock, digests the last two
minutes, and then shakes his head as if trying to understand
why he just sent her back to Jean Paul before--

                              JOSH (OS)
                         (calling)
                    I'm not wearing any socks over here!

                              CHARLIE
                         (calling back)
                    Yeah yeah.

And CHARLIE heads back to JOSH as we

                                                            CUT TO:

25aA   **INT. SITUATION ROOM - NIGHT**   25aA

LEO, FITZ, NANCY, a few others. Very informal. It's the end of
a day.

                              NANCY
                         (getting off the phone)
                    Well the FBI's got the crew of the
                    container ship accounted for.

                              LEO
                         (just out of curiosity)
                    What're the rules on questioning foreign
                    nationals?

                              NANCY
                    I think we can keep 'em for up to seven
                    days, isolation, well-lit room.

                              LEO
                    What's the well-lit room for?

                                                            (CONTINUED)

25aA CONTINUED: 25aA

> FITZWALLACE
> Sleep deprivation.

> LEO
> All right, let's go around the table one
> last time. Where are we with this, what
> kind of day has it been?

CUT TO:

25A **INT. JOSH'S BULLPEN - NIGHT**   25A

DONNA's the only one working there. AMY comes in with a note
she was about to leave at DONNA's desk--

> DONNA
> You're here late.

> AMY
> I can't believe *you're* here, I was gonna
> leave a note on your desk.

> DONNA
> I had a thing cancel, so I'm catching up.

> AMY
> I just wanted to let you know the
> Wellingtons are back on.

> DONNA
> For APEC?

> AMY
> Yeah.

> DONNA
> It's gonna be a problem.

> AMY
> I know, but Human Rights Watch, Amnesty,
> we need their help three times a week. Is
> there a side meeting they can play a role
> in?

> DONNA
> There might be, that's a good idea.

> AMY
> You got a few minutes to work with me?

(CONTINUED)

25A   CONTINUED: 25A

                          DONNA
                    Yeah.

                                                        CUT TO:

25B   **EXT. TECHNO CLUB/BACK - NIGHT**   25B

                          MOLLY
                    (into her sleeve)
                    There are 132 cars parked there.

                                                        CUT TO:

25C   **EXT. TECHNO CLUB/FRONT - NIGHT**   25C

                          WESLEY
                    (into sleeve)
                    You counted the cars?
                    (beat, into sleeve)
                    Randy, Molly counted the cars. Do you
                    believe that?

                                                        CUT TO:

26   **INT. TECHNO CLUB - NIGHT**   26

The place is jam packed and thumping. RANDY looks around, then
talks into her sleeve.

                          RANDY
                    (into sleeve)
                    All right, she's clear.

ZOEY comes in alone and is immediately met with shrieks from
her GIRLFRIENDS as they all hug each other--

                          JEAN PAUL
                    Now when is it my turn?

                          ZOEY
                    Hi, I'm sorry I'm late.

                          JEAN PAUL
                    Yes, where were you, you've been missed.

                          ZOEY
                    I was at the National Arboretum if you
                    can believe that.

                          JEAN PAUL
                    As long as you're here now.

                                                        (CONTINUED)

26   CONTINUED: 26

                    ZOEY
          Can we talk for a minute?

                    JEAN PAUL
          Of course.

                                              CUT TO:

27   **INT. JOSH'S BULLPEN - NIGHT**   (**FORMERLY EXT. TECHNO CLUB**)   27

DONNA's at her desk and AMY's gotten a couple of bottles of
beer.

                    DONNA
          There's a side meeting, closed to the
          press, on Agricultural concentration.

                    AMY
          I was thinking more in the human rights
          family.

                    DONNA
          A group session on displaced workers.

                    AMY
          What about prison labor?

                    DONNA
          No, but labor law enforcement, a joint
          DOL/USTR session.

                    AMY
          Sold.

                    DONNA
          There it is.

                    AMY
          I'm not gonna get an answer about what I
          said to Josh, am I? It's just eating at
          me.

                    DONNA
          I don't know why.

                    AMY
          'Cause it's eating at *him* and *I* don't
          know why.

                    DONNA
          Really?

                                              CUT TO:

27A   **INT. SITUATION ROOM - NIGHT**   27A

                         NANCY
             Well there was a credit card charge at a
             Mobile station in La Grande, Oregon to
             John H. Fajid which is an a/k/a used by
             Salam Mohammed. Local law enforcement's
             sending a sketch from the gas attendant.

                         FITZWALLACE
             What'd they buy?

                         NANCY
             I don't know.

                         LEO
             How the hell *did* we lose these people?

                         NANCY
             I don't know.

                         LEO
             All right, but one of these days the
             President's gonna need a better answer
             than that.

                         FITZWALLACE
                  (reading)
             Gas, Fritos and a Yoo-Hoo.
                  (beat)
             What John Fajid bought at the Mobile
             station.

                                                      CUT TO:

28   **INT. TECHNO CLUB - NIGHT**   28

     ZOEY and JEAN PAUL in a dark corner with two drinks. A good
     eye would notice that ZOEY's face is starting to look
     overheated.

                         JEAN PAUL
             Well three months is a long time. Maybe
             you just come for a few weeks, we go to
             some parties, and then you decide.

                         ZOEY
                  (beat)
             Maybe...but then I guess the whole point
             was to...was to check out, so...going
             just for parties doesn't seem--

                                                  (CONTINUED)

28 CONTINUED: 28

                              JEAN PAUL
                    The parties are at night, you can't check
                    out during the day?

                              ZOEY
                    I'm sorry, we're having this conversation
                    and I'm just feeling a little light-
                    headed. I had champagne before and now
                    I'm mixing it with this.

                              JEAN PAUL
                    Well light-headed is good. Better than
                    the opposite.

                                                       CUT TO:

29   **INT. PRESS BRIEFING ROOM - NIGHT**   **(FORMERLY EXT. STREET)**   29

DANNY's in his cubicle tapping away. C.J. comes in from the
far end to retrieve something at the podium, then sees him.

                              C.J.
                         (calling)
                    Danny?

                              DANNY
                         (still typing)
                    Yeah.

                              C.J.
                    What are you doing here, why aren't you
                    asleep?

                              DANNY
                         (still typing)
                    I really don't know.

                              C.J.
                    Well what are you writing?

                              DANNY
                         (still typing)
                    A volume of springtime haiku.

                              C.J.
                    Three days, Daniel.

                              DANNY
                    I'm filing in three days, I've still
                    gotta write it.

                                                      (CONTINUED)

29   CONTINUED: 29

> C.J.
> The President's speech was good this
> afternoon, didn't you think?

> DANNY
> You wanna comment on a wire report that
> says the President lifted his gown and
> groped himself during the Invocation?

> C.J.
> Yeah, that was a troubling moment but he
> had to get his napkins.

> DANNY
> All right, then you want to comment on a
> Gulfstream jet flown by--

> C.J.
> Madras Research Project. That's what
> we'll call it for a few days.

                                                CUT TO:

30   **OMITTED (MOVED TO SCENE 32B)**   30

31   **EXT. TECHNO CLUB - NIGHT**   31

JOSH, in dry clothes now, is leaning up against WESLEY's car
and drinking a beer.

> JOSH
> We *scaled* the wall, we didn't hop it, it
> was like 30 feet high, it was like a
> castle gate and we took it.
>   (beat)
> Buzzards and wilderness life everywhere.

> WESLEY
>   (into sleeve)
> Someone give me a SitRep, please, anyone,
> I'll take any news at all.

> JOSH
> But it was at the pricker bushes I became
> a man.

                                                CUT TO:

32   **OMITTED**   32

32A   **INT. JOSH'S BULLPEN - NIGHT**   32A

> AMY
> I understand why Josh may have been
> offended by what I said, even though it
> was misinterpreted, but what I don't
> understand is that both times we've
> spoken about it it seemed like you were
> too.

> DONNA
> No, I understood what you were saying.

> AMY
> Why doesn't Josh? Why does he take these
> things so seriously?

> DONNA
> He worked for Hoynes for a long time,
> there was a reason.

> AMY
> He left him.

> DONNA
> And if you think *that* was easy, you're
> crazy, Josh doesn't leave people.

CUT TO:

32B   **INT. TECHNO CLUB - NIGHT**   **(FORMERLY SCENE 30)**   32B

The dark corner with JEAN PAUL and ZOEY...

> ZOEY
> I don't want to lie to you...but I don't
> want to--I'm sorry, I meant, I don't want
> to hurt you, but I shouldn't lie to you,
> either. Yes, I, yes, I...
> (beat)
> ...I obviously have, still have feelings
> for Charlie. And my father, you know, he
> won't say so, but I think--did you put
> ecstasy in my drink?

> JEAN PAUL
> No.

> ZOEY
> I feel very strange.

> JEAN PAUL
> You're drunk, enjoy it?

(CONTINUED)

32B CONTINUED: 32B

             ZOEY
You didn't put--

          JEAN PAUL
I put a little bit, I put a half.

             ZOEY
       (pause)
Wow. I kinda wish you hadn't done that.

          JEAN PAUL
You're not sick, it's how you're supposed
to be feeling. Listen to the music.

             ZOEY
       (pause)
Yeah, I'm okay. I'm gonna go to the
restroom and put some water on my face.
We should--I don't want to hurt you.

ZOEY heads off and disappears as we

                              CUT TO:

32C **INT. PRESS BRIEFING ROOM - NIGHT**   32C

            DANNY
I'm gonna need the following five
questions answered to start with, you
wanna write these down?

            C.J.
I don't want to write anything down right
now.

            DANNY
Was Madras Research retaliatory or
preemptive. Were any allies in the Arab
world, or Israel for that matter,
notified either before or after. How
involved were Congressional leaders and
how involved will they be in the next few
days.

            C.J.
I don't know, but the answer to the last
two questions'll be the same.

            DANNY
Especially in the absence of Executive
Orders rendering them legal--

                         (CONTINUED)

32C   CONTINUED: 32C

                         C.J.
          There was an NSC Decision Directive.

                         DANNY
          --does this create a precedent for
          future...Madras Research Projects.

                         C.J.
          That was four, what's the fifth?

                         DANNY
          Does the President or his national
          security advisers fear attempts at
          retribution?

                                                        CUT TO:

33   **INT. JOSH'S BULLPEN - NIGHT (FORMERLY EXT. TECHNO CLUB)**   33

                         AMY
          I get that he was close to Hoynes, what I
          don't get--

                         DONNA
          You have to get Josh. His sister died in
          a fire while she was babysitting him. She
          tried to put it out and he ran outside.
          He went off campaigning and his father
          died. He wakes up in a hospital and
          discovers the *President*'s been shot. He
          goes through every day worried that
          someone he likes is gonna die and it's
          gonna be his fault. What do you think
          makes him walk so fast?

                         AMY
                    (pause)
          Does he really think that if he'd never
          left Hoynes he could've stopped it from
          happening?

                         DONNA
          Without question he does. And he would
          have. Anyway, when you looked at the list
          of replacements and said, "That's a
          windfall", what he heard was "Thank you,
          Josh, you did it again. More for us."

                         AMY
                    (pause)
          You said, "You have to get Josh."

                                                    (CONTINUED)

33 CONTINUED: 33

                         DONNA
                    (pause)
              Yeah, that was, I didn't mean to say that
              you don't...
                    (pause)
              ...get him.

                         AMY
              Are you in love with Josh?

                                                        CUT TO:

34   **EXT. WESLEY'S CAR - NIGHT**   34

                         JOSH
              It's true, though. You adapt to the
              terrain. For instance, after a little
              while I just said to hell with it and
              took my pants off.

                         WESLEY
                    (into sleeve)
              Randy, does it look like she's thinking
              about leaving?

                                                  INTERCUT WITH:

35   **INT. TECHNO CLUB - NIGHT**   35

       JAMIE and RANDY are at two different positions. JAMIE's
       looking across the crowded sea of heads and the back of one
       looks like ZOEY.

                         RANDY
              Well she's still in the restroom.

                         JAMIE
              No, she's not, I got her right here.

                         RANDY
              You have her?

                         JAMIE
              No, check that, I'm wrong.

                         WESLEY
              Oh come on, people, get past the first
              day kinks.

                         RANDY
              I think she's still in the restroom.

                                                  (CONTINUED)

35   CONTINUED: 35

And now we're with WESLEY on the street. He wanted something
more definitive in that last report.

But nothing's coming...And in the silence, JOSH even seems to
have a canine sense that something's not right...

                    WESLEY
          All right, I want a 20 on Bookbag right
          now.

                    RANDY
          I'll go into the restroom.

                    WESLEY
          No, keep your distance, let her get
          pissed at me.

And WESLEY goes across the street and heads into--

36   **INT. TECHNO CLUB - NIGHT**   36

--as WESLEY comes in. He takes the arm of a WAITRESS--

                    WESLEY
          Excuse me, I'm with the Secret Service,
          do you work here?

                    WAITRESS
          Yeah, is something wrong?

                    WESLEY
          No. Would you mind going into the ladies
          room for me please and checking to see if
          anyone's in there.

                    WAITRESS
          Yeah.

WESLEY follows the WAITRESS into--

36A   **INT. BACK CORRIDOR/RESTROOM AREA - CONTINUOUS**   36A

The WAITRESS heads into the ladies room. A moment later she
comes out.

                    WAITRESS
          There's no one in there.

                    WESLEY
          Would you mind checking again?

The WAITRESS goes back in again and comes out--

                                                        (CONTINUED)

36A   CONTINUED: 36A

                         WAITRESS
                    No.

                         WESLEY
                    (into sleeve)
                    P2, Molly, did she come out back, are
                    there people back there?
                    (pause)
                    Molly, are you reading this?
                    (to the WAITRESS)
                    This is the fire alley?

                         WAITRESS
                    (nervous now)
                    Yeah.

WESLEY goes through a fire door and into--

36B   **EXT. ALLEY - CONTINUOUS**   36B

                         WESLEY
                    (into sleeve)
                    P2, Molly, what's your position?

And then he sees it. A dark object on the ground. He picks it
up. It's ZOEY's panic button with her keys attached.

And no sooner does he quickly register that, then he sees
MOLLY, the one who flipped him this morning, lying on the
ground with a bullet in her head.

                         WESLEY
                    (into sleeve)
                    Bookbag's been taken, she's been taken
                    and I've got an agent down. Go to black,
                    we're black. Close the streets and keep
                    the planes on the ground.

                                                          CUT TO:

37   37
and   **OMITTED**   and
38   38

38A   **INT. SITUATION ROOM - NIGHT**   38A

LEO, FITZWALLACE and NANCY. It's been a long day. NANCY hangs
up the phone.

                         NANCY
                    FBI Field Office has all 98 members of
                    the *Agile* crew at Sheridan Federal Prison
                    for interrogation.

                                                       (CONTINUED)

38A CONTINUED: 38A

FITZWALLACE is dead tired and that struck him as amusing...

                    NANCY
          It's not funny, apparently the Captain's
          scared to death. *His* manifest only says
          45 containers, he swears it's a typo.

                    LEO
               (rolling down his sleeves and
                putting on his jacket)
          Well if it turns out we closed the Port
          of Portland because of a typo it's only
          gonna fuel Margaret's insanity. I'm gonna
          go home for a few hours. Call me if
          something happens.

LEO walks outside into--

38B **INT. CORRIDOR - CONTINUOUS**   38B

--where he's immediately confronted by the rapid footfalls of
BUTTERFIELD and two other AGENTS as they rush down the stairs--

                    LEO
          Ron?

                    BUTTERFIELD
          We have a situation. We're up at black
          and procedurally, the Chief of Staff is
          told before--

                    LEO
          What's happened?

                    BUTTERFIELD
          Zoey Bartlet's missing and there's a dead
          agent at the scene.

LEO looks at BUTTERFIELD for the longest time, and then he
does something we've never seen him do...he starts to run. He
runs up--

38C **INT. STAIRWAY - CONTINUOUS**   38C

--and into--

38D **INT. CORRIDOR - CONTINUOUS**   38D

--where two AGENTS fall in with him on his way through--

39   **INT. OVAL OFFICE - CONTINUOUS**   39

--where he heads onto--

40   **EXT. PORTICO - CONTINUOUS**   40

--where a few more AGENTS join him from FIDERER's office and
the Mural Room and he turns the corner and heads into--

41   **INT. THE GREAT HALL - CONTINUOUS**   41

--a place we've never been before. A huge and beautiful
hallway connecting the West Wing to the East Wing. And as LEO
runs down the hall, a few more AGENTS fall in behind him and
we

                                    BLACKOUT.

<u>END OF SHOW</u>

TWENTY FIVE

TRACY

It's out. Access Hollywood has it, you have to tell them now.

ME

Fuck.

This wasn't the plan. Tommy and I had wanted to take the show to its 100th episode (the 12th of Season 5) before handing it over to John, Chris, Alex and Kevin and riding into the sunset. But for various reasons of no interest it was not to be.

So on a morning in the first week of May, Tommy and I were on a conference call with our agent, Ari Emanuel; my lawyer, Rich Heller; and my publicist, Tracy Shaffer. We'd been seriously mulling our resignations for the past few days after semi-seriously mulling them for the previous six weeks and twelve hours earlier we'd made our decision and written a press release.

Tracy was to wait for a call from me saying that everyone had been told and the release could go out but somehow the news got out and it was truly only a matter of minutes before the cast and crew were hearing it from someone else, and we didn't want that.

Tommy and I went over to the stage where the entire cast, with the exception of Janel, was shooting a scene on the Oval Office set. We took them into another room.

"Neither Tommy or I will back next season," I said.

I don't remember anything that happened after that. From the cast and crew, from Kevin and the staff, from Chris and Alex and from Tommy, I couldn't have gotten a nicer parting gift than these final two episodes of the fourth season.

Here's *Twenty Five*.

The West Wing

25

WHITE 2 REVISIONS:	05/05/03
CHERRY REVISIONS:	04/29/03
SALMON REVISIONS:	04/28/03
BUFF REVISIONS:	04/28/03
GREEN REVISIONS:	04/25/03
YELLOW REVISIONS:	04/21/03
PINK REVISIONS:	04/21/03
BLUE REVISIONS:	04/21/03

THE WEST WING

"Twenty Five"

Written by
Aaron Sorkin

Directed by
Christopher Misiano

PRODUCTION #175-323
Episode Twenty-Two

JOHN WELLS PRODUCTIONS
in association with
WARNER BROS. TELEVISION
4000 Warner Blvd.
Burbank, CA 91522

Final Shooting Script
April 20, 2003
Copyright © 2003
Warner Bros. Television
All Rights Reserved

DATE	COLOR	PAGES
04/21/03	BLUE PAGES	5,46,47-50
04/21/03	PINK PAGES	CAST,SETS,4-5,10,18,29, 43
04/21/03	YELLOW PAGES	CAST,6,6A,21
04/25/03	GREEN PAGES	CAST,4-5,18,43,55,56,58, 59,60,61,62,63
04/28/03	BUFF PAGES	CAST,31,31A
04/28/03	SALMON PAGES	39,39A,40,40A,41,42,42A
04/29/03	CHERRY PAGES	52,59,59A,60,61,61A
05/05/03	WHITE 2 PAGES	CAST,31

SET LIST

INTERIORS
WHITE HOUSE
Bartlet Family Room
Corridors
Situation Room
C.J.'s Office
C.J.'s Outer Office
Press Briefing Room
Communications Bullpen
Toby's Office
Josh's Bullpen
Oval Office
Leo's Office
Lobby
Outside Situation Room
Stairway
Cabinet Room

MAKESHIFT INTERROGATION
ROOM

HOSPITAL
Maternity Ward/Nurses Stat.
Hospital Room
Corridor

CAPITOL BUILDING
Corridor

EXTERIORS
TECHNO CLUB - NIGHT

PORTICO - NIGHT

WHITE HOUSE/BACK ENTRANCE -
NIGHT

CAPITOL BUILDING/BASEMENT
ENTRANCE - NIGHT

PENNSYLVANIA AVENUE (MOTOR-
CADE) - NIGHT

THE WEST WING

"Twenty Five"

CAST LIST

PRESIDENT JOSIAH BARTLET
LEO McGARRY
JOSH LYMAN
SAM SEABORN
TOBY ZIEGLER
C.J. CREGG
CHARLIE YOUNG
DONNA MOSS
ABIGAIL BARTLET
AMY GARDNER

WESLEY DAVIS
JAMIE REED
BUTTERFIELD
MIKE CASPER
FITWALLACE
NANCY MCNALLY
RANDY WEATHERS
JEAN PAUL
CAROL

WILL BAILEY	TV #3 *
MARK	TV #4 *
KATIE	CONTROLLER #1 (V.O.)
STEVE	CONTROLLER #2 (V.O.) GEN-
GINGER	ERAL
MARGARET	PILOT (V.O.)
	BEECH
PEGGY	NURSE
JILL	AGRICULTURE SECRETARY
GWEN	LABOR SECRETARY
JERRY	INTERIOR SECRETARY
JAY	HUD SECRETARY
ANDREW	VET AFFAIRS SECRETARY
BANKS	TREASURY SECRETARY
PARAMEDIC	GLENALLEN WALKEN
LYLE	JUSTICE SHARON DAY
DR. WELLMAN	GERI
TV #1 *	AGENT #2
TV #2 *	AGENT #3

506

"25"

FADE IN:

1   **INT. BARTLET FAMILY ROOM - NIGHT**   1

Jazz plays and drinks are being consumed as BARTLET and ABBEY
are entertaining three other couples, all parents of friends
of Zoey's at Georgetown.

ABBEY's with the wives...

                    PEGGY
          My husband's been having some empty nest
          problems.

                    JILL
          David's been sighing all week, has the
          President been sighing?

                    ABBEY
          Please, Jed's been sighing, he's been
          sighing in all kinds of dead languages.

                    GWEN
          Those pearls really are beautiful.

                    ABBEY
          Thank you.
              (beat)
          Yeah, the men aren't taking this well.

ABBEY's talking about the husbands, who are sitting on the
other side of the room, their heads down in their drinks like
they're at a wake. BARTLET's got a photo album that's got a
lot of pictures that haven't been pasted into place, and he's
got a bourbon on the rocks.

                    ABBEY
              (calling)
          Fellas, you know, we're all having a good
          time over here.

                    BARTLET
              (calling back)
          We're having a good time here too.

                    ABBEY
          Doing what?

                                              (CONTINUED)

1   CONTINUED: 1

> BARTLET
> Talking about the too rapid passage of
> time and, you know, grieving.

> ABBEY
> He's scheduling nine White House visits
> to France over the next three months,
> he's gonna accept every invitation, he'll
> be a judge at the Cannes Film Festival.

> BARTLET
> (tossing a photo on the table)
> I told you it was this one. That's the
> day we brought her home from the
> hospital. Tell me that wasn't a *month*
> ago. What the hell is she doing
> graduating summa cum laude from
> something.

And with that, LEO appears in the door, BUTTERFIELD and the
AGENTS somewhere behind him. LEO must've slipped and hit
something on his run to the residence, 'cause his jacket's a
little torn and his face might be scratched.

> JERRY
> Remember the ride home from the hospital?
> The scariest drive of your life?

BARTLET sees LEO and immediately takes in that something very
wrong has happened. He gets up and goes to the doorway,
mindlessly carrying the photobook and the drink with him as
the conversation between the husbands continues.

> JAY
> Seven miles an hour with the hazard
> lights on all the way home.

> ANDREW
> I can't even remember, did we have baby
> seats then or did we just hold on very
> tight?

> JAY
> Oh yeah, they had these--honey, were
> there baby seats when Jackie was born?

> PEGGY
> Yes, of course there were baby--there
> were baby seats, indoor plumbing--

> JAY
> It was 21 years ago, I can't remember
> what hotel we stayed at last night.

                                                    (CONTINUED)

1   CONTINUED: (2)   1

                    GWEN
          I wore all my jewelry to the hospital
          when George was born, I don't know why.

                    ANDREW
          To show off?

                    GWEN
          Just out of curiosity, what exactly out
          of my fine *collection* at the time would I
          have been showing off?

Of course we're not paying attention to any of this. What
we're watching, but not able to hear, is BARTLET maybe
starting to ask what happened to LEO's face or jacket but
before he can get very far, LEO says something to him quickly.
Then something else, then BUTTERFIELD speaks, and then we see
about 30 loose photographs fall to the floor, followed by the
photo album and the bourbon glass crashing.

Which makes ABBEY's head whip around and BARTLET's staring
dead at her and we

                                              SMASH CUT TO:

MAIN TITLES

                        END OF TEASER

ACT ONE

FADE IN:

2   **OMITTED**   2

3   **EXT. TECHNO CLUB - NIGHT**   3

Cars are screeching around the corner and unloading law
enforcement and investigators. SWAT teams are hurrying out of
vehicles. Yellow police tape is being run around the area.
Control of the crime scene is being taken over as WESLEY comes
out of the club and starts talking to an FBI AGENT as he walks--

                    WESLEY
          They know there are two more exits on the
          South side?

                    FBI AGENT
          They're sealed.

TITLE:
                         Hour 1

                    WESLEY
          We're prioritizing staff and bystanders
          for interviews.

                    FBI AGENT
          Yeah.

                    WESLEY
          And Harbor Patrol's got the Potomac?

                    FBI AGENT
          Yes sir.
               (shouting out)
          Forensics!

JOSH and CHARLIE are together and have no idea what's
happening. JOSH sees WESLEY--

                    JOSH
               (calling)
          Wes, what the hell is going on?

                    WESLEY
          She's been taken.

                    JOSH
               (pause)
          What?

                                                   (CONTINUED)

3   CONTINUED: 3

                          CHARLIE
              What are you talkin' about?

                          AGENT #2
                    (shouting over)
              Wes, how many?

                          WESLEY
                    (shouting back)
              188, 24 staff.

                          CHARLIE
              What are you talking about?

                          WESLEY
              Zoey's been taken. We had her going into
              the bathroom and she's gone.

                          JOSH
              I don't understand.

                          WESLEY
              Somebody took her near the bathroom, they
              used force.

                          CHARLIE
              She's messin' with you.

                          WESLEY
              No--

                          AGENT #3
                    (shouting)
              There's local news over there--

                          WESLEY
                    (shouting back)
              There were here for--it doesn't matter,
              we moved 'em away. Charlie--

                          CHARLIE
              Wes, she's messin' with you, I'm telling
              you, she's at a Baskin-Robbins with her
              girlfriends right now, you gotta call
              these people off.

                          WESLEY
              They shot one of my agents.
                    (beat)
              Charlie. Molly's dead, they shot Molly.

                          CHARLIE
              Molly's dead?

                                              (CONTINUED)

3   CONTINUED: (2)   3

There's a long silence as JOSH and CHARLIE begin to understand what's unfolded...

Then CHARLIE turns to head off down the street--

> CHARLIE
> Well they couldn't have--

> WESLEY
> Charlie--

> CHARLIE
> They couldn't have gotten very far, how long--

> WESLEY
> Charlie, you gotta stay here.

> CHARLIE
> My car's around the corner.

> JOSH
> We need to stay here. They're gonna need to--

> CHARLIE
> No, I'm gonna drive around.

> JOSH
> They're gonna need to talk to us.

> CHARLIE
> How far could they have--they couldn't have gotten--

> JOSH
> We have to--

> CHARLIE
> Get offa me.

> JOSH
> Listen to me, they've already dropped a net on the city, they've already dropped a net. These guys aren't gettin'
> *anywhere.*
>> (beat)
> They're not gonna let us leave right now, we were the last people to see her before she went in the club, they're gonna want to have a word with us.

JOSH waits a moment before...

                                        (CONTINUED)

3   CONTINUED: (3)   3

                              JOSH
                    Wes, we need to be interviewed *now*, we
                    have to get back to the President.

                                                                  CUT TO:

4   **INT. WHITE HOUSE HALLS - NIGHT**   4

BARTLET, LEO, BUTTERFIELD and a few AGENTS are making quick
time to the Situation Room. BUTTERFIELD's on a secure phone
and reports on the conversation he's listening to.

                              BUTTERFIELD
                    Metro Police and the FBI have roadblocks
                    around Georgetown and they've already
                    closed down Key Bridge and Memorial
                    Bridge and Route 29.

                              LEO
                    FBI's putting up a command post at OEOB?

                              BUTTERFIELD
                    Yes.

                              LEO
                    CIA and Diplomatic Security are getting
                    briefed?

                              BUTTERFIELD
                    Right now, and they're wired to the Ops
                    Center.

                              BARTLET
                    Do you have my other daughters, do you
                    have Ellie and Elizabeth?

                              BUTTERFIELD
                    Yes sir.

They walk into--

5   **INT. SITUATION ROOM - CONTINUOUS**   5

The room has started to fill up. FITZWALLACE, NANCY and CASPER
are there and several others are working phones. It's the
loudest and most disorderly we've ever seen the room, and
doesn't quiet down all that much even after Bartlet enters.
The ship's been hit and people are working.

                                                            (CONTINUED)

5   CONTINUED: 5

>   LEO
> There's no need to keep this a secret in
> fact we want to get it out there quickly
> and *massively*, Mike, right, turn all the
> lights on?
>
>   CASPER
> Secret Service put themselves onto police
> frequencies so anyone with a scanner has
> it, everyone's comin' in.
>
>   LEO
> Major, I need C.J. Cregg.
>   (to the room)
> Are we being attacked?
>
>   FITZWALLACE
> We don't know.
>
>   LEO
> Then tell me what you think.
>
>   FITZWALLACE
> I think we're being attacked, but this is
> gonna take some time.
>
>   LEO
> How much time?
>
>   FITZWALLACE
> 45 minutes to assemble and evaluate known
> threats and another hour to cross check
> with the Secret Service familiar faces
> list.
>
>   BUTTERFIELD
> Another two hours for the interviews at
> the club.
>
>   LEO
> Related incidents.
>
>   CASPER
> We don't believe any of the three high
> profile abductions last week are related.
> The Mexican CEO or the two DEA agents in
> Peru.
>
>   LEO
> Patterns.

                                                        (CONTINUED)

5   CONTINUED: (2)   5

                              CASPER
              INS says three separate groups of Qumari
              nationals, 17 people all together, flew
              back today, 11 out of JFK and 6 out of
              Dulles and traffic lights went out at
              Wisconsin and M four minutes after Wes
              Davis called in the AOP.

                              BARTLET
              What is it they're gonna want.
                    (beat)
              What is it they're gonna want, Bahji
              prisoners freed, we get outa Qumar, we
              get outa Kundu?

                              FITZWALLACE
              Well they're gonna let us know, sir, in a
              typical kidnapping--

                              NANCY
              It's not a typical kidnapping.

                              FITZWALLACE
              They're gonna let us know what--

                              LEO
              Wait, Nancy, what did you say?

                              NANCY
              Is there anyone here who thinks this
              sounds like a typical kidnapping so far?
              Could this have been any more low-tech? A
              plan based on knowing when someone's
              gonna need to use the bathroom?

                              FITZWALLACE
              17 Qumari nationals leave the country?

                              NANCY
              Out of 10,000 in the U.S.

                              FITZWALLACE
              Every rental car agency is out of vans
              and U-Hauls.

                              NANCY
              It's graduation weekend, every kid in the
              mid-Atlantic is moving right now. We shut
              down the airports, either they didn't
              know we were gonna do that or they didn't
              care, either way, Mike, does this seem
              like a James Bond operation to you?

                                              (CONTINUED)

5   CONTINUED: (3)   5

                              CASPER
              I don't know what it is yet, Dr. McNally.

                              LEO
              I want to stop hearing that answer soon.

                              BARTLET
              And Union Station, too? We shut down
              Union Station?

                              BUTTERFIELD
              Yes sir.

                              BARTLET
              I'm gonna check on Abbey.

BARTLET exits...

                              NANCY
              Leo, whoever took her doesn't know what
              they're doing, it was an absurd
              kidnapping, she's not gonna turn up in a
              Bahji camp, she's gonna turn up in the
              back of a muffler shop.

                              FITZWALLACE
              Well I'm looking at Syria moving 20,000
              troops closer to Lebanon today and
              Pakistan testing a long range missile so
              I'm not sure about that.

                              CASPER
                       (getting off the phone)
              They've set up command at OEOB.

LEO, CASPER and BUTTERFIELD head out the door as we

                                                          CUT TO:

6   INT. MAKESHIFT INTERROGATION ROOM - NIGHT   6

In one corner, an AGENT's talking to three of ZOEY's
girlfriends from the party, in another an AGENT's talking to
two bartenders and in another, BANKS is talking to JOSH and
CHARLIE. WESLEY, JAMIE and RANDY are listening in.

                              JOSH
              I didn't see her at the Arboretum, I was
              at the Arboretum but I didn't see her.

                              BANKS
              I don't understand.

                                                        (CONTINUED)

6   CONTINUED: 6

                              JOSH
          This part doesn't matter.

                              BANKS
          We don't know what matters.

                              JOSH
          You're right, I'm sorry. We went there
          together, we hopped the wall, and then
          when we realized Zoey was also there, I
          stayed with Agent Reed--

                              JAMIE
          He did.

                              JOSH
          --and Charlie went to--

                              CHARLIE
          We buried a bottle of champagne out there
          three and a half years ago and we were
          drinking it to celebrate graduation.

                              BANKS
          Where's out there?

                              CHARLIE
          At a spot between two--in the Asian
          Garden.

                              BANKS
          How much champagne did she have?

                              CHARLIE
          I don't know, maybe a third of the
          bottle, I don't know.

                              WESLEY
          Charlie, there's no evidence of a
          struggle at the club. None. All she had
          to do was press a panic button and she
          didn't, in fact it was on the ground.
          It's graduation night, she's going to
          France tomorrow, you guys are feeling
          good at the Arboretum, you didn't do
          anything? Vicadin, valium, ecstasy--

                              CHARLIE
          Ecstasy.

                              BANKS
          She took ecstasy?

                                             (CONTINUED)

6   CONTINUED: (2)   6

CHARLIE jumps out of his chair toward--

                    CHARLIE
          Jean Paul--

                    BANKS
          You need to siddown, son.

                    CHARLIE
          Did you--she said you wanted her to take
          ecstasy with you tonight, did you give
          some to her?

                    RANDY
          He's completely out of it, Charlie, he's
          high.

And he is, by the way. He can't keep his head up anymore and
he's stopped trying. His eyes are sort of open but he's only
got maybe another three minutes of consciousness left.

                    CHARLIE
          Did you give her ecstasy, did you put it
          in her drink or something, just tell me.

                    WESLEY
          This guy isn't--
               (to JEAN PAUL)
          --look at me for a second--
               (to an AGENT)
          --this guy isn't high on X. Get a
          paramedic.
               (to JEAN PAUL)
          Who's your dealer, who'd you buy it from,
          gimme a name? Listen to me, you're gonna
          be fine, you are the key witness to the
          end of the world, we are gonna keep you
          alive, you have to tell me who you got
          this from.

JEAN PAUL is only able to look at him and then mutters
something unintelligible.

A PARAMEDIC runs in with his orange box--

                    PARAMEDIC
          What's wrong with him?

                    WESLEY
          Who gives a damn, get a blood sample to a
          lab right now.

The PARAMEDIC gets to work...

                                                    (CONTINUED)

6   CONTINUED: (3)   6

                         JOSH
             Hey, Wesley, I know you guys have to do
             your job but I can't imagine what's going
             on in the White House right now and I was
             wondering--

                         WESLEY
             You guys are done.

                         JOSH
                (beat)
             Listen...I don't know what to say about
             Molly.

                         WESLEY
             Go back to the White House, Josh, stand
             your post. Charlie--

                         CHARLIE
             We're all gonna make it through this
             night.

                         WESLEY
             Well I don't see how we possibly can, but
             I like your spirit.

As JOSH and CHARLIE are exiting, WESLEY starts calling out
instructions--

                         WESLEY
                (calling out)
             Every kid in the club, where do you get X
             on campus, start with the chemistry
             majors.

JEAN PAUL says something to JOSH as he passes--

                         JOSH
             What?

                         JEAN PAUL
             I don't know what we took.

                         JOSH
             Well we're gonna know soon enough, I'm
             sure they're gonna pump your stomach.

And JOSH and CHARLIE exit as we

                                              CUT TO:

7   **INT. C.J.'S OFFICE/OUTER OFFICE/CORRIDORS - NIGHT**   7

It's moments before the biggest press conference of the
Bartlet Administration and C.J.'s getting loaded up with some
last minute things.

                         CAROL
             No law enforcement issues from the
             podium, you refer 'em to the FBI. The
             crime scene's still being secured,
             there's no press on the scene.

                         C.J.
             I heard there was.

                         CAROL
             It was local news 'cause they were at the
             party but they got 'em out of there.

                         LEO
             C.J.--excuse me, Carol.

                         CAROL
             Yes sir.

CAROL disappears...

                         LEO
             Do not--do *not* get into a discussion of
             the President's emotional state.

                         C.J.
             Yeah.

                         LEO
             You *have* to pivot whatever you get to
             Commander-in-Chief.

                         C.J.
             Yeah.

                         LEO
             Congressional leadership's been notified,
             we'll have statements inside an hour.

                         C.J.
             Carol gave me that.

WILL comes along--

                         WILL
             Excuse me.

                                              (CONTINUED)

7   CONTINUED: 7

                              LEO
                  We're in control, the government is
                  functioning, this is the most important
                  press conference of your life.

LEO takes off--

                              WILL
                  Has anyone heard from Toby?

                              C.J.
                  I haven't, you haven't?

                              WILL
                  The last time I saw him was this morning
                  and then he went with Andy to the house.
                  I have to write a statement from the
                  President and I don't even know where to
                  start.

                              C.J.
                  He'll answer his page.

                              WILL
                  Listen--

                              C.J.
                  Yeah.

                              WILL
                  Nothing.

                              C.J.
                  What?

                              WILL
                  There's no Vice President.

                              C.J.
                      (beat)
                  What does that have to do with this?

                              WILL
                  Are we really expecting him to get on the
                  phone with somebody and say we don't
                  negotiate with terrorists?

                              C.J.
                  One step at a time.

                              WILL
                  Good luck.

                                                        (CONTINUED)

7   CONTINUED: (2)   7

                         C.J.
          Thanks.

     C.J. walks into--

8   **INT. PRESS BRIEFING ROOM - CONTINUOUS**   8

     --where she's met by the biggest crowd that's ever been in
     there. Bright camera lights in her face and flashbulbs and
     noise and calls of "C.J.!".

     She takes the podium and stands still till it quiets down...

                         C.J.
               At 11:21 pm, Special Agent Wesley Davis
               of the U.S. Secret Service called in an
               AOP, which means "Attack on the
               Principal."

                                             FADE TO BLACK:

                    <u>END OF ACT ONE</u>

ACT TWO

FADE IN:

9   **INT. PRESS BRIEFING ROOM - NIGHT**   9

The briefing's been underway for about an hour.

                    C.J.
          As I said, they're obviously examining
          any tape from security cameras that may
          have picked her up at the club but we
          don't have a photograph of what she was
          wearing. I'm gonna repeat again what
          witnesses have told us:

TITLE:

                    Hour 2

                    C.J.
          Black pants, black high heeled boots and
          a black tank top over a red tank top
          which makes it seem from a distance that
          the black top has red piping. Walking
          into the club she was wearing a multi-
          colored, silk Chinese jacket but it
          appears that she may have taken the
          jacket off. I know this feed is being
          carried live right now by all the
          networks and I'd just like to remind the
          news directors to keep the 800 number, to
          keep the tip line bannered on your air,
          please. Two more questions. Mark.

                    MARK
          Has the President expressed personal
          frustration?

                    C.J.
          Again, as I've said, the President and
          First Lady are obviously deeply concerned
          to say the least, as any parent would be,
          and he'll be meeting with his law
          enforcement, Secret Service and national
          security teams throughout the night and
          until the situation is resolved. Katie?

                    GERI
          But surely he's not reacting as if this
          is someone else's kid?

                                        (CONTINUED)

9   CONTINUED: 9

                       LYLE
           Is there a concern that she's being
           raped?

                       C.J.
           Lyle, for the sake of a number of
           distraught people I'm gonna ask you not
           to publicly speculate on what's going on.
           Katie, then I've gotta go.

                       KATIE
           Is there a concern that this could
           exacerbate his MS?

                       C.J.
           No. Thank you, I'll brief again in an
           hour.

                       STEVE
           When will you release the name of the
           Secret Service agent?

                       C.J.
           Just as soon as we can locate her family.

C.J. exits into--

10   **INT. CORRIDOR - CONTINUOUS**   10

--where TOBY's just shown up.

                       C.J.
           Where have you been?

                       TOBY
           All of Northwest is shut down.
           Pennsylvania Avenue and Connecticut
           Avenue are shut down, I wouldn't be
           surprised if Pennsylvania and Connecticut
           were shut down. There are no cabs, the
           metro's closed. Metro police took me to
           18th Street and then it took me 15
           minutes to get in with a hard pass.

They walk into--

11   **INT. COMMUNICATIONS BULLPEN - CONTINUOUS**   11

--where WILL's coming out of his office--

                       WILL
           Where've you been?

                                 (CONTINUED)

11   CONTINUED:

> TOBY
> I'm not repeating all that again, do you
> have a statement?

> WILL
> Right here.

TOBY starts reading and JOSH comes in--

> GINGER
> You've got about a hundred phone
> messages, how do you want 'em?

> TOBY
> I want them to stay in your hand for a
> moment.
> (reading)
> "...in this difficult time, we are grateful
> for the support of the American--", we're
> not asking for fruit baskets. It's gotta
> say, "Our youngest daughter has been
> abducted. She will be found, brought home
> safely, and her abductors caught and
> punished."

> JOSH
> "While we work for her safe return--"

> C.J.
> Yes.

> JOSH
> "The world community must know that this
> country will *not* be taken hostage, that
> our efforts toward peace and freedom
> continue unabated."

> TOBY
> Good.

It's TOBY, JOSH, C.J., WILL, GINGER and BONNIE.

> TOBY
> (pause)
> Everybody take a breath.
> (pause)
> Take another one.
> (to JOSH)
> How is he?

> JOSH
> I haven't seen him.

(CONTINUED)

11   CONTINUED: (2)

                    TOBY
What about Abbey?

                         C.J.
Someone's looking in on her and they want
a doctor to see the President too.

                    TOBY
He's not gonna allow himself to be
sedated right now, it's a waste of time
and I don't want that story leaked.

                         C.J.
It's not for a sedative.

                    TOBY
MS?

                         C.J.
Yeah.

                    TOBY
          (pause--then to JOSH)
Where's Leo on the stock exchange?

                    JOSH
We haven't had time to talk about it yet,
but I think if we don't have her by six,
we gotta recommend that Leo instruct the
Treasury Department to suspend trading.

                    WILL
That the *President* instruct the Treasury--
Listen to me, there is no mechanism,
none, there is no mechanism for
Presidential recusal. Leo can't give an
order to the Treasury Secretary and the
Treasury Secretary can't follow it.

                    TOBY
All right. Listen this is--everybody. A
world event has occurred. But this is
what we gear up for, we know how to do
this. We haven't rehearsed this
particular one but we know how to do
this.
          (pause--then to C.J.)
I heard most of your briefing on the
radio, you did great. For the rest of the
night they need to get their information
from us and not the agencies, I don't want
it like she's on a milk carton. Josh--

                                              (CONTINUED)

11   CONTINUED: (3)

                  JOSH
I've already started the calls.

                  TOBY
535 Congressmen and Senators you've gotta
call, you're gonna need a posse. State's
gotta call the Ambassadors and Will
you've gotta be a lawyer. Sit in on all
the meetings tonight in the Counsel's
office and report back to Josh right
away, he's not gonna have time to wait
for a memo. Let's go.
    (beat)
Oh. Hey. This is--by the way, this is--
the babies were born.

                  C.J.
    (beat)
What babies?

                  TOBY
The twins. Andy had the babies. That's
where I was, I was at the hospital.

                  C.J.
Oh my God--

                  JOSH
Are you kidding?

                  TOBY
No, it just happened. Ten days early.

                  WILL
Are they okay?

                  TOBY
Yeah, they're great. Six pounds, one
ounce. Each.

                  JOSH
    (beat)
God, mazel tov, Toby.

They hug--

                  WILL
Mazel tov.

                  C.J.
Toby--

                    (CONTINUED)

11   CONTINUED: (4)   11

                              JOSH
              Oh wait, wait, do they have names?

                              TOBY
              The boy does. He's named after Andy's
              grandfather.

                              JOSH
              What's his name?

                              TOBY
              Huck.

                              C.J.
              Huck. What a great name for a boy.

                              TOBY
              We've gotta get to work.

                              JOSH/WILL
              Yeah.

And they take off--

                              C.J.
              Toby--

And all C.J. can do is move her arms around to indicate that
it's horrible that something so good had to happen tonight...

                              C.J.
                        (for no reason)
              ...okay.

And C.J. goes off...TOBY heads into--

12   **INT. TOBY'S OFFICE - CONTINUOUS**   12

--where he sits at his desk. This day and night is an
incredible struggle for him. He gets it together and calls
out--

                              TOBY
                        (calling)
              Ginger, you can bring me those calls now.

And we

                                                        CUT TO:

13   **INT. BARTLET FAMILY ROOM - NIGHT**   13

Back where we were at in the teaser, only a much different
atmosphere. BARTLET sits on the edge of a table with one of
his sleeves rolled up so a doctor can take his blood pressure.
We'll now start to be aware that this is 24 hour news and
we'll be seeing it with banners like *Crisis at the White House*
on every TV monitor and soon TV monitors are gonna be
everywhere.

                    WELLMAN
      This is high, I'm a little concerned.

                    BARTLET
      You and me both.

CHARLIE steps in--

                    CHARLIE
      Mike Casper.

                    BARTLET
      Yeah.

                    WELLMAN
      I just want to test some cognitive
      abilities, sir, repeat what I'm about to
      say. 13, 5, 3, 11, 7.

CASPER comes in--

                    BARTLET
      What do you have?

                    CASPER
      They've found a tire track in the alley
      and they should have a make and model
      soon.

                    BARTLET
      What about ballistics?

                    WELLMAN
      Sir, I'm sorry--

                    BARTLET
      Mike?

                    CASPER
      The accuracy of the shots and the fact
      that nobody heard it means it was
      suppressed fire from about 30 yards away.
          (MORE)

                            (CONTINUED)

13   CONTINUED: 13

                        CASPER (cont'd)
            The barrel threading and velocity suggest
            an SV 98 which is a Russian sniper rifle.

                        BARTLET
            Wait, what about 30 yards away, was there
            an apartment, a bakery--

                        CASPER
            No, just the parking lot, the shot came
            from a car or a van.

                        WELLMAN
            Sir--

                        BARTLET
            13, 5, 3, 11, 7, they're all prime
            numbers and add up to 39, I'm fine,
            George.

                        WELLMAN
            Yes sir.

    CHARLIE comes in...

                        CHARLIE
            Mr. President?

                        BARTLET
            Yeah.

                        CHARLIE
            They've located Molly O'Connor's parents,
            they're on the phone now.

                                                    CUT TO:

14   **INT. JOSH'S BULLPEN - NIGHT**   14

    DONNA is pulling a huge pile of faxes out of a fax machine
    that's been pouring out paper for well over an hour and it'll
    continue for the rest of the night.

                        JOSH
            How many people are in the building right
            now?

                        DONNA
            Including press?

                        JOSH
            Not including press.

                                              (CONTINUED)

14   CONTINUED: 14

                              DONNA
               Not many, anyone who left town can't get
               back.

                              JOSH
               Why did people leave town in the first
               place.

                              DONNA
               It's the weekend, they went crazy.

                              JOSH
               We're gonna need some people.

                              DONNA
               Do you know how many faxes we've gotten
               and do you know how many of them are from
               your insane groupies? The LymanHos have
               chosen this time to let you know via fax
               that should you be needing any *physical*
               comforts during this horrible time--read
               that.

     JOSH takes the fax--

                              DONNA
               Do you like that, is that what turns you
               on, you sicky.

                              JOSH
               I didn't write this.

                              DONNA
               Yeah, but they must *sense* it in you.

                              JOSH
               What are the others?

                              DONNA
               I just picked them up, it's gonna be
               more...thoughts and prayers, good wishes.

                              JOSH
               That's nice.

                              DONNA
               And bus station skanks.

     WILL's come in--

                              WILL
               Do you need help with these calls?

                                                         (CONTINUED)

                         JOSH
          Yeah, but you've gotta sit with Babish
          and his guys.

                         DONNA
          The Spreklettes of Ames Iowa hope we
          don't exploit this to make another
          irrational argument about taking their
          guns.
               (beat)
          The Spreklettes of Ames have weighed in.

                         WILL
          Yeah, I was gonna say the speechwriting
          interns are here.

                         JOSH
          They got in?

                         WILL
          No, they've been here.

                         JOSH
          You had them in on a Saturday night?

                         WILL
          It was a character building exercise.

                         JOSH
               (to DONNA)
          You hear that?

                         DONNA
          Hang on.

                         JOSH
          What?

                         DONNA
               (pause)
          That's one tank top on top of another
          tank top. This is a polaroid of Zoey.

     A photograph's been faxed at the top of a piece of paper
     filled with Arabic writing.

                         WILL
          That's a ransom note.

                                                         CUT TO:

15   **EXT. PORTICO - NIGHT**   15

BARTLET, CHARLIE and CASPER bust out onto the portico and
start heading to the Oval Office when BUTTERFIELD comes out of
the Mural Room--

> BUTTERFIELD
> Sir--

> BARTLET
> Blood tests?

> BUTTERFIELD
> They found GHB, gamma hydroxy butyrate.

> CASPER
> It's degreasing solvent mixed with drain
> cleaner. It's a clear liquid that mixes
> in a drink and in low doses--

CASPER stops himself and CHARLIE gives him a look behind
BARTLET's back that says 'have a heart'. CHARLIE knows what
it's used for...

> BARTLET
> In low doses it's a date rape drug.

> CASPER
> Yes sir.

> BARTLET
> What about the boy?

> BUTTERFIELD
> They believe he'll be conscious in an
> hour or so.

They walk into--

16   **INT. OVAL OFFICE - CONTINUOUS**   16

--where LEO, FITZWALLACE, NANCY and MILITARY and CIVILIAN
PERSONNEL are standing and waiting.

> BARTLET
> Where is it?

LEO hands BARTLET two pieces of paper--

> LEO
> This is the translation.

(CONTINUED)

> BARTLET
> We think this is Zoey?

> LEO
> It's a fax quality picture, but the left shoulder...

> BARTLET
> Where was it faxed from?

> LEO
> A Kinko's self-serve in Dover. A security camera got a partial license plate, it's a mini-van rented to a Shahab Kaleel and there's an FBI APB out.

> BARTLET
> (reading)
> "Release Uzma Kalil, Ahmed Mansour and Barmak Essa from the Islamabad Maximum Security Prison. The President will announce on television that the United States will abandon its military presence in Qumar."

> LEO
> Now the analysts say Qumar's Mufti made a call for "martyrdom operations" last week using phrasing that's almost identical to the next passage and named those three prisoners. Two years ago a Bahji cell kidnapped the sons of the Prime Minister of Eritrea in exchange for close to a hundred of their prisoners.

> BARTLET
> (to FITZWALLACE)
> Where are you?

> FITZWALLACE
> I want to prepare to attack the following targets. The Bahji C3I, Communications, Command/Control and Intelligence, I want to move the C-130s and the Blackhawks and I want to move the Washington carrier group into the Gulf to strike three Bahji camps in Qumar.

> NANCY
> And I believe that we cannot move into position yet, this will escalate, this will get worse before it gets better.
> (MORE)

(CONTINUED)

16   CONTINUED: (2)   16

                         NANCY (cont'd)
          Sir, that kid's gonna be conscious in an
          hour and we have a good chance of finding
          the dealer once he does.

                         LEO
          We're gonna find the dealer, Nancy, but
          he's gonna be dead when we do.

                         BARTLET
          Move the Fifth Fleet into the Gulf.

                         FITZWALLACE
          Yes sir.

                                             FADE TO BLACK:

                         END OF ACT TWO

ACT THREE

FADE IN:

17 **INT. LEO'S OFFICE - NIGHT**   17

Four TVs are going at once as LEO and TOBY watch the talking
heads. TOBY will switch sound from one to the next.

                    TV #1
          --and there's no way to know that right
          now, it could be a small group of people
          acting alone, but the reason the First
          Family has Secret Service protection
          isn't to protect *them*, it's to protect
          the country from blackmail.

TITLE:
                         Hour 5

                    TV #2
          Well they're not about to announce
          military moves to the press but in rooms
          at the Pentagon and the White House
          they're war gaming this right now. There
          will be terrible reprisals if this is the
          work of terrorists. Certainly we can't
          allow the children of government leaders
          to be--

                    TV #3
          --no, and I think we should be careful
          about saying that but certainly it's easy
          to imagine how this escalates to a
          military situation, under any number of
          scenarios that are perfectly justified--

                    TV #4
          --non-governmental elements in Pakistan,
          Iran, Saudi Arabia, the former Soviet
          Union--

                    TV #1
          --all of Washington D.C. virtually sealed
          off, all air traffic grounded--

                    LEO
               (pause)
          Huck?

                    TOBY
          Yeah.

                                        (CONTINUED)

17 CONTINUED: 17

                         LEO
                    (beat)
          That's nice, I like that.

                         TOBY
          It's her grandfather's.

                         LEO
                    (remembering)
          Hey.
                    (beat)
          Hey, the house. What happened?

                         TOBY
          Hm?

                         LEO
          What happened at the house, did you
          propose?

                         TOBY
          Yeah. I did. We tabled it though, 'cause,
          you know--

                         LEO
          You had to go to the hospital.

                         TOBY
          Yeah.

                         LEO
          Was there time to tell her you bought her
          the house?

                         TOBY
          Yeah, I told her about the house and
          everything.

                         LEO
          What did she say?

                         TOBY
                    (beat)
          This doesn't really feel like the night
          to, you know--

                         LEO
          What did she say?

                         TOBY
          She said no.

(CONTINUED)

17   CONTINUED: (2)   17

                    LEO
       (beat)
Well...I mean, that'll change, right?

                    TOBY
Hey lemme ask you something. When Jenny
was pregnant with Mallory, you were
nervous, right?

                    LEO
Yeah.

                    TOBY
Me too.

                    LEO
Every father.

                    TOBY
Yeah, but I think I was nervous for a
different reason.

                    LEO
What?

                    TOBY
I think I was nervous I wasn't gonna love
my kids as much as other fathers love
theirs.

                    LEO
Why?

                    TOBY
I don't know.
       (pause)
I don't know. For nine months you're
hearing how this is gonna change your
life and you've never loved anything like
this and my God, the love, and nothing is
gonna be important anymore and it's just
never really felt to me like I was
someone who had the capacity for those
feelings. Plus I like what's important to
me, I want it to stay important, I want
to be able to do it well.

                    LEO
What do you mean you don't have the
capacity?

                    TOBY
You know what I mean.

                              (CONTINUED)

17   CONTINUED: (3)   17

>   LEO
>   I don't know what you mean.
>
>   TOBY
>   Anyway, I was just curious.
>
>   LEO
>   Of course you're gonna be a great father,
>   of course you're gonna love your kids the
>   way you're supposed to, the way other
>   fathers--
>
>   TOBY
>   God, Leo, we look around and we see
>   that's not true, it's not automatic.
>
>   LEO
>   I'm not saying it's automatic, I'm not
>   talking about everybody, I'm talking
>   about you and I'm telling you it's a
>   mortal lock, it's guaranteed.
>   (pause)
>   Listen, you can go back to the hospital,
>   you know, we'll send you in a car, you
>   can get right back here when--
>
>   TOBY
>   Nah, she needs to sleep now.
>
>   LEO
>   You could see the babies.
>
>   TOBY
>   They can't really do anything yet.
>   (beat)
>   You know, and I'm not really someone
>   who's comfortable talking out loud to
>   them.
>
>   LEO
>   (pause)
>   Toby, what went on at the house?

TOBY waves it off and turns the sound back on--

>   TV #1
>   --wait, wait, it's not known whether the
>   President has been sedated, we know the
>   First Lady was given--

>   CUT TO:

18   **INT. LOBBY - NIGHT**   18

Obviously there's an increased security presence. People who
are talking are talking in small groups and hushed tones.

AMY's sitting on the couch, taking the first moment she's had
to herself all night. She rubs her eyes and tries to regroup
when--

--down the corridor comes ABBEY with some AGENTS. ABBEY only
thinks she's shaken off the sedative but she hasn't. She's
dizzy, she can't think clearly and she's irritable.

> AMY
> Mrs. Bartlet? Ma'am?

But ABBEY's not paying attention as she continues down--

19   **INT. CORRIDOR - CONTINUOUS**   19

--toward the Briefing Room with AMY hurrying after her--

> AMY
> Mrs. Bartlet?

> ABBEY
> I'm gonna make a direct appeal. They'll
> turn on the cameras when I go in the
> briefing room and I'll make a direct
> appeal.

> AMY
> Ma'am, you can't.

> ABBEY
> From the mother.

> AMY
> You can't.

> ABBEY
> I don't know why I waited this long, I
> screwed up.

> AMY
> Let's siddown for a minute.

> ABBEY
> Get away from me.

> AMY
> You can't go in the press room, it'll
> undermine--

(CONTINUED)

19 CONTINUED: 19

                          ABBEY
                I've seen mothers do it.

C.J. sees that ABBEY's heading toward the press room and
immediately understands the situation and hurries--

                          C.J.
                Abbey--

                          AMY
                She wants to--

                          C.J.
                Abbey, you can't go in the press room.

                          ABBEY
                I'm gonna make a direct appeal. I don't
                know why I waited this long, I should've--

--and C.J. and AMY try to stop her but she opens the door to--

20 **INT. PRESS BRIEFING ROOM - CONTINUOUS**   20

--and takes a few steps in while she's talking--

                          ABBEY
                --I've seen mothers do this--

--and the stadium-sized crowd sees this instantly and lights
are everywhere and--

                          REPORTERS
                MRS. BARTLET!

--and they're shouting as C.J. and AMY are trying to keep
ABBEY from the stage and this thing's gone from 0 to 60 in ten
seconds--

                          C.J.
                AH, GUYS GIVE HER A BREAK!

--and they get ABBEY back out the door and into--

21 **INT. CORRIDOR - CONTINUOUS**   21

...where they catch their breath for a moment...

                                              (CONTINUED)

21   CONTINUED: 21

                         AMY
                    (pause)
              It can be seen as negotiating with
              them...and it could undermine the
              military threats that the President is
              making...and if the goal is to
              destabilize our government, they're going
              to see you and know they're succeeding.
                    (beat)
              You can't go in the press room.

                         ABBEY
                    (pause)
              I know...I'd just seen other mothers do
              it. I screwed up.

                         C.J.
              Abbey, come sit on my couch for a minute.

                         AMY
                    (quietly)
              I'm gonna call the doctor.

C.J. nods that she should--

                         ABBEY
              Tell him I want whatever Zoey got.

                         C.J.
              Come sit on my couch.

ABBEY follows C.J. and AMY heads into--

22   **INT. JOSH'S BULLPEN - CONTINUOUS**   22

--where AMY steps into the nearest empty cubicle, picks up the
phone and hits three numbers.

                         AMY
                    (into phone)
              Yeah, she's all right, she's fine. If you
              could just step into the Press
              Secretary's office. Thank you.

She hangs up the phone...

                         DONNA
              Is she all right?

                         AMY
              Yeah.

                                                          (CONTINUED)

22   CONTINUED: 22

                           DONNA
                         (pause)
                    Are *you* all right?

                           AMY
                    Yeah.

                           DONNA
                    That was probably hard just now.

                           AMY
                    Did I ask you if you were in love with
                    Josh a few hours ago? Was that really
                    tonight, is this the same night?

                           DONNA
                         (pause--then smiles with
                          recognition)
                    I know exactly how you feel.

She starts to walk away, then over her shoulder--

                           DONNA
                    Yeah, you did.

                                                           CUT TO:

23   **INT. SITUATION ROOM - NIGHT**   23

BARTLET's getting a briefing with the accompanying bells and
whistles on the big board.

                           FITZWALLACE
                    Syria and Nigeria have launched Damman-
                    Class torpedo boats, a Madina Class
                    frigate and they've activated their
                    Panzer-SI anti-aircraft system. The
                    Yemeni have scrambled six MiG-29
                    Fulcrums.

                           NANCY
                    Mr. President, have Leo meet with the
                    Qumari Ambassador, have him do it before
                    the sun comes up. Let's try the
                    diplomatic route before this gets outa
                    hand, sir.

                           FITZWALLACE
                    Before it gets outa hand? I want to get
                    the planes in the air now, sir, if we're
                    gonna end up striking bases near Tamar
                    and Laddi we're gonna need some element
                    of surprise.

                                                      (CONTINUED)

23   CONTINUED: 23

                              NANCY
              Chairman, do I need to remind you Qumar's
              an ally.

                              FITZWALLACE
              You don't, but I need to ask you what
              good is an ally if their citizens are
              capable of waging war on their own?

LEO hurries in--

                              LEO
              Excuse me, sir, we have a problem.

                              BARTLET
              One?

                              LEO
                   (picking up a phone)
              There's an airplane up there.
                   (into the phone)
              Captain, give us the controller's
              transmission please.
                   (to the room)
              An unidentified Beech Baron 58, it's a
              twin prop plane, is in the air over
              Richland, Washington and it hasn't
              acknowledged radio communications from
              Air Traffic Control. They're 90 miles
              from the Saw Mill River Nuclear Reactor.

                              CONTROLLER #1 (VO)
              Beech 0827, do you respond, over? Beech
              0827, this is Air Route Traffic Control
              Center Seattle. Do you respond, over?

                              LEO
              We scrambled the jets?

                              GENERAL
                   (ear to a phone)
              Two F-15s outa Portland, they're on
              either side, they're over water, they
              have clear shots.

                              BARTLET
              When do you want me to give the order, 70
              miles from the target, 60, 50?

                              GENERAL
              I'm sorry Mr. President, which target are
              you talking about?

                                              (CONTINUED)

23   CONTINUED: (2)   23

                              LEO
              He meant the nuclear plant.

                              BARTLET
              How far away do I--

                              CONTROLLER #2 (VO)
              Has the transponder been dialed to 7700?

                              CONTROLLER #1 (VO)
              Negative, no signal.

                              BARTLET
              7700's an emergency frequency?

                              LEO
              If you lose your radio, you set your
              transponder to 7700. 7500 means you've
              been hijacked. These guys aren't
              signaling anything.

                              BARTLET
              Fellas we got confusion in here, when do
              I give the order?

                              CONTROLLER #1 (VO)
              Beech 0827, this is Air Route Traffic
              Control Center Seattle, do you respond,
              over?

                              LEO
                   (to GENERAL)
              70 miles but they're gonna be over
              population in about a minute.

                              BARTLET
                   (to LEO)
              Talk to me.

                              LEO
              General?

                              CONTROLLER #1 (VO)
              Beech 0827--

                              PILOT (VO)
              Beech 0827, this is U.S. Air Force F-15
              five-six, I'm a half-mile back on your
              right side and I have missile lock.
              Switch to frequency 121.5 and stand-by
              for slow flight.

              Silence...then--

                                                          (CONTINUED)

23   CONTINUED: (3)   23

> BEECH (VO)
> *Yeah, this is Beech 0827. Sorry about*
> *that, we were having a problem with*
> *the...with the thing--*

And everyone throws up their arms--they can't believe this
night. NANCY slumps back in her chair...the GENERAL replaces
the phone...

BARTLET starts to head out--

> FITZWALLACE
> Mr. President--

> BARTLET
> I know you want to get the planes in the
> air. Lemme think about it a minute, okay?

> FITZWALLACE
> Of course, sir.

BARTLET and LEO head out into--

24   **INT. OUTER AREA - CONTINUOUS**   24

--and then they start up--

25   **INT. STAIRWAY - CONTINUOUS**   25

--and BARTLET stops about halfway up and sits on the stairs.
Not because he's tired, though he is, but because walls and
offices have stopped having any importance to him for the
night. Also, he needs to just stop for a second.

> BARTLET
> I don't know what to do about the
> military options, Nancy's making good
> points.
>   (beat)
> I'm sorry about the confusion in there, I
> know we've practiced that.

LEO sits on the next step up...

> LEO
> We're doing fine.

> BARTLET
> I don't think so.
>   (beat)
> I need you to tell me now, do you think
> she's already dead?

(CONTINUED)

25   CONTINUED:

> LEO
> I absolutely do not.

> BARTLET
> If they show me a picture of her alive
> and tell me to aim Cruise Missiles at Tel
> Aviv, they're counting on the fact that a
> father--

Now the scene starts to pick up some urgency, with LEO trying
to calm it down.

> LEO
> But you wouldn't.

> BARTLET
> I might.

> LEO
> There are people around you who won't let
> you.

> BARTLET
> How 'bout a picture they've got a
> knife to her throat, get out of Saudi
> Arabia.

> LEO
> You shouldn't think of images like that.

> BARTLET
> All I *can* think of are images like that.

> LEO
> Sir--

> BARTLET
> Leo, please listen to me. Did Fitz give
> me target recommendations a little while
> ago.

> LEO
> Yes sir, he wants to attack--

> BARTLET
> I don't remember having the conversation
> and I don't know what targets he wants
> to hit, *did I greenlight the targets?!*

> LEO
> Of course not. Mr. President, no one is
> expecting you to keep the United States
> out of a war tonight.
> (MORE)

(CONTINUED)

25   CONTINUED: (2)   25

> LEO (cont'd)
> Me and Nancy and Fitz are standing right
> next to you when you get information, you
> don't need to remember it. And we're
> standing right next to you when you give
> orders, you're not gonna hurt anybody.

> BARTLET
>   (pause)
> I know it's a strange time to bring this
> up, but I forecasted this once. I made
> up a scary story a few years ago for
> Zoey so that she'd take her protection
> seriously and I went too far and I
> scared her and she cried. This was the
> story.
>   (pause)
> Leo, the people you just named don't
> have the legal authority to stop me from
> doing certain things. And some of them
> would go to jail if they didn't follow
> my orders.
>   (pause)
> Very quietly. I want you to assemble the
> Cabinet. I want you to call the Speaker
> of the House.

FADE TO BLACK:

<u>END OF ACT THREE</u>

43.

FADE IN:

26   **INT. MATERNITY WARD/NURSES STATION- NIGHT**   26

TOBY steps quietly out of Andy's room, which is right across
from the Nurses Station, and closes the door behind him.

> NURSE
> Is she asleep?

> TOBY
> Hm? Yeah.

TITLE:

Hour 7

TOBY stands at the window of the nursery and looks in on five
or six babies, two of which are his.

> NURSE
> (pause)
> You know, these people went home last
> night. If you like, I can bring the
> babies in there, you can have a few
> minutes with--

> TOBY
> Oh no. Thank you, no, that's okay.
> (beat)
> Okay, yeah sure.

TOBY watches as the NURSE picks up two tiny babies who are
pretty well swaddled and takes them into--

27   **INT. HOSPITAL ROOM - CONTINUOUS**   27

--where she sets them down on the bed. The TV up in the corner
has the news on with the sound off.

> NURSE
> They need to be fed in a few minutes so
> I'll come back.

> TOBY
> Thank you.

The NURSE exits...TOBY's silent for a long moment, then--

> TOBY
> I didn't realize babies came with hats.
> (pause)
> You guys crack me up.
> (MORE)

(CONTINUED)

27   CONTINUED: 27

> TOBY (cont'd)
> You don't have jobs, you can't walk or
> speak a language, you don't have a dollar
> in your pockets but you got yourselves a
> hat so everything's fine.
>   (pause)
> I don't want to alarm you or anything,
> but...I'm Dad.
>   (beat)
> And son, for you, this'll be the last
> time I pass the buck but I just think it
> should be clear from the get-go that it
> was Mom who named you Huckleberry. I
> guess she was feeling like life doesn't
> present enough challenges to overcome on
> its own. And honey, you've got a name now
> too. Your mom and I named you after an
> incredibly brave, uh, incredibly brave
> woman, really not all that much older
> than you. Your name is Molly.
>   (beat)
> Huck and Molly.
>   (beat)
> I know you can't understand me, but it's
> the deepness of my voice--
>   (deepening his voice)
> --I read that the deepness of my voice is
> appealing...
>   (beat)
> Did you just smile when I said 'deepness
> of my voice'?
>   (pause)
> So what do *I* do? Well you're gonna need
> food and clothes and doctors and
> dentists, so there's that. Also, should
> you have any questions along the way. And
> I'll be doing stuff like this, Huck,
> 'cause you're leaking a little bit out of
> your mouth there.

TOBY dabs his handkerchief around HUCK's mouth...and now
TOBY's son does something that knocks him out...

> TOBY
> You holding my finger, son?
>   (pause)
> Molly, your brother's holding my hand,
> you wanna hold my hand?

TOBY gives his other hand to MOLLY...

> TOBY
> Hm.
>   (beat)
>   (MORE)

(CONTINUED)

27   CONTINUED: (2)

> TOBY (cont'd)
> This isn't gonna mean anything to
> you...but Leo was right.
>   (beat)
> Leo was right.

The NURSE steps back in...

> NURSE
> Mr. Ziegler.

> TOBY
> Yeah.

TOBY's still on the kids...

> NURSE
> It's nice when they look at you like
> that, isn't it?

> TOBY
> Yeah.

> NURSE
> Oh. Look how sweet they are together.

And at first TOBY probably thinks she meant HUCK and MOLLY,
but he sees that she's looking at the TV news which is showing
a Bartlet Archive home movie of a five year old ZOEY being
taught to play chess by her father.

> NURSE
> They've been showing old home videos on
> the news, I don't know why they do that.

The little girl is giggling and having a great time. Then TOBY
sees the father's hand reach in with his handkerchief and wipe
something from the little girl's face...and for TOBY, the
penny now fully drops.

> NURSE
> She can't be more than five years old
> here.

> TOBY
> I have to go back to my office now.

> NURSE
> Mr. Ziegler, would you convey to the
> President and Mrs. Bartlet that the
> prayers of everyone at this hospital and,
> well, everyone are with them tonight?

                                        (CONTINUED)

27   CONTINUED: (3)   27

> TOBY
> Of course I will and they'll both
> appreciate that. I'm writing down my
> pager number if Andy needs me or they do
> anything new.

> NURSE
> New?

> TOBY
> Yeah.

> NURSE
> Like what?

> TOBY
> You never know.

And TOBY jogs down--

28   **INT. HOSPITAL CORRIDOR - CONTINUOUS**   28

--where he jumps and slaps a red-lit exit sign on his way to
the elevators and we

                                                        CUT TO:

29   **OMITTED**   29

30   **EXT. PORTICO - NIGHT**   30

LEO's reading something that's bound and just a few pages
long. MARGARET comes out with some coffee.

> LEO
> Thank you.

> MARGARET
> Charlie's on his way.

> LEO
> Thanks.

> MARGARET
> Zoey's now been spotted in over 400
> places, including a dinner theatre in
> suburban Arizona, where a patron was
> certain he was watching Zoey play Tuptim
> in *The King and I*.

> LEO
> Isn't Tuptim a man?

                                                    (CONTINUED)

30   .CONTINUED: 30

                              MARGARET
                    That's the part of the story you found
                    strangest? How can we possibly have the
                    resources--especially when guys like the
                    King and I man have deputized themselves--

                              LEO
                    I think that's probably not a lead
                    they're gonna spend a lot of time running
                    down.

                              MARGARET
                    I think you should sleep for a few hours.

                              LEO
                    I'll sleep when he sleeps but you should
                    sleep for a few hours.

                              MARGARET
                    I'll sleep when you sleep.

                              LEO
                    Well this is gonna be interesting 'cause
                    we're gonna have a small band of
                    dedicated people who can't lift their
                    arms.

CHARLIE steps out--

                              CHARLIE
                    Yes sir.

MARGARET gives CHARLIE an affectionate pat as she exits.

                              LEO
                    I guess if I told *you* to get some sleep,
                    it wouldn't do much good.

                              CHARLIE
                    I'm fine.

                              LEO
                    Tell the Staff Secretary's office I'm
                    gonna freeze all non-essential paper for
                    Executive signature. All non-essential
                    Executive Orders, all non-essential
                    correspondence, all legislation.
                         (beat)
                    You understand?

                              CHARLIE
                         (pause)
                    Until when?

                                                      (CONTINUED)

                       LEO
Until further notice.

CHARLIE looks at the cover of what LEO was reading at the table: *The Constitution of the United States*...LEO sees him do this...

                       LEO
I need you to get a Federal Judge here right away.

JOSH, C.J. and WILL step out onto the portico...

                       CHARLIE
Yes sir.

CHARLIE exits. After a moment...

                       JOSH
Donna's paging Toby.

                       LEO
Margaret says Zoey's been spotted near Phoenix playing the ingenue in a Rodgers and Hammerstein musical.
        (beat)
Don't think I'm not questioning the theatre owner with the next free minute I have.

LEO takes a sip of coffee.

                       LEO
I just ordered Charlie to have the Staff Secretary's office hold all non-essential paper for Executive signature.

                       JOSH
Why?

                       LEO
It's one in a series of steps I'm taking tonight to temporarily but dramatically downsize the scope of the Oval Office.

                       JOSH
        (beat--he knows why)
Why?

                       LEO
The Cabinet's meeting in a few minutes.

                                      (CONTINUED)

30   CONTINUED: (3)   30

                         C.J.
               Leo--

                         LEO
               He's invoking the 25th Amendment, he's
               invoking 25.

          Silence...

                         JOSH
                    (pause)
               Really.

                         LEO
               Yes.

                         C.J.
                    (pause)
               Is his mind made up?

                         LEO
               He's with the Cabinet now.
                    (pause)
               You must've speculated on this
               possibility.

                         C.J.
               Yeah.

                         LEO
               Where did everyone come down?

                         C.J.
               Josh and I were on the fence, we don't
               know what Will thinks.

                         WILL
               Of the President temporarily handing over
               power to his political enemy? I think
               it's a fairly stunning act of patriotism.
               And a fairly ordinary act of fatherhood.

                         LEO
                    (beat)
               Yeah, I do too.
                    (beat)
               What does Toby think?

                                                            (CONTINUED)

30   CONTINUED: (4)   30

                         JOSH
          Well I haven't spoken to him in the last
          hour but the last time we talked about it
          he said, "We worked our asses off winning
          two elections I'm not gonna recommend
          that the President get out of the West
          Wing."

TOBY hurries out onto the Portico, a little winded from what's
still an obstacle course outside--

                         C.J.
          Toby--

                         TOBY
          Yeah, the President's gotta get outa the
          West Wing, I don't know what we've been
          thinking.

                         LEO
          Why are you out of breath?

                         TOBY
          I ran here very fast and there were some
          obstacles.

                         LEO
          The babies are okay?

                         TOBY
          Yeah, they're great, and if somebody was
          hurting 'em I'd drop napalm on
          Yellowstone to get 'em to stop--lettin'
          some prisoners out of jail wouldn't be
          nothing--and I've known my kids for about
          45 minutes.

                         LEO
          He's invoking the 25th.

                         TOBY
          He is.

                         LEO
          Yes.

                         TOBY
          When?

                         LEO
          Now.

                                              (CONTINUED)

30   CONTINUED: (5)   30

                              C.J.
                 Now.

                              LEO
                 Well once you decide you're gonna do this
                 you don't wait.

                              TOBY
                 Good.

                                                            CUT TO:

31   **INT. CAPITOL CORRIDOR - NIGHT**   31

      --as six pairs of footsteps emerge from an office and begin
      down the marble hallway. We can see that the large door reads
      OFFICE OF THE SPEAKER OF THE HOUSE and we see on a couple of
      the men the tell-tale earpieces of Secret Service Agents as we

                                                            CUT TO:

32   **INT. CABINET ROOM - NIGHT**   32

      The CABINET members are in their seats, BARTLET's standing at
      his--he doesn't feel like sitting--and reads from a piece of
      paper--

                              BARTLET
                         (reading)
                 "...availing myself of the Constitutional
                 option offered to this Office by Section
                 3 of the 25th Amendment, which permits
                 through written declaration to
                 temporarily transfer all powers of the
                 Presidency to the next in the
                 Constitutional line of succession."

                                                            CUT TO:

33   **EXT. PORTICO - NIGHT**   33

                              JOSH
                         (to TOBY)
                 It's just that we're elevating the most
                 powerful Republican in the country.

                              LEO
                 That's just a political reality.

                              JOSH
                 It's *just* a political reality?

                                                            CUT TO:

52.

34   **INT. CABINET ROOM - NIGHT**   34

                          BARTLET
              The Article doesn't require the unanimous
              consent of the Cabinet but I want it, I
              want it clear as can be that this
              Administration stands shoulder-to-
              shoulder behind the Acting President.

                                                          CUT TO:

35   **EXT. CAPITOL BASEMENT ENTRANCE - NIGHT**   35

A five car motorcade with an emergency vehicle and motorcycle
escort is waiting as the half-dozen pairs of feet emerge from
the building. The door to a sedan is being held open as the
silhouette of a large man climbs in the back and we

                                                          CUT TO:

36   **EXT. PORTICO - NIGHT**   36

                          JOSH
              We're giving Walken the Republican
              nomination.

                          LEO
              Yes we are.

                          JOSH
              It doesn't say, "I can't handle this"?

                          TOBY
              It says I <u>am</u> handling this.

                          C.J.
              It does.

                                                          CUT TO:

37   **EXT. PENNSYLVANIA AVENUE - NIGHT**   37

--as the motorcade rolls up the street toward the White House
and we

                                                          CUT TO:

53.

38   **INT. CABINET ROOM - NIGHT**   38

               AGRICULTURE SECRETARY
Mr. President, my concern is this. If you
and the Acting President were to give
contradictory orders, Leo McGarry would
be put in an impossible position which
could lead to extraordinary chaos.

               BARTLET
I won't be giving *any* orders.

               LABOR SECRETARY
But if you <u>did</u>...I think there are those
in this room, myself included, who would
want to follow those orders. And now we
have two governments.

               BARTLET
Leo would know what to do.

               INTERIOR SECRETARY
Would he?

               BARTLET
Yes.

                                   CUT TO:

39   **EXT. PORTICO - NIGHT**   39

               JOSH
What if he changes his mind and starts
giving orders?

               TOBY
Leo'll know what to do.

                                     CUT TO:

40   **INT. CABINET ROOM - NIGHT**   40

               BARTLET
Secretary of Labor.

               LABOR SECRETARY
Aye.

               BARTLET
Secretary of the Interior.

                              (CONTINUED)

40   CONTINUED: 40

                         INTERIOR SECRETARY
              Aye.

                                                        CUT TO:

41   **EXT. BACK ENTRANCE - NIGHT**   41

      --the motorcade's pulled up and the half dozen pairs of
      footsteps get out and we

                                                        CUT TO:

42   **INT. CABINET ROOM - NIGHT**   42

                         BARTLET
              Secretary of Housing and Urban
              Development.

                         HUD SECRETARY
              Aye.

                         BARTLET
              Secretary of Veterans Affairs.

                         VET AFFAIRS SECRETARY
              Aye.

                                                        CUT TO:

43   **INT. WHITE HOUSE CORRIDORS - NIGHT**   43

      --the enemy's at the gate and we

                                                        CUT TO:

44   **INT. CABINET ROOM - NIGHT**   44

                         BARTLET
              Secretary of the Treasury.

                         TREASURY SECRETARY
              Aye.

                         BARTLET
              Secretary of Defense.

                                                        CUT TO:

45   **EXT. PORTICO - NIGHT**   45

      LEO, TOBY, JOSH, C.J. and WILL just stand and wait. Nothing
      but crickets.

                                                        (CONTINUED)

45 CONTINUED: 45

Then the door at the other end opens with a thud and from the
other end of the Portico we see the doors to the East Wing
open and the half-dozen pairs of shoes coming down the walk.
And as they turn the corner, we see for the first time,
GLENALLEN WALKEN, the Speaker of the House. He's perfectly
affable, but mysterious and tends not to give anything away.
He's well aware that he's in the locker room of the enemy at
certainly their lowest moment, but that's gonna have to be
small potatoes right now. As matter of fact, even relaxed, as
he may seem, he's determined not to fail at what he's been
asked to do.

WALKEN and the AGENTS come to a stop in front of LEO and the
staff. There's silence. WALKEN takes in the tension and finds
it un-useful. So he says, simply--

                    WALKEN
               (pause)
          Relax everybody.
               (beat)
          Breathe regular.
               (pause--then to his AGENTS)
          You too.

                    LEO
               (pause)
          Mr. Speaker.

                    WALKEN
          Leo.

                    LEO
          Let's go inside.

They walk into--

46 **INT. OVAL OFFICE - CONTINUOUS**   46

--where FITZWALLACE and NANCY are coming in from the corridor.

                    WALKEN
          How's Mrs. Bartlet?

                    LEO
          Well she's very upset.

                    WALKEN
          Yeah.

                                              (CONTINUED)

46   CONTINUED:

                 LEO
         (pause)
Mr. Speaker, C.J., Josh, Toby, Will
Bailey, they're just getting this news
now, and they're among the first--they
haven't put anything together yet, but
we'll do a joint press conference, you
and the President, in probably two hours
or so and in that time you'll receive the
first of your briefings which'll--

               WALKEN
What was the Beech Baron doing?

                 LEO
         (beat)
I'm sorry?

               WALKEN
What did it end up that the two guys in
the Beech Baron were doing?

                 LEO
They were frat guys and they were drunk.
They were playing chicken.

               WALKEN
Really.

                 LEO
Yeah. The briefings are gonna--

               WALKEN
With the Air Force?

                 LEO
What?

               WALKEN
         (to FITZWALLACE now)
They were playing chicken with the Air
Force?

             FITZWALLACE
Yes sir.

               WALKEN
Unidentified aircraft get one warning and
then I don't care if my mother's on the
plane going to visit *her* mother.

BARTLET comes in--

                     (CONTINUED)

46   CONTINUED: (2)   46

                              BARTLET
                    Mr. Speaker.

                              WALKEN
                    Mr. President.

There's an awkward moment, and then they shake hands, and then
BARTLET can't help it, he says--

                              BARTLET
                    I find out the gun that killed Molly
                    O'Connor was bought through a loophole,
                    so *help me mother of God, Glen*--

                              LEO
                         (stopping him)
                    Mr. President.

A scary moment...this hasn't started off promisingly...

CHARLIE steps in--

                              CHARLIE
                    Excuse me. Madam Justice Sharon Day.

                              LEO
                    Come in.

JUSTICE DAY, still in her raincoat, comes in with a Bible and
stands off to the side.

                              WILL
                    Mr. Speaker?

                              WALKEN
                    Yeah.

                              WILL
                    You need to resign.

                              BARTLET
                    Does he?

                              JOSH
                    He's right.

                              WALKEN
                    Yeah, it's against the law to work for
                    two branches of government at the same
                    time.
                         (to WILL)
                    You got a piece of paper?

                                                        (CONTINUED)

46   CONTINUED: (3)   46

                              LEO
             Hang on. Glen, if you resign from
             Congress you can't just go back, you have
             to be elected again in two years.

                              WALKEN
             I was gonna have to be elected again in
             two years anyway, right?
                    (to WILL)
             Witness this.

He quickly signs his name and WILL nods.

BARTLET looks at TOBY, smiles, and maybe steps toward TOBY so
he knows this is just for him in the middle of all this.

                              BARTLET
             Huck?

                              TOBY
             And Molly.

                              BARTLET
             Nice.
                    (beat)
             So what do you know now that you didn't
             know before.

                              TOBY
             Babies come with hats.

                              BARTLET
             Yeah, they also come with those little
             theft protection devices, those little
             lojacks on their ankles so they can't be
             boosted from the hospital. Man, don't
             ever let them take it off.

                              TOBY
             There's no one in this room who wouldn't
             rather die than let you down you know.

BARTLET nods...

                              BARTLET
             All right, let's get organized. I've got
             two letters. One removing me from power
             and the other reinstating me. I'll sign
             the first and the Justice'll swear in the
             Speaker and then I think Leo's right, the
             first thing is how do we announce this.

                                              (CONTINUED)

46   CONTINUED: (4)   46

                        C.J.
          Well the President and the Speaker have
          to make clear to the country that there's
          someone in charge.

                        JOSH
          I'd argue that we first have to make
          clear to the *world* that there's someone
          in charge--

                        WILL
          I'd make it clear to Bahji that there's
          someone in charge.

                        WALKEN
          Franz Ferdinand, who was the nephew of
          the Austro-Hungarian Emperor, was killed
          by a group called the Black Hand, and
          because they were a Serbian Nationalist
          society, the Empire declared war on
          Serbia. Then Russia, which was bound by a
          treaty, had to mobilize which meant
          Germany had to declare war on Russia. And
          France declared war on Germany, that was
          World War I. Because the Emperor's nephew
          was killed. I thought all of your
          suggestions were good but I think first
          we should make it clear that someone's in
          charge in this *room*.

                        BARTLET
          Glen, they've been up all night.

                        WALKEN
          You're relieved, Mr. President.

          No one's ever witnessed anything like this...BARTLET looks at
          LEO...

                        LEO
          You're relieved, sir.

                        BARTLET
                (pause--then to the JUSTICE)
          Swear him in.

                        JUSTICE
          Will you place your right hand on the
          Bible, raise your left hand toward God
          and repeat after me. I, Glenallen Walken
          do solemnly swear.

          And as WALKEN takes the oath, BARTLET signs the first letter--

                                                          (CONTINUED)

> WALKEN
> I, Glenallen Walken, do solemnly swear.

> JUSTICE
> That I shall faithfully execute the
> Office of President of the United States.

> WALKEN
> That I shall faithfully execute the
> Office of President of the United States.

And they watch as BARTLET slips out the door and into the
darkness--

> JUSTICE
> And I will, to the best of my ability,
> preserve, protect and defend the
> Constitution of the United States.

                                                      BLACKOUT:

                          END OF SEASON IV

Emmy® Awards, Best Drama Series, September 22, 2003

ABOUT THE AUTHOR

AARON SORKIN
(Executive Producer/Creator)

Aaron Sorkin graduated from Syracuse University in 1983 with a Bachelor of Fine Arts in Theatre. In 1989, he received the Outer Critics Circle award as Outstanding American Playwright for *A Few Good Men* and followed that with the off-Broadway comedy *Making Movies*. His screen adaptation of *A Few Good Men* was nominated for four Academy Awards and five Golden Globe Awards, including Best Picture and Best Screenplay.

Sorkin received his second Golden Globe nomination for *The American President*, and his screenplay for *Malice* was nominated for the Edgar Allen Poe Award by the Mystery Writer's Association of America. He is a founding member of the Playwrights Unit of Playwrights Horizons.

Sorkin was also creator and executive producer of the award-winning television series *Sports Night* which aired on ABC for two seasons (1998-99, 1999-2000). Sorkin's work on *Sports Night* earned the series the Television Critics Award for Best Comedy Series, The Viewers for Quality Television Award for Best New Comedy Series, and The Humanitas Prize.

Sorkin's work on *The West Wing* garnered 24 Emmys including four consecutive Awards for Best Drama Series. *The West Wing* also won a Golden Globe Award for Best Television Drama Series, two consecutive Peabody Awards for Broadcast and Cable Excellence, two Humanitas Prizes as well as Television Critics Awards for Best Drama Series, New Program of the Year and Program of the Year. In 2001, Sorkin won the Writer of the Year Award from the Caucus for TV Producers, Writers, and Directors. Sorkin was also the recipient of the Producers Guild Award, in addition to the People for the American Way's Spirit of Liberty Award.

To date, two collections of *West Wing* Script Books have been published by Newmarket Press, introduced and selected by Aaron Sorkin. *The West Wing Script Book* contains six teleplays from Seasons 1 & 2, including the pilot. *The West Wing Script Book: Seasons 3 & 4* contains eight additional teleplays.